CliffsTestPrep®

Praxis II®: Social Studies
Content Knowledge Test (0081)

by

Shana Pate, Ph.D.

WILEY

Wiley Publishing, Inc.

About the Author

Shana Pate, Ph.D. is an Associate Professor of Curriculum and Instruction at Texas State University-San Marcos at the Round Rock Higher Education Center (RRHEC) in Round Rock, Texas. She teaches teacher preparatory courses and graduate courses in Elementary Education.

Publisher's Acknowledgments

Editorial

Acquisitions Editor: Greg Tubach

Project Editor: Lynn Northrup

Composition

Proofreader: John Greenough

Wiley Indianapolis Composition Services

CliffsTestPrep® Praxis II®: Social Studies Content Knowledge Test (0081)

Published by:
Wiley Publishing, Inc.
111 River Street
Hoboken, NJ 07030-5774
www.wiley.com

Copyright © 2006 Wiley, Hoboken, NJ

Published by Wiley, Hoboken, NJ
Published simultaneously in Canada

Library of Congress Cataloging-in-Publication Data

Pate, Shana, 1968-
 CliffsTestPrep Praxis II : social studies content knowledge / by Shana Pate.
  p. cm.
 Includes bibliographical references.
 ISBN-13: 978-0-471-79412-7 (pbk.)
 ISBN-10: 0-471-79412-0
1. Social sciences--Examinations, questions, etc.--Study guides. 2. National teacher examinations--United States--Study guides. 3. Teaching--United States--Examinations--Study guides. I. Title.
 H62.5.U5P366 2006
 300.76--dc22

2006015196

ISBN-10: 0-471-79412-0

ISBN-13: 978-0-471-79412-7

1O/RV/RR/QY/IN

WILEY

Table of Contents

PART II: FULL-LENGTH PRACTICE TESTS

Introduction

You are going to be a social studies teacher! You have chosen an admirable, rewarding, challenging profession, and for that you should be congratulated. To be a professional, however, you must be licensed. If you are sick, you go to a licensed doctor; if you need legal help, you go to a licensed attorney; if you need a haircut, you go to a licensed cosmetologist; if you want an education, you go to a licensed teacher. So, let's get you licensed! One step in the licensing process is to pass your state's required Praxis II: Social Studies Content Knowledge Test. This book will help you prepare for that test.

About the Exam

The Social Studies Content Knowledge Test is designed to determine your knowledge and skills—the knowledge and skills that are necessary for a beginning teacher of social studies in a secondary school. The test requires you to understand and apply social studies knowledge, concepts, methodologies, and skills across the fields of world history (22 percent of the exam); United States history (22 percent); government/political science/civics (16 percent); geography (15 percent); economics (15 percent); and the behavioral science fields of sociology, anthropology, and psychology (10 percent).

A number of the questions are interdisciplinary, reflecting the complex relationships among the social studies fields. Answering the questions correctly requires knowing, interpreting, and integrating history and social science facts and concepts.

Some questions are based on knowledge. Some questions are based on interpreting material such as written passages, maps, graphs, tables, cartoons, and diagrams. Some questions contain content reflecting the diverse experiences of people in the United States as related to gender, culture, and/or race, and/or content relating to Latin America, Africa, Asia, or Oceania.

The test and this book use the chronological designations B.C.E. (before the common era) and C.E. (common era). These labels correspond to B.C. (before Christ) and A.D. (anno Domini), which are used in some world history textbooks.

How to Use This Book

This book is divided into two sections. Part I contains the subject review material. Each of the six major areas is presented in an easy-to-understand summary format. Part II contains two complete practice tests of 130 questions each, with answers and explanations. You should take each section as you would an actual test. Each section is timed, and it would be helpful to take the tests in a quiet room, with no distractions. The purpose of taking these practice tests is to help you become familiar with the types of questions you will encounter on the Social Studies Content Knowledge Test. Complete the practice tests, self-correct, and then study the explanations.

Frequently Asked Questions

Q. How do I register for the test?

A. Contact the Education Testing Service (ETS) at www.ets.org/praxis.

Q. How do I know which test to take?

A. Contact the State Department of Education for the state for which you seek teacher licensure. Use your favorite search engine to locate your State Department of Education's teaching certification office.

Q. What score do I need to pass the test and earn my teaching license?

A. Each State Department of Education sets its passing score. You should contact your State Department of Education for this answer.

Q. Do all states require the test for teacher licensure?

A. No, but several do. Some states have created their own licensure test. Some states use other Praxis II tests. Again, contact your State Department of Education for specifics.

Q. What materials should I take to the test?

A. Be sure to take with you your admission ticket, some form of photo and signature identification, several sharpened number 2 pencils with good erasers, and a watch to help pace yourself during the test. You may also want to dress in a way that you can adapt to the temperature of the room. No scratch paper, books, or other aids will be permitted in the exam center.

Q. Should I guess on the test?

A. YES! There is no penalty for guessing, so guess if you have to. On the multiple-choice section, first try to eliminate some of the choices to increase your chances of choosing the right answer. But do not leave any of the answer spaces blank.

Q. What, generally, are the questions like?

A. The multiple-choice questions will be based on best practices (what you learned in your university courses, not *always* what you have seen in public schools). Typically, one of the choices will be borderline ridiculous. The other three choices will be pretty good, but one of the three will be best—it will answer the question *exactly*, whereas the other two may not address the question thoroughly. This idea will be addressed later in this introduction.

Q. How long does it take to get my scores back?

A. ETS usually gets your scores to you in four to six weeks.

Q. Are there any modifications available to test takers?

A. Yes. Test takers with disabilities and those whose primary language is not English may apply for test-taking modifications. More information is available at www.ets.org/praxis or in the Praxis series registration booklet.

Q. What's the best way to prepare for the Social Studies Content Knowledge Test?

A. You're doing it! Become familiar with the format of the test, the types of questions, and the content of the test. After you're familiar with what will be on the test, it's best to complete the two practice tests in this book. Go back and review the specific content if you answer a question incorrectly, and then analyze why the right answer is the right answer and the wrong answers are the wrong answers.

Test-Taking Tips

Once you have studied the subject areas and taken the practice tests in this book, and then reviewed necessary content, you should be ready to take the test. Here are some tips for your last-minute preparation:

- Make sure you know where you will be going to take your test, and know how long it will take to get there. Allow yourself plenty of driving time.
- Get a good night's sleep the night before the test.
- Eat a balanced breakfast the morning of the test.
- Take plenty of sharpened number 2 pencils with good erasers.
- Dress in layers in case you get hot or cold in the exam room.
- Bring along some mints or gum to enliven you during the test if need be.
- Once you have been given your test, begin to work. Try to avoid getting too bogged down in any one question. Remember the way the Praxis is written. Make sure you choose the answer that *best fits* the question.

How to Approach the Multiple-Choice Questions

In the Social Studies Praxis, there are 130 multiple-choice questions, each with four answer choices. Answering multiple-choice questions is a skill, and the better you are at it, the better you will do on this test. There are some things about the Praxis test, though, that will help you answer the questions:

- Keep in mind that the test is based on "best practices" and "best answers." So, remember the things you have been taught in your content areas and your preparatory classes to become a teacher. As you're deciding on your answers to the multiple-choice question, refer to the question and make sure your answer correlates to the question.

- Remember that often all four answer choices, if looked at independently of the question, may seem like best practices. You must refer back to the question and see which answers tie in with the question. Read and reread the question.

- Once you have read the question, try to formulate an answer in your head before you even look at the answer choices. Then see if one of the answer choices matches your answer. If you know the answer, of course, finding the correct answer will be easy.

- If, when you read the question, you are unable to formulate an answer, look at the answer choices. If you know the material *fairly* well, the correct answer will probably be clear to you. If it is not immediately clear to you, a little thought and reflection may sift out the right answer.

In many cases you can use the process of elimination to answer a question correctly. This process involves eliminating the wrong answers so that you're left with the correct one, or at least you've narrowed down the answer choices. Multiple-choice tests like the Praxis follow patterns in their answer choices. There is the correct answer, and then there are "distracters." Usually, there is one choice that is completely incorrect—almost laughable—and you can quickly eliminate that choice. Then there will be two choices that are pretty good choices, but not the *best* answer for that particular question, and there may be clues in the answers that make them incorrect. The question setup may be something like this:

1. Question

   A. Totally incorrect choice
   B. Almost but not quite correct
   C. Correct choice
   D. Good, best-practices answer, but doesn't address the question

Look for giveaway words such as *always, never,* or *not*. Most things in the world are not *always* or *never*, and you should be careful if a question asks, "Which of the following is NOT ..."

By using the process of elimination, you increase your chances of getting the right answer. Remember that you are not penalized for incorrect answers on the test, so it's worth taking a chance. What this means is that if you just guess, you have a one in four chance—25 percent—of guessing correctly. But if you are able to eliminate one of the choices because it was so wrong, it made you laugh, you have a one in three chance of selecting the correct answer. That's 33 percent—better odds than one in four! If you can narrow it down to only two choices, you have a 50–50 chance.

Different Types of Multiple-Choice Questions

Complete the Statement

In this type of question, you are given an incomplete statement, and you must choose the answer that makes the completed statement correct.

1. The legal basis for the escalation of United States involvement in the Vietnam War was the

   A. declaration of war by Congress.
   B. passage of the Gulf of Tonkin Resolution by Congress.
   C. United Nations' resolution condemning the North Vietnamese invasion of South Vietnam.
   D. Mutual defense provisions of the North Atlantic Treaty Organization (NATO).

Which of the Following...

The best way to answer this type of question is to replace "which of the following" with the words in the answer choices and figure out which "fits" the best.

1. In which of the following fields did Islamic civilization most influence Europeans at the time of the Crusades?

   A. Music
   B. Theology
   C. Mathematics
   D. Law

Roman Numeral Choices

In this format, more than one correct answer is in the list, and you must select the answer choice that includes the two correct answers.

1. The following graph indicates that rapid population growth is most likely to occur in

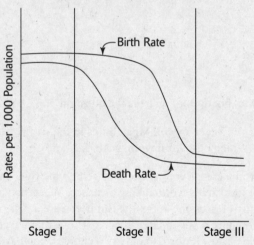

DEMOGRAPHIC TRANSITION

   A. stage I only.
   B. stage II only.
   C. stages I and III only.
   D. stages II and III only.

Questions Containing "NOT," "LEAST," or "EXCEPT"

In this type of question, you must select the answer that does *not* fit. Be careful with this type of question—it is easy to forget that you are selecting the *exception*. Always refer to the question.

1. On the following map, which number indicates a region that was NOT a center of early urban civilization?

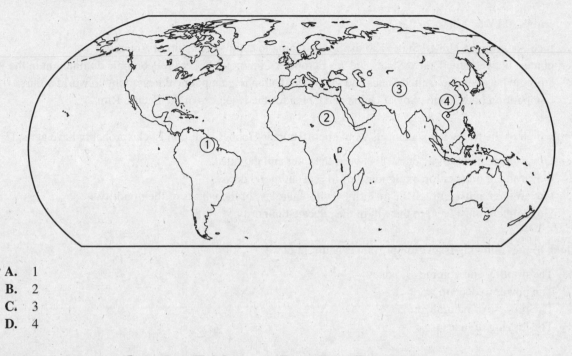

    A. 1
    B. 2
    C. 3
    D. 4

Questions About Graphs, Tables, or Reading Passages

In questions about graphs, tables, or reading passages, you should provide only the information that is asked for in that question. You may want to read the questions first and then look at the map or graph. Again, always refer to the question.

Practice the Multiple-Choice Questions

For ease, we will use the previous questions along with some additional questions. Use these practice questions to become familiar with the various types of multiple-choice questions. The answer explanations follow the questions.

1. President Abraham Lincoln's Emancipation Proclamation declared free only those slaves who

    A. were living in the areas still in rebellion.
    B. were serving in the Union armies.
    C. were living in the border states.
    D. had escaped to Northern states.

2. The legal basis for the escalation for United States involvement in the Vietnam War was the

    A. declaration of war by Congress.
    B. passage of the Gulf of Tonkin Resolution by Congress.
    C. United Nations' resolution condemning the North Vietnamese invasion of South Vietnam.
    D. mutual defense provisions of the North Atlantic Treaty Organization (NATO).

3. In which of the following fields did Islamic civilization most influence Europeans at the time of the Crusades?

   A. Music
   B. Theology
   C. Mathematics
   D. Law

4. The term "Cold War" refers to the

   A. race between the United States and the Soviet Union to claim ownership of Antarctica.
   B. contest between the United States and the European Common Market for economic domination in the West.
   C. struggle between the United States and the Soviet Union to gain political hegemony in world affairs.
   D. competition between the Soviet Union and China for the resources of the Pacific Rim.

5. With which of the following statements would both Thomas Hobbes and John Locke probably have agreed?

   A. Government exists as a contract between the ruler and the ruled.
   B. Government must enforce religious law to prevent moral decay.
   C. Government must enforce the majority's will regardless of the wishes of the minority.
   D. Government must bend to the will of the educated minority.

6. Which of the following is an example of a concurrent power?

   A. The printing and coining of money
   B. The power to declare war
   C. The process of naturalization
   D. The levying of taxes

7. According to Erik Erikson, the primary dilemma faced in adolescence is

   A. industry vs. inferiority.
   B. identity vs. identity confusion.
   C. generativity vs. stagnation.
   D. integrity vs. despair.

8. The following map shows which of the following to be true about precipitation in China?

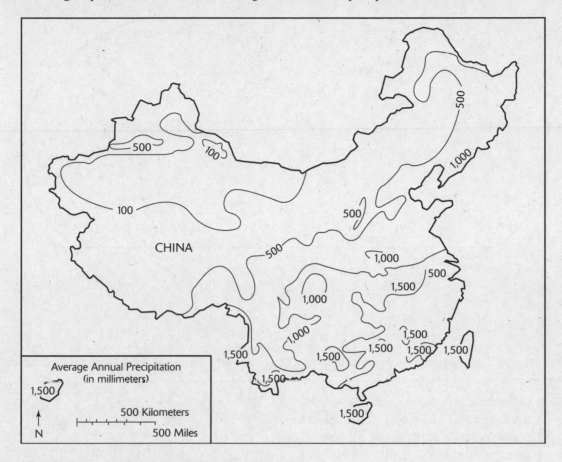

A. The North receives more precipitation than the South.
B. The driest region is the Northeast.
C. The Southeast receives the most precipitation.
D. The West receives more precipitation than the East.

9. If the tax rate for a single person with $25,000 in taxable income is 24 percent, and the tax rate for a single person with $20,000 in taxable income is 20 percent, the tax rate over this income range is

A. regressive.
B. progressive.
C. proportional.
D. revenue-neutral.

10. On the following map, which number indicates a region that was NOT a center of early urban civilization?

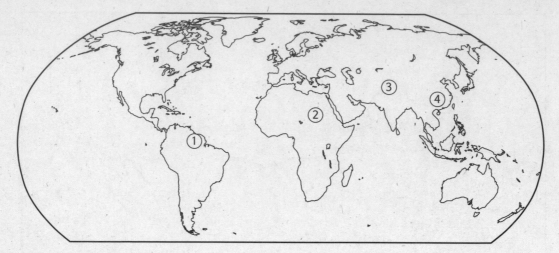

    A. 1

    B. 2

    C. 3

    D. 4

11. Which of the following people would benefit most if the value of the United States dollar increased relative to the Japanese yen?

    A. A United States car dealer importing Japanese cars

    B. A Japanese tourist vacationing in the United States

    C. A worker in the United States beer industry

    D. A Japanese baker buying United States wheat

12. The following graph below indicates that rapid population growth is most likely to occur in

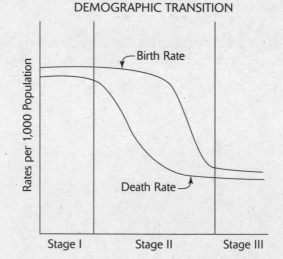

    A. stage I only.

    B. stage II only.

    C. stages I and III only.

    D. stages II and III only.

Answer Explanations

1. A. The Emancipation Proclamation freed only those slaves who were living in the states or parts of states still in rebellion. Lincoln feared that complete emancipation would cost the Union the loyalty of the border states (Missouri, Kentucky, Maryland, and Delaware), slave states that remained loyal to the Union. Moreover, Lincoln did not believe he had the constitutional authority to declare free those slaves living in areas loyal to the Union.

2. B. There was no declaration of war by Congress. However, Congress did pass the Gulf of Tonkin Resolution, which authorized the president to "take all necessary measures to repel any armed attack against the forces of the United States and to prevent further aggression."

3. C. At the time of the Crusades, when contact increased between Europe and the Islamic world, Islamic mathematicians were using sophisticated mathematical tools and concepts (algebra, zero, Arabic numerals) that were unfamiliar to Europeans. In the twelfth century, European scholars became more aware of and interested in the contributions of Islamic mathematicians, and they made this knowledge available to the West in Latin translations.

4. C. The term "Cold War" is used to describe the tense relationship that developed between the United States and the Soviet Union in the years immediately following World War II. During the Cold War, both the United States and the Soviet Union sought to extend their economic, diplomatic, and, at times, military influence in many parts of the world. Beginning in the late 1980s, dramatic changes in the Soviet Union and eastern Europe led to a reduction in U.S.-Soviet tension and the end of the Cold War.

5. A. Hobbes and Locke both agreed that a contract existed between the governed and those governing, although their views on the nature of the contract differed.

6. D. A concurrent power is a power shared by the federal and state governments. Both the federal and state governments have the power to levy taxes. The powers described in choices A, B, and C are reserved for the federal government alone.

7. B. Erikson stated that an adolescent needs to integrate previous experiences in order to develop a sense of "ego identity."

8. C. The map shows that the greatest amount of precipitation (1,500 millimeters on average) is in southeast China, compared to other areas that receive far less precipitation (less than 500 millimeters on average).

9. B. A progressive tax rate is one in which the tax rate increases as income rises. In this example, someone earning $25,000 a year is taxed at a higher rate than someone earning a lower income; thus, the tax rate is progressive.

10. A. Early city civilizations developed along the Nile River, the Sindhu (Indus) River, and the Tangtze, but not along the Amazon.

11. A. Appreciation in the value of the dollar results in a decline in the relative cost of importing foreign goods. An importer of foreign goods would thus benefit. U.S. goods would be relatively more expensive, so choices B and D are incorrect. C is also incorrect; a change in the value of the dollar would have no beneficial effect on a worker in the U.S. beer industry.

12. B. In stages I and III, birth and death rates are approximately equal. Therefore, the rate of natural increase (population growth) would be quite low, even in the first stage in which the birth rate is high. In stage II, a decline in the death rate precedes a decline in the birth rate. It is in this middle stage that rapid and dramatic population growth would occur.

PART I

SUBJECT AREA REVIEW

World History

The following topics are covered in the World History portion of the test:

- Prehistory to 500 C.E.
- India and China (3000 B.C.E.-500 C.E.)
- Ancient Greece (1900-133 B.C.E.)
- Rome and the rise of Christianity (600 B.C.E.-500 C.E.)
- The world of Islam (600-1500 C.E.)
- Early African civilizations (2000 B.C.E.-1500 C.E.)
- The Asian world (400-1500 C.E.)
- Emerging Europe and the Byzantine Empire (400-1300 C.E.)
- Europe in the Middle Ages (1000-1500)
- The Americas (400-1500 C.E.)
- Renaissance and Reformation (1350-1600)
- The age of exploration (1500-1800)
- Crisis and absolutism in Europe (1550-1715)
- The Muslim Empires (1450-1800)
- The East Asian world (1400-1800)
- Revolution and the Enlightenment (1550-1800)
- The French Revolution and Napoleon (1789-1815)
- Industrialization and nationalism (1800-1870)
- Mass society and democracy (1870-1914)
- The height of imperialism, East Asia under challenge (1800-1914)
- War and revolution (1914-1919)
- The west between the wars, nationalism around the world (1919-1939)
- World War II (1939-1945)
- Cold war and postwar changes (1945-1970)
- The contemporary Western world (1970-present)

Prehistory to 500 C.E.

Paleolithic peoples learned how to adapt to their nomadic lifestyle, improve on their primitive tools, and use fire to their advantage, thus enabling them to create a more sophisticated human culture. The agricultural revolution of the Neolithic Age gave rise to more complex human societies that become known as the first civilizations. In this time period, there were significant cultural change, movement, and technological innovations. Early humans learned how to control fire and make tools, caves were painted with religious and decorative art, Neolithic peoples domesticated animals, and early agricultural villages evolved into highly complex societies. Early humans migrated to warmer climates during the Ice Ages, and Neanderthals inhabited Europe and Asia.

The Sumerians in Mesopotamia were among the first groups to build a civilization, and they were the first to develop a system of writing. Due in large part to the Nile, early Egyptian civilization was stable and prosperous. Massive monuments, the pyramids, were built to honor the deaths of the pharaohs. The Israelites emerged as a distinct people. Of the other empires that came into being in Southwest Asia, the longest lasting and most powerful were the Assyrian and Persian Empires. The peoples of this time period utilized their environment and invented new technologies:

Environment: Egypt used floodwaters for farming; Phoenicia set up a trading empire on the sea; Mesopotamia created irrigation and flood control systems.

Cooperation: Assyria developed an empire-wide communication system; Mesopotamia built temples and houses for religious leaders; Palestine adhered to sacred law to maintain separateness.

Cultural Diffusion: Assyria acquired iron making from the Hittites; Persia acquired architecture from the Assyrians, Babylonians, and Egyptians; Egypt acquired bronze making from the Hyssops.

Innovation: Mesopotamia invented the arch, dome, wheel, and system of writing; Phoenicia invented an alphabet; Persia created a standing army.

India and China (3000 B.C.E.-500 C.E.)

Buddhism, Hinduism, Confucianism, Daoism, and Legalism profoundly affected the way of life of the early Indians and Chinese. The Silk Road provided a means for prosperous trade. The ruler of the Zhou overthrew the Shang dynasty and established the longest-lasting dynasty in Chinese history. The Great Wall of China was built to keep out enemies.

Chinese and Indian civilizations were remarkable for their achievement and innovation. The key elements of their culture included the following:

In India:

Religion/Philosophy: Hinduism, Buddhism

Key People: Siddhartha Gautama, Asoka, Chandragupta II

Innovation: Iron plow, caste system, concept of zero, decimal system

Literature: *Mahabharata, Ramayana, Arthasastra,* Vedas

Government/Society: Patriarchal, monarchy

In China:

Religion/Philosophy: Confucianism, Daoism, Legalism

Key People: Confucius, Laozi, Qin Shihuangdi

Innovation: Bronze casting, crossbow, paper, iron plowshare, silk

Literature: *Analects,* Confucian classics, *Tao Te Ching,* poetry

Government/Society: Patriarchal, monarchy

Ancient Greece (1900–133 B.C.E.)

Athens and Sparta emerged as the leading Greek city-states. The Greek military defeated the Persian army. Greek theater, arts, and architecture flourished during the Classical Age. Greek philosophers such as Socrates, Plato, and Aristotle established the foundations of Western philosophy. Although Greek civilization had unique problems, all four groups of Greek cultures—the Minoans, the Myceneans, the Spartans, and the Athenians—faced common challenges in several areas, as summarized in the following table.

	Minoans	Mycenaeans	Spartans	Athenians
Environment				
a. Location	a. Crete	a. Peloponnesus	a. Peloponnesus	a. Attica
b. Factors	b. Tidal waves	b. Earthquakes	b. Farming	b. Lack of fertile land
Movement				
a. Origin	a. Unknown	a. Indo-European	a. Greek-speaking invaders	a. Greek-speaking invaders
b. Trade	b. Sea trading empire	b. Pottery	b. Trade discouraged	b. Pottery
Regionalism				
a. Government	a. King	a. Monarchies forming a loose alliance of independent states	a. Military state, oligarchy	a. Oligarchy, direct democracy
b. Values, interests, beliefs	b. Sports, nature	b. Heroic deeds	b. Discipline, military arts	b. Philosophy, art, theater, architecture
Conflict				
a. With other Greeks	a. Invaded by Mycenaeans	a. Conquered Minoans	a. Conquered other Greeks, fought Athenians	a. Fought Spartans
b. With foreign invaders		b. Fell to Greek-speaking invaders	b. Fought Persians, Macedonians	b. Fought Persians, Macedonian

Rome and the Rise of Christianity (600 B.C.E.–500 C.E.)

Romans overthrew the last Etruscan king and established a republic. Romans crushed Hannibal and won the Second Punic War. Augustus became the first emperor, signifying the beginning of the Roman Empire. Constantine proclaimed official tolerance of Christianity. Germanic tribes defeated the Romans, and the empire fell.

A series of causes and effects shaped historical events of ancient Rome:

Cause: Rome defeated Carthage and took Sicily.

Effect: Hannibal brought the Second Punic War into Italy, defeating the Romans at Cannae.

Cause: Marius recruited armies by promising them land. He required an oath of loyalty to him.

Effect: The Roman army was no longer under government control; military power rested in the hands of individual generals.

Cause: Sulla used his army to seize governmental power.

Effect: Sulla restored power to the government with a strong Senate, but his actions set the precedent for military coups.

Cause: Julius Caesar filled the Senate with his own supporters.

Effect: The power of the Senate was weakened. Julius Caesar was assassinated in 44 B.C.E.

Cause: Economic and social policies of Diocletian and Constantine were based on control and coercion.

Effect: The policies of these two emperors contributed to the empire's eventual collapse.

The World of Islam (600-1500 C.E.)

Muhammad and his followers spread the beliefs and practices of Islam. At its peak, the Arab Empire extended west and north through Spain and into France. In the seventh century, a split in Islam created two groups, the Shiite and the Sunni Muslims.

Islamic civilization was renowned for the following:

- **Innovation:** Irrigation; astrolabe; algebra; large-scale paper manufacturing
- **Movement:** Trade routes; Arab expansion in Africa, Asia, and Europe; movement of Arab center of power from Makkah to Baghdad to Cairo
- **Cultural Diffusion:** Bureaucracy relied on non-Arabs; Arabs translated Greek philosophers; Ibn Sina's medical textbook was standard in Europe

Early African Civilizations (2000 B.C.E.-1500 C.E.)

The continents' immense size and distinct geographical and climatic zones influenced where civilizations developed and how they survived. The introduction of Christianity and Islam affected the way civilizations developed and interacted. The development of trade led to the exchange of goods and cultural ideas.

African civilizations did not develop in a vacuum. As far back as the ancient Egyptians, African civilizations were open to contact with outside groups. Contact came about either through trade, migration, or war, and led to the introduction of new ideas, new ways of living, and the development of multicultural societies. The major concepts associated with cultural diffusion and contact were trade, migration, and warfare:

Trade:

Ghanaian gold was exchanged for salt from the Sahara.

Muslim traders brought cotton, silk, and Chinese porcelain from India to East Africa.

Malian farmers produced surplus crops for export.

Ivory and gold from inland Africa were brought to East Africa.

Cotton cloth, brass, copper, and olive oil were imported by Axum.

The Kingdom of Mali (one of the greatest trading societies in West Africa which rose in place of Ghana) became rich from the profitable salt and gold trades.

Migration:

Bantu peoples slowly migrated into East Africa.

Arab merchants settled along the east coast of Africa.

Islamic scholars moved to Timbuktu, a new center for learning.

Warfare:

Kushites conquered Egyptians.

Muslim merchants gained control of Axum's trade.

Moroccan armies occupied Songahi's gold-trading centers.

Assyrians drove the Kushites out of Egypt.

The Asian World (400-1500 C.E.)

Innovations in agricultural production, the reemergence of trade routes, and a unified central government allowed China to prosper under the Sui, Tang, and Song dynasties. Japan's geography isolated it from other countries and caused the island nation to develop its own unique culture. The Muslim expansion made both Islam and Hinduism powerful religions in the Indian subcontinent. Because of the geography of the region, Southeast Asian countries developed into a series of separate states with their own culture, religion, and language. In the Asian world, countries developed different political systems and forms of government. Each country, however, had strong leaders:

China: Sui, Tan, and Song dynasties; Mongols

Japan: Yamato and Fujiwara clans; Kamakura shogunate; Ashikaga family

Korea: Koryo and Yi dynasties

India: Mahmud; Timur Lenk

Southeast Asia: Vietnam—emperors; Angkor—Jayavarman; Thailand and Burma—kings; Malay—overlords

Emerging Europe and the Byzantine Empire (400-1300 C.E.)

The new European civilization was formed by the coming together of three major elements: the Germanic tribes, the Roman legacy, and the Christian church. The collapse of a central authority in the Carolingian Empire led to feudalism. In the 1100s, European monarchs began to build strong states. While a new civilization arose in Europe, the Byzantine Empire created its own unique civilization in the eastern Mediterranean.

Europe and the Byzantine Empire changed and developed during the Middle Ages in many ways:

- **Movement:** Anglos and Saxons settled in England. Monks came to England to convert the Anglo-Saxons to Christianity. Vikings, Magyars, and Muslims invaded areas of Europe.
- **Cooperation:** The Frankish ruler Clovis converted to Christianity and gained the support of the Roman Catholic Church. Benedictine rule emphasized the need for monks to work together within the monastery. The system of feudalism, based on the granting of land to nobles in exchange for military service, spread throughout Europe.
- **Conflict:** Charlemagne's death led to the decline and division of the Carolingian Empire. Schism divided the Eastern Orthodox Church and the Roman Catholic Church. William the Conqueror defeated Harold Godwinson in the Battle of Hastings.
- **Uniformity:** The emperor Justinian restored the Roman Empire in the Mediterranean. Eastern Orthodox Christianity became the state religion of Kiev. The Magna Carta guaranteed rights to all English freemen.

Europe in the Middle Ages (1000-1500)

The revival of trade led to the growth of cities and towns, which became important centers for manufacturing. The Catholic Church was an important part of people's lives during the Middle Ages. During the fourteenth and early fifteenth centuries, Europeans experienced many problems including the Black Death, the Hundred Years' War, and the decline of the Church.

The Middle Ages was a period marked by cultural diffusion, innovation, and conflict:

- The Crusades increased the exchange of goods and ideas between European and non-European cultures. European monarchs gained strength through new taxes and through the new armies required for the Crusades. Increased trade, especially of luxury goods, led to new importance for Italian cities. Classical texts were translated and reintroduced into Europe, leading to a revival in learning.

- The rise of towns and the middle class led to advances in all areas of society. As trade increased, the importance of towns and guilds grew. A money economy replaced bartering. Universities were founded. Literature and poetry flourished and were increasingly written in the vernacular rather than in Latin. The Romanesque style of architecture gave way to the Gothic style.
- The Hundred Years' War and the Great Schism strengthened the authority of some and weakened the authority of others. After the Hundred Years' War, the French monarchy gained power. Conflict within the English monarchy led to the War of the Roses. Conflict, corruption, and challenges by reformers weakened the authority of the Catholic Church.

The Americas (400-1500 C.E.)

The early inhabitants of the Americas probably traveled from Asia across a Bering Strait land bridge produced by the Ice Age. The Mayan, Aztec, and Incan civilizations developed and administered complex societies. Diseases that Europeans brought to the Americas contributed to the downfall of several cultures.

The following table summarizes the factors that helped shape early cultures in the Americas.

Location	People	Economics	Architecture
Eastern Woodlands	Mound Builders, Iroquois	Hunting and gathering, some agriculture	Longhouses, some urban centers
Central Plains	Plains	Hunting and gathering	Tepees
Southwest	Anasazi	Extensive farming	Cliff dwellings
Mesoamerica	Olmec, Maya, Aztec	Farming, trade	Large cities, religious and political structures
South America	Moche, Inca	Farming, trade	Large cities, religious and political structures

Renaissance and Reformation (1350-1600)

Between 1350 and 1550, Italian intellectuals began to reexamine the culture of the Greeks and Romans. Historians later referred to this period of European history as the Renaissance. Martin Luther's break with the Catholic Church led to the emergence of the Protestant Reformation. During the period known as the Catholic Reformation, the Catholic Church enacted a series of reforms that were successful in strengthening the Church.

The Renaissance was a period of great intellectual and artistic achievement. Religious rebirth followed in the 1500s. Italy experienced an artistic, intellectual, and commercial awakening. Ideas quickly spread from Italy to northern Europe. Protestant reformers began to challenge both secular and religious rules and practices. In response, the Catholic Church enacted reforms to reform the papacy and reaffirm traditional Catholic teachings, spreading Catholicism throughout Europe.

The Age of Exploration (1500-1800)

Europeans risked dangerous ocean voyages to discover new sea routes. Early European explorers sought gold in Africa then began to trade slaves. Trade increased in Southeast Asia, and the Dutch built a trade empire based on spices in the Indonesian Archipelago. The age of exploration brought the peoples of Europe, Asia, the Americas, and Africa into direct contact for the first time and led to a transfer of ideas and products. However, the European colonization took a great toll in human life and often had a negative impact on cultures that were conquered.

Crisis and Absolutism in Europe (1550-1715)

The French religious wars of the sixteenth century pitted Protestant Calvinists against Catholics. From 1560 to 1650, wars, including the devastating Thirty Years' War, and economic and social crises plagued Europe. European monarchs sought economic and political stability through absolutism and the divine right of kings. The rulers of Europe during the sixteenth, seventeenth, and early eighteenth centuries battled to expand their borders, power, and religion.

Conflict:

Spanish and English monarchs engaged in a dynastic struggle.

Philip II, a champion of Catholicism, resented English tolerance of Protestants.

The defeat of the Spanish Armada in 1588 meant that England would remain Protestant.

Dynastic and religious conflicts divided the German states.

Two German states, Prussia and Austria, emerged as great powers in the seventeenth and eighteenth centuries.

Prussia built an army to protect its borders. Austria was diverse with no common culture or political rule.

Change:

Tudor monarchs brought stability and prosperity to England.

The Act of Supremacy was passed.

Foreign policy was moderate. Queen Elizabeth Tudor tried to keep Spain and France from becoming too powerful by balancing power.

Spain hoped to successfully invade England, overthrow Protestantism, and begin a return to Catholicism. The Spanish Armada, however, was defeated by England in 1588.

Uniformity:

France's Louis XIV strengthened absolute monarchy in France and limited the rights of religious dissenters.

He removed nobles and princes from royal council and kept them busy with court life.

He bribed people to make sure his policies were followed in the provinces.

Innovation:

Peter the Great attempted to modernize Russian society by introducing Western customs, practices, and manners.

He wrote a Russian book of etiquette to teach Western manners, and he mixed the sexes for conversation and dancing.

The Muslim Empires (1450-1800)

Muslim conquerors captured vast territory in Europe and Asia using firearms. Religion played a major role in the establishment of the Ottoman, Safavid, and Mogul Empires. Trade and the arts flourished under the Muslim Empires.

The following table shows the characteristics of the Ottoman, Safavid, and Mogul Empires.

	Ottomans	*Safavids*	*Moguls*
Warfare	Trained janissaries Conquered Constantinople	Battled Ottomans Allied with European states	Conquered India Battled Persians and British
Arts	Made magnificent mosques, pottery, rugs, and jewelry	Blended Persian and Turkish influences Excelled at carpet making and painting	Combined Persian and Indian motifs Excelled at architecture and painting
Government	The sultan governed through local rulers called pashas	The shah trained administrators	The emperor controlled semi-independent states
Trade	Merchants were the privileged class	Geography limited trade	Traded with Europeans
Religion	Sunni Muslim Religious tolerance	Shiite Muslim Religious orthodoxy	Muslim, Hindu Religious tolerance
Women	Social restrictions Can own land, inherit property, seek divorce, and hold senior government posts	Social restrictions Were kept secluded and made to wear veils	Some social restrictions Served as warriors, landowners, political advisors, and businesspeople

The East Asian World (1400–1800)

China closed its doors to the Europeans during the period of exploration between 1400 and 1800. The Ming and Qing dynasties produced blue-and-white porcelain and new literary forms. The Chinese viewed Europeans as barbarians. Both sides, however, benefited from the early cultural exchange. The Qing rulers eventually attempted to limit contact with European traders. The Qing government tried to preserve its distinct identity within Chinese society. However, the Qing brought Chinese into the top ranks of the imperial administration, sharing important government positions equally with them. Emperor Yong Le began renovations on the Imperial City, which was expanded by succeeding emperors. By the nineteenth century, Japanese and Chinese societies had changed as a result of the decisions and policies of their leaders.

Revolution and the Enlightenment (1550–1800)

The ideas of the Scientific Revolution and the Enlightenment laid the foundation for a modern worldview based on rationalism and secularism. Enlightenment was a movement of intellectuals who were greatly impressed with achievements of the Scientific Revolution. Enlightenment thought led some rulers to advocate such natural rights as equality before the law and freedom of religion. The American colonies formed a new nation and ratified the Constitution of the United States. As the Scientific Revolution and the ideas of the Enlightenment spread across Europe, innovations based on science and reason came into conflict with traditional beliefs.

The French Revolution and Napoleon (1789–1815)

The fall of the Bastille marked the beginning of the French Revolution. The Committee of Public Safety began the Reign of Terror. Napoleon Bonaparte created the French Empire. Allied forces defeated Napoleon at Waterloo. The French Revolution was one of the great turning points in history. The years from 1789 to 1815 in France were chaotic, and change came about in unexpected ways. Some of the major changes from this time period were:

- From the meeting of the Estates-General, the creation of the National Assembly
- From the Great Fear, the adoption of important reforms by nobility in the National Assembly
- From the Declaration of Rights, the spread of liberal beliefs
- From the March on Versailles, the return of Louis XVI to Paris
- From the Reign of Terror, the Fall of Robespierre and establishment of the Directory
- From Napoleon's coup d'etat, the creation of the French Empire
- From the Battle of Trafalgar, the safety of Great Britain and birth of the Continental System
- From the Invasion of Russia, the deaths of hundreds of thousands and the downfall of Napoleon

Industrialization and Nationalism (1800-1870)

The Industrial Revolution saw a shift from an economy based on farming and handicrafts to an economy based on manufacturing by machines and industrial factories. Three important ideologies—conservatism, nationalism, and liberalism—emerged to play an important role in world history. Romanticism and realism reflected changes in society in Europe and in North America.

During this period, there were developments from industry to art, faith to science, liberalism to conservatism.

Advances:

Steam and coal became new sources of power.

Higher-quality iron led to better railroads.

Conflict:

Nationalism and liberalism became forces for change.

Conservatives attempted to suppress nationalism.

Change:

People moved to cities for factory work.

Italy unified.

Germany emerged as a strong European power.

Reaction:

Russian czars opposed the forces of liberalism and nationalism.

Science had a greater impact on people, undermining religious faith.

Diversity:

Austria-Hungary contained many different ethnic groups seeking self-rule.

Romanticism and realism were opposite artistic styles.

Mass Society and Democracy (1870-1914)

The Second Industrial Revolution resulted in changes in political, economic, and social systems. After 1870, higher wages and improved conditions in cities raised the standard of living for urban workers. The late 1800s and early 1900s were a time of political conflict that led to the Balkan crises and, eventually, World War I. New discoveries radically changed scientific thought, art, architecture, and social consciousness between 1870 and 1914.

Innovations in technology and production methods created great economic, political, social, and cultural changes between 1870 and 1914. The development of a mass society led to labor reforms and the extension of voting rights. New scientific theories radically changed people's vision of the world. Change also brought conflict as tensions increased in Europe and new alliances were formed.

Economics:

The Second Industrial Revolution, combined with the growth of transportation by steamship and railroad, fostered a true world economy.

Industrial growth and the development of new energy resources led to increased production of consumer goods.

Politics:

Growth of mass politics led to the development of new political parties.

Labor leaders used ideas of socialism and Marxism to form unions.

Society:

Women fought for equal rights.

Society adopted middle-class values.

Unions fought for labor reforms.

Mass leisure developed because people had more money.

Culture:

Many artists rejected traditional styles and developed new art movements.

New scientific ideas radically changed people's perception of the world.

Conflict:

Nationalism and imperialism created conflict in the Balkans and eventually led to World War I.

Growth of nationalism led to increased anti-Semitism.

The Height of Imperialism, East Asia Under Challenge (1800-1914)

Competition among European nations led to the partition of Africa. Colonial rule created a new social class of Westernized intellectuals. British rule brought order and stability to India, but with its own set of costs. The United States practiced many of the same imperialist policies as European nations.

The imperialist powers of the nineteenth century conquered weaker countries and carved up the lands they seized. Their actions had a lasting effect on the world, especially the conquered peoples of Asia and Africa. There were four themes surrounding these events:

- **Movement:** Imperialistic nations set up colonies and protectorates. Christian missionaries preached in Africa and Asia. British policy in South Africa was influenced by Cecil Rhodes, who made a fortune in South Africa by founding diamond and gold companies. He gained control of a territory north of the Transvaal, which he named Rhodesia, after himself.
- **Change:** Ferdinand de Lesseps completed the Suez Canal in 1869. King Leopold II of Belgium colonized the Congo Basin. The United States gained new territory after the Spanish-American War. The Panama Canal opened in 1914.
- **Reaction:** The British East India Company controlled India. Afrikaners set up independent republics.
- **Nationalism:** The United States created the Monroe Doctrine in 1823. In May 1857, the sepoys rebelled against British commanders. Afrikaners fought the British in the Boer War from 1899 to 1902.

Western nations used political persuasion and military strength to gain trading privileges with China and Japan. China's internal problems made it easier for Western nations to penetrate the country and strengthen their influence. Japan's ability to adopt Western ways and to maintain its own traditions enabled it to develop into a modern, powerful nation.

Imperialist powers advanced into China and Japan in the nineteenth century. China's government fell, but Japan's modernized and endured.

- **Movement:** British secured trade outlets at five coastal ports in China. Commodore Perry sailed into Edo Bay. Japan invaded Port Arthur, Manchurai.
- **Change:** Japan's Tokugawa shogunate and China's Qing dynasty collapsed. Meiji reformers instituted compulsory military service in Japan. John Hay, U.S. secretary of state, proclaimed that all major states with economic interests in China had agreed that the country should have an Open Door policy. The Open Door policy reflected American concern for the survival of China.
- **Reaction:** Tai Pin Rebellion broke out in China. Sat-Cho leaders demanded the resignation of Japan's shogun. Boxer Rebellion occurred in China.
- **Nationalism:** Meiji government reformed Japan. Japan adopted the Meiji constitution. Sun Yat-sen established the Republic of China.

War and Revolution (1914-1919)

Archduke Francis Ferdinand was assassinated by a Serbian nationalist. Militarism, nationalism, and alliances drew nations into war. The United States' entry into the war helped the Allies. The impact of the war at home led to an increase in the federal government's powers and changed the status of women. The Russian Revolution ended with the Communist Party in power. Peace settlements caused lingering resentment. The League of Nations was formed. Four themes emerged during this time period:

- **Cooperation** (Alliance System): Two loose alliances formed in Europe: the Triple Alliance (Germany, Austria-Hungary, and Italy) and the Triple Entente (France, Great Britain, and Russia). Alliances drew France and Great Britain into a conflict in which they had no direct interest.
- **Conflict** (World War I): Combat took the forms of trench warfare on the Western Front, a war of movement on the Eastern Front, and German submarine warfare in the waters surrounding Great Britain. For the first time in history, airplanes were used for reconnaissance, combat, and bombing.
- **Revolution** (Russian Revolution): Military and economic crises led to a spontaneous revolution that ended the reign of the czars. The Bolsheviks overthrew the provisional government and established a communist regime.
- **Internationalism** (Peace of Paris): The peace was a compromise between international and national interests. Germany's reparation payments, military reduction, and territorial losses created a lasting bitterness that helped spark World War II.

The West Between the Wars, Nationalism Around the World (1919-1939)

Europe faced several economic problems after World War I, including inflation and the Great Depression. Dictatorial regimes began to spread into Italy, Germany, and across eastern Europe. The uncertainties and disillusionment of the times were reflected in the art and literature of the 1920s and 1930s. Between 1919 and 1939, the West experienced great economic and political challenges.

Political and Economic Changes:

- In Britain, the Conservative Party implemented traditional economic policies.
- In the United States, President Roosevelt developed the New Deal, a policy of active government intervention in the economy.
- In France, the Popular Front established the French New Deal, which promoted workers' rights.

Rise of Totalitarianism:

- In Italy, Mussolini led the Fascists to power.
- Stalin became dictator of the Soviet Union and purged the Communist Party of Old Bolsheviks.
- In Germany, Adolf Hitler established a totalitarian Nazi regime and started the large-scale persecution of Jews.

Innovations and Ideas:

- The artistic movements of Dadaism and surrealism reflected the uncertainty of life created by World War I.
- Radio and film transformed communications and entertainment.
- Literary techniques reflected an interest in the unconscious.
- Werner (Karl) Heisenberg's uncertainty principle suggested that physical laws are based on uncertainty.

The Balfour Declaration issued by the British foreign secretary in 1917 turned Palestine, a country with an 80 percent Muslim population, into a homeland for the Jews. Chian Kai-shek positioned his nationalist forces against Mao Zedong's communists. Key oil fields were discovered in the Persian Gulf area in 1938.

Between the two World Wars, a growing sense of nationalism inspired many countries to seek their independence from foreign rulers:

- **Middle East:** The decline of the Ottoman Empire resulted in the emergence of many new Arab states.
- **African and Asia:** Black Africans who fought in World War I became more politically active. They organized reform movements, then called for independence.
- **China:** In 1923, the nationalists and the communists formed an alliance to oppose the warlords and drive the imperialist powers out of China.
- **Latin America:** After the Great Depression, Latin American countries worked to become economically independent by creating new industries to produce goods that were formerly imported.

World War II (1939-1945)

Adolf Hitler's philosophy of Aryan superiority led to World War II in Europe and was also the source of the Holocaust. Two separate and opposing alliances, the Allies and the Axis Powers, waged a worldwide war. World War II left lasting impressions on civilian populations.

World War II was the most devastating total war in human history. Events engaged four continents, involved countless people and resources, and changed subsequent history. The following table summarizes some of the themes and developments.

Country	Movement	Cooperation	Conflict
United States	Retook Japanese positions in Southeast Asia	Relaxed neutrality acts Met with Allies at Tehran, Yalta, and Potsdam	Led war effort Conducted island-hopping counterattacks Dropped atomic bombs on Japan
Great Britain	Made huge troop movements in Dunkirk and Normandy	Met with Allies at Tehran, Yalta, and Potsdam	Stopped Rommel at El Alamein Withstood heavy German bombing
Soviet Union	Occupied Kuril and Sakhalin Islands Took control of much of eastern Europe	Met with Allies at Tehran, Yalta, and Potsdam	Defeated Germany and Stalingrad Forced Germany to fight war on two fronts

Country	Movement	Cooperation	Conflict
Germany	Took over Austria, Poland, and Sudetenland	Formed Rome-Berlin Axis Signed Anti-Comintern Pact	Used blitzkrieg tactics Conducted genocide of Jews and others Besieged Leningrad
Italy	Invaded Ethiopia	Formed Rome-Berlin Axis	Became German puppet state (northern Italy)
Japan	Seized Manchuria and renamed it Manchukuo Invaded China	Signed Anti-Comintern Pact	Attacked Pearl Harbor Conquered Southeast Asia from Indochina to Philippines

Cold War and Postwar Changes (1945-1970)

At the end of World War II, the United States and the Soviet Union engaged in a Cold War that was fought around the globe. The two new superpowers competed for political domination of the world. The United States fought in Korea and Vietnam to prevent the spread of communism. The Soviet Union used armies to maintain Soviet regimes in eastern Europe. The creation of NATO and the European Economic Community helped western Europe move toward political and economic unity during the Cold War. Some changes/conflicts and their results are listed in the following table.

	Conflict/Crisis	Significant Event(s)	Result(s)
Greece (1944-1949)	Civil war erupted	Great Britain aided government forces against communism	United States created Truman Doctrine
Berlin (1949)	Soviets and Western powers divided Germany	Western powers airlifted supplies to Soviet-blockaded West Berlin	Blockade was lifted
Korea (1950-1953)	Civil war began when North Korea invaded South Korea	United Nations forced fight to save South Korea from communism	United States extended military alliances around the world
Berlin (1961)	Refugees escaped from East to West Berlin	Soviets built Berlin Wall	Berlin Wall became symbol of divided Germany
Cuba (1962)	Soviets supported Castro's totalitarian regime in Cuba	United States invaded Bay of Pigs; Soviets placed nuclear missiles in Cuba; United States blockaded Cuba	Soviets withdrew missiles; hotline was established between Moscow and Washington, D.C.
Vietnam (1964-1973)	Civil war erupted between North and South Vietnam	United States intervened to prevent North Vietnam from taking over South Vietnam	United States withdrew from Vietnam; Vietnam was reunited by communists

The Contemporary Western World (1970-Present)

Political and social changes led to the end of the Cold War and the fall of communism in eastern Europe and the Soviet Union. Economic challenges helped bring about and accompanied these sweeping political and social changes. Society and culture reflected these changes with the advent of the women's movement, the growth of technology, and a rise in terrorism.

The end of the Cold War brought dramatic economic, political, and social changes to Europe and North America. Many of these changes can be understood through the themes of conflict, change, regionalism, and cooperation. Some of the major events in postwar society are categorized according to these themes:

Conflict:

> Serb forces carried out "ethnic cleansing" of Muslims.
>
> Terrorism became a regular aspect of modern society.
>
> Soviet troops crushed a reform movement in Czechoslovakia.
>
> Nicolae Ceausescu was arrested and executed.

Change:

> The Soviet Union adopted a policy of perestroika under Gorbachev.
>
> Lech Walesa became the first freely elected president of an eastern European nation in 40 years.
>
> The national debt tripled in the United States during Ronald Reagan's presidency.
>
> Television, movies, and music spread American culture throughout the world.

Regionalism:

> Ethnic Albanians declared Kosovo an independent province.
>
> Bosnia Serbs fought Bosnia Muslims and Croats.
>
> Bands of German youths attacked immigrants.
>
> Intense fighting broke out between Protestants and Catholics in Northern Ireland.

Cooperation:

> British women protested against nuclear weapons.
>
> East Germany and West Germany were reunited into one nation.
>
> The Soviet Union and the United States signed the INF Treaty.

Latin America (1945-Present)

Many Latin American nations have experienced severe economic problems, and their governments have been led by military dictators. Successful Marxist revolutions in Cuba and Nicaragua fed fears in the United States about the spread of communism in the Americas.

Africa and the Middle East (1945-Present)

From the 1950s to the 1970s, most African nations gained independence from colonial powers. Israel declared statehood on May 14, 1948, creating conflict and struggle between the new state and its neighbors.

Asia and the Pacific (1945-Present)

Communists in China introduced socialist measures and drastic reforms under the leadership of Mao Zedong. After World War II, India gained its independence from Britain and divided into two separate countries, India and Pakistan. Japan modernized its economy and society after 1945 and became one of the world's economic giants.

Challenges and Hopes for the Future

Today's world faces the challenges of protecting and preserving the environment, addressing economic and social changes, implementing new technologies, resolving political conflicts, and eliminating international terrorism. The world's inhabitants must adopt a cooperative global vision to address the problems that confront all humankind. At the beginning of the twenty-first century, the world has become a global society. Nations are politically and economically dependent on one another, and the world's problems are of a global nature:

Cultural Diffusion:

Jumbo jetliners transport passengers around the world.

Many corporations have offices in more than one country.

Advances in communication, such as the Internet, connect people around the globe.

Technological Innovation:

The science of ecology is born.

American astronauts landed on the moon in 1969, and exploration of space continues to be a world-changing development.

Super strains of corn, rice, and other grains produce greater crop yields.

Health care advances prolong lives.

Developments in transportation and communication transform the world community.

Cooperation:

The Earth Summit met in Rio de Janeiro in 1992, to examine the challenges to the environment and propose new solutions.

Nations enact recycling programs and curb the dumping of toxic materials.

The United Nations promotes world peace.

Nongovernmental organizations advocate social and environmental change.

Conflict:

Massive growth in world population causes overcrowding and hunger in many countries.

Regional, ethnic, and religious differences continue to produce violence around the world.

International terrorists remain a threat to peace and security.

United States History

The following topics are covered in the United States History portion of the test:

- Physical geography of North America
- Native American peoples
- European exploration and colonization
- American Revolution
- Establishing a new nation: early years and continued development
- Civil War era
- Emergence of the modern United States
- Progressive Era and World War I through the New Deal
- World War II
- Post-World War II period
- More recent developments

Physical Geography of North America

The last Ice Age made the sea level drop to reveal the land bridge between Asia and America. The Bering Strait that now separates Alaska and Siberia was dry land. Across this so-called land bridge, bands of fur-clad hunter-gatherers from Asia trekked to the northwestern corner of North America.

Settlers may have made their way to the Americas other ways: From northeast Asia, people traveled by boat along the coastline to North and South America; people from southeast Asia crossed the Pacific Ocean, hopping from island to island; people from southwestern Europe crossed the North Atlantic, passing by Iceland and Greenland; and people migrated from Africa.

Native American Peoples

The Native Americans of what is today the United States had diverse social structures and religions. Different Native American groups lived in different regions in North America. In the West were the Zuni, Hopi, and other Pueblo peoples. They depended on corn to survive. In the lands bordering the Pacific Ocean, there were the Tlingit, Haida, Kwakiutls, Nootkas, Chinook, and Salish peoples. They relied on fish from the coastal waters and deer, roots, and berries from the Rocky Mountains for their survival.

In the Great Plains, the Sioux followed the migrating buffalo herds and lived in tepees. Life for the Sioux changed dramatically after they began taming horses.

Two different Native American groups made their homes in the Far North. The Inuit and Aleut depended upon hunting seals, walruses, whales, polar bears, and caribou for their survival.

East of the Mississippi lay almost a million square miles of woodlands. Most of the peoples of the Northeast were divided into two major language groups—those who spoke Algonquian languages and those who spoke Iroquoian languages. Many peoples in the Northeast, including the Algonquians of New England and the Iroquoians of New York, practiced slash-and-burn agriculture. The early peoples of the Northeast used several types of houses. Many villages, enclosed by wooden stockades, had large rectangular longhouses with barrel-shaped roofs covered in bark. Others built wigwams, which were either conical or dome-shaped, and were made using bent poles covered with hides or bark. The Iroquois League was formed by five Native American groups to keep the peace. According to Iroquois tradition, Dekanawidah, a shaman or tribal elder, and Hiawatha, a chief of the Mohawk, founded the League.

Almost all of the people in the Southeast lived in towns. The Cherokee were the largest Native American group in the Southeast.

By the 1500s, Native Americans had created a wide array of cultures and languages. They had also developed economies and lifestyles well suited to the geography and climate of their particular corners of North America.

European Exploration and Colonization

Pope Urban II's call to arms launched nearly two centuries of armed struggle to regain the Holy Land. The expeditions were called the *Crusades,* from the Latin word *crux,* meaning "cross." The Crusades helped pry western Europe out of centuries of isolation and triggered a series of events that revolutionized European society and encouraged a new desire for exploration. For centuries the Roman Empire had dominated much of Europe, imposing a stable social and political order. By 500 C.E. the Roman political and economic system had collapsed, isolating western Europe from the rest of the world. Trade declined. Cities, bridges, and roads fell into disrepair. Law and order vanished, and money was no longer used. For most people, life did not extend beyond the tiny villages where they were born, lived, and died. This period, lasting roughly from 500 to 1400 C.E., is known as the Middle Ages. With the weakening of central government, a new political system known as *feudalism* developed in western Europe. By 1100 C.E. feudalism had spread throughout much of Europe.

The Crusades broadened European horizons and stimulated interest in luxury goods. Monarchs of new states wanted to acquire gold to strengthen their rule. The Renaissance promoted a scientific and practical view of the world. New technology such as the compass and astrolabe made exploration possible. With these changes, an exchange of goods and ideas between Europe and the Americas began. However, European diseases devastated Native American populations, American diseases spread to Europe, and Europeans became increasingly involved in the West African slave trade.

The political and economic changes that encouraged western Europeans to begin exploring the world would not have mattered had they not had the technology necessary to launch their expeditions. They needed navigational instruments that would enable sailors to travel out of sight of land and still find their way home. They also needed ships capable of long-distance travel across the ocean. By studying Arab texts, western Europeans learned about the astrolabe, a device invented by the ancient Greeks and refined by Arab navigators. They also acquired the compass from Arab traders. In the 1400s a Portuguese ship called the caravel incorporated all the necessary technology for long sailing trips. The Portuguese explorers became the first Europeans to find a sea route to Asia.

Christopher Columbus sought financial backing for a sea route to Asia. In 1492, King Ferdinand and Queen Isabella of Spain agreed to give Columbus the funding to reach Asia by going east around Africa, so he and his three ships—the *Nina,* the *Pinta,* and the *Santa Maria*—finally left Spain.

The arrival of European colonists in the Americas set in motion a series of complex interactions between peoples and environments. Native Americans taught the Europeans local farming methods and introduced them to new crops. The Europeans introduced Native Americans to wheat, oats, barley, rye, rice, coffee, dandelions, onions, bananas, and oranges, and other new citrus fruits, none of which existed in North America.

The French colonies were established to expand fur trade. The colonization effort grew slowly. The population of New France was increased by promotion of immigration. Enslaved Africans were imported to work plantations in Louisiana.

The Spanish colonies were established to gain wealth and spread Christianity and European culture. Their structured society was based on birth, income, and education. The economy was dominated by mining and ranching.

The Dutch colonies were founded to make money in the fur trade. Settlers from many countries populated New Netherlands. The need for laborers led to Dutch involvement in the slave trade. The territory eventually surrendered to Britain.

The British colonies were established as places to earn profits and to practice religion freely. They provided a place for the poor to start a new life. They offered the right to elect legislative assembly. The colonies were used as a source of raw materials and markets for British goods.

The New England Colonies

New Hampshire, Connecticut, Rhode Island, Massachusetts

In the 1600s, English Puritans feeling religious persecution and economic difficulties founded several colonies in New England. Puritan religious beliefs shaped the cultural history of the New England colonies.

Geography: Coastal areas with good natural harbors; inland areas with dense forests; poor rocky soil and short growing season.

Economy: Small farms, lumber mills, fishing, shipbuilding, and trade flourished; cities developed along the coast.

People and Society: Most people organized as congregations lived on farms; in the cities merchants controlled trade, artisans made goods, unskilled workers and enslaved Africans provided labor.

The Middle Colonies

New York, New Jersey, Pennsylvania, Delaware

After the English Civil War, economic, strategic, and religious factors led to the founding of seven new English colonies along the Atlantic seaboard. The middle colonies were part of these new colonies. A diverse economy supported many large port cities.

Geography: Fertile soil and long growing season; rivers ran into backcountry.

Economy: Colonies grew large amounts of rye, oats, barley potatoes, and wheat as cash crops to sell; cities developed on the coast.

People and Society: Wealthiest people owned large farms and other businesses. Most farmers produced a small surplus. Tenant farmers rented land from large landowners or worked for wages.

The Southern Colonies

Maryland, Virginia, North Carolina, South Carolina, Georgia

The southern colonies developed labor-intensive agricultural economies that relied heavily upon enslaved labor.

Geography: Favorable climate and soil for agriculture; wide rivers made cities unnecessary.

Economy: Tobacco, rice, and indigo grown on large plantations emerged as cash crops.

People and Society: Wealthy elite controlled most of the land. Cash crops required a large amount of labor, which was supplied on large farms by indentured servants and enslaved Africans.

American Revolution

In the early colonial period, roughly 1754 to 1763, the colonies grew accustomed to running their own affairs. When Britain tried to reestablish control, tensions mounted over taxes and basic rights. In 1775 these tensions led to battle, and in 1776 the colonists declared their independence from Britain. With the help of France and Spain, the colonists defeated the British in 1781. The Treaty of Paris in 1783 formally ended the war.

The American Revolution changed American society in a variety of ways. The following timeline highlights major events before and during the American Revolution:

1763: French and Indian War ended; Proclamation of 1763 issued. The Proclamation drew a line from north to south along the Appalachian Mountains and declared that colonists could not settle west of the line without the British government's permission. This enraged many farmers and land speculators, who wanted access to the land.

1764: Sugar Act and Currency Act passed. The Sugar Act changed the tax rates levied on raw sugar and molasses imported from foreign colonies. It also placed new taxes on silk, wine, coffee, pimentoes, and indigo. The Currency Act banned the use of paper money in the colonies, because it tended to lose its value very quickly. The act angered colonial farmers and artisans. They liked paper money precisely because it lost its value quickly. They could use paper money to pay back loans, and since the money was not worth as much as when they borrowed it, the loans were easier to pay back.

1765: Stamp Act passed; colonists staged protests. The Stamp Act required stamps to be placed on most printed materials, including newspapers, pamphlets, posters, wills, mortgages, deeds, licenses, and even diplomas, dice, and playing cards. The stamp tax was different from other taxes the colonies had paid to Britain. Parliament had imposed many taxes on trade, but the stamp tax was the first direct tax Britain had ever placed on the colonists.

1766: Stamp Act repealed; Declaratory Act asserted Parliament's supremacy. The Declaratory Act asserted that Parliament had the power to make laws for the colonies.

1767: Townshend Acts passed. The Townshend Acts were a series of new regulations and taxes.

1768-1769: Colonists boycotted British imports to protest the Townshend Acts. During the winters of 1767 and 1768, John Dickinson published a series of essays in which he reasserted that only assemblies elected by the colonists had the right to tax them. Additionally, Dickinson called on the colonies to become "firmly bound together" to "form one body politic" to resist the Townshend Acts. Less than a month later, the Massachusetts assembly began organizing resistance against Britain. Among the leaders was Sam Adams, a passionate defender of colonial rights and cousin of John Adams, who would become the nation's second president. Sam Adams was particularly skilled in uniting Bostonians of different social classes. The merchants of Boston and New York signed nonimportation agreements, promising not to import any goods from Britain. Philadelphia's merchants joined the boycott. As the boycott spread throughout the colonies, Americans stopped drinking British tea or buying British cloth.

1770: Boston Massacre; Townshend Acts repealed. In the fall of 1768, Britain dispatched roughly 1,000 troops to Boston to maintain order. On March 5, 1770, a crowd of colonists began taunting and throwing snowballs at a British soldier. The troops began firing into the crowd. When the smoke cleared, three people lay dead, six others were wounded, and two more died later. The shooting became known as the Boston Massacre. A few weeks later, Britain repealed almost all of the Townshend Acts. Parliament kept one tax—the tax on tea.

1773: Tea Act passed; Boston Tea Party held in protest. The Tea Act refunded four-fifths of the taxes the company had to pay to ship tea to the colonies, leaving only the Townshend tax. East India Company tea could now be sold at lower prices than smuggled Dutch tea. The act also allowed the East India Company to sell directly to shopkeepers, bypassing American merchants who normally distributed the tea. The Tea Act enraged colonial merchants, who feared it was the first step by the British to squeeze them out of business. In December 1773, tea ships arrived in Boston Harbor. On the night before customs officials planned to bring the tea ashore, approximately 150 men boarded the ships. Several thousand people on shore cheered as the men dumped 342 chests of tea into the harbor. The raid came to be called the Boston Tea Party.

1774: Coercive Acts passed; First Continental Congress met. The Coercive Acts were four new laws that were intended to punish Massachusetts and end colonial challenges to British authority. The first act shut down Boston's port until the city paid for the tea that had been destroyed during the Boston Tea Party. The second act required all council members, judges, and sheriffs in Massachusetts to be appointed by the governor instead of being elected. The third act allowed the governor to transfer trials of British soldiers and officials to England to protect them from American juries. The final act required local officials to provide lodging for British soldiers at the scene of a disturbance, in private homes if necessary. The First Continental Congress met in Philadelphia on September 5, 1774. The 55 delegates to the Congress represented 12 of Britain's North American colonies. The delegates were searching for compromise.

1775: Battles of Lexington and Concord; Second Continental Congress met. Americans who backed Britain came to be known as Loyalists, or Tories. Those who believed the British had become tyrants were known as Patriots, or Whigs. On April 19, 1775, fighting began on Lexington Common; eight Americans died and ten more were wounded. Paul Revere was captured, and William Dawes, a fellow Patriot, turned back. At Concord's North Bridge, colonial militia inflicted 14 casualties on the British. In retreat to Boston, the British suffered over

250 casualties and Americans suffered 95. Three weeks after the battles at Lexington and Concord, the Second Continental Congress met in Philadelphia. The first issue was defense. On June 15, 1775, the Congress appointed George Washington as general and commander in chief of the new army.

1776: Declaration of Independence signed. Despite the fighting, many Americans were not prepared to break away from Great Britain. However, as the fighting continued, more and more Patriots began to think the time had come to declare independence. On July 4, 1776, the Continental Congress issued the Declaration of Independence, declaring themselves the United States of America. The American Revolution had begun.

1778: On February 6, 1778, the United States signed the first of two treaties. In the first, France became the first country to recognize the United States as an independent nation. The second treaty was an alliance between the United States and France.

1781: War of Independence ended when General Cornwallis surrendered at Yorktown. In the spring of 1781, Cornwallis decided to invade Virginia. As long as the Americans controlled Virginia, he believed, new troops and supplies would keep coming south. In late April 1781, Cornwallis marched into Virginia, where he linked up with forces under the command of Benedict Arnold. They began to conquer Virginia. Cornwallis retreated to the coastal town of Yorktown. His retreat created an opportunity for the Americans and their French allies. When he learned of the French fleet, Washington canceled the attack on New York and led his forces to Yorktown. As the American and French troops raced south, the French fleet grew closer. With the French fleet nearby, Cornwallis could not escape by sea or receive supplies. On September 28, 1781, American and French forces surrounded Yorktown and began to bombard it. Cornwallis began negotiations to surrender, and on October 19, 1781, approximately 8,000 British troops marched out of Yorktown and laid down their weapons.

1783: Treaty of Paris signed. In the Treaty of Paris, signed on September 3, 1783, Britain recognized the United States of America as a new nation with the Mississippi River as its western border. Britain also gave Florida back to Spain. France received colonies in Africa and the Caribbean that the British had seized from them in 1763. On November 24, 1783, the last British troops left New York City. The Revolutionary War was over, and the creation of a new nation was about to begin.

1786: Virginia Statute for Religious Freedom introduced. The statute declared that Virginia no longer had an official church and that the state could not collect taxes for churches.

Establishing a New Nation: Early Years and Continued Development

After the American Revolution, the new nation struggled to draw up a plan for government. Americans wanted to make sure the government did not have too much power. Eventually they came up with a way to balance federal and state power and to divide federal power into three branches. Promising to add a bill of rights helped win approval for the Constitution.

There were several challenges—and subsequent solutions—with establishing a new nation:

Problem: The newly independent colonies needed a central government.

Solution: The Articles of Confederation were adopted as the country's first constitution.

Problem: The weak central government created by the Articles led to diplomatic problems with other nations. The states began to act as independent countries to protect their trade rights.

Solution: Delegates at the Constitutional Convention adopted the Virginia Plan, which proposed the creation of a new federal government.

Problem: Opponents of the proposed new federal government feared that it would become too powerful.

Solution: The Constitution divided power between the federal government and the state governments and established three branches of power in the federal government.

Problem: Constitutional delegates feared that one branch of the federal government would become too powerful.

Solution: The Constitution gave each branch of the federal government the ability to limit the power of the other branches.

Problem: Delegates realized that the Constitution might need to be changed over time.

Solution: A system for making amendments was added, and the Constitution was ratified.

In the first government under the Constitution, important new institutions included the cabinet, a system of federal courts, and a national bank. Political parties gradually developed from the different views of citizens in the Northeast, West, and South. The new government faced special challenges in foreign affairs, including the War of 1812 with Great Britain.

Some of the more noteworthy figures of the new government included the following men:

- *George Washington:* Established legitimacy of the new government, created executive departments, favored neutrality, used troops to stop Native American resistance in the West.

- *Thomas Jefferson:* Republican leader; worked to limit power of national government, favored land ownership for all people, supported farmers over commerce and trade, negotiated purchase of the Louisiana Territory.

- *John Adams:* Federalist leader in favor of strong national government, supported neutrality; negotiated treaties with Britain and France to avoid war, angered farmer and landowners with taxes; angered political opponents with Alien and Sedition Acts.

- *James Madison:* Republican who favored neutrality, asked Congress to declare war on Britain to protect trade interest in the East and farmers and settlers in the West. Under his administration, the War of 1812 generated feelings of nationalism, and the Treaty of Ghent established fishing rights and boundaries with Canada.

Nationalism

After the War of 1812, a new spirit of nationalism took hold in American society. A new national bank was chartered, and Supreme Court decisions strengthened the federal government. The building of new roads and canals helped connect the country. Industry prospered in the North, while an agricultural economy dependent on slavery grew strong in the South. Regional differences began to define political life.

Americans developed powerful feelings of patriotism and national unity after the War of 1812. American leaders prepared an ambitious program to bind the nation together. The program included creating a new national bank, protecting American manufacturers from foreign competition, and building canals and roads to improve transportation and link the country together. The judicial philosophy of the Chief Justice of the United States, John Marshall, provided another boost to the forces helping unify the nation after the war. The wave of nationalism within Congress and among voters influenced the nations' foreign affairs as well. Feeling proud and confident, the United States under President Monroe expanded its borders and asserted itself on the world stage. The following key events helped establish nationalism in government:

- War of 1812 sparked national pride.
- Second Bank of the United States and protective tariffs were set up to promote the nation's economy.
- Supreme Court rulings gave federal government power over states.
- Spain ceded Florida.
- Monroe Doctrine established foreign policy.

Beginning in the early 1800s, revolutions in transportation and industry brought great changes to the North and nationalism in society was strengthened. Along with dramatic changes in transportation, a revolution occurred in business and industry: the Industrial Revolution. The following key events contributed to nationalism in society:

- Steamboats and railroads linked the nation's regions.
- The telegraph established fast, long-distance communication.
- Rural farmers and immigrants came together in northern cities to find work.

Sectional disputes eroded the spirit of nationalism that swept the country after the War of 1812. The rise of a new political party represented a disagreement between those who wanted to expand federal power and those who wanted to limit it. The following key events led to sectionalism in the country:

- South's agricultural economy relied on slavery.
- Northern leaders viewed slavery as morally wrong.
- Missouri Compromise pitted Northern leaders against Southern leaders.
- Disputed election of 1824 led to return to two-party political system.
- Congress voted almost strictly along sectional lines.

Reform

Reform was a key theme of the 1830s and 1840s. Political reform came with the growth of popular democracy. President Jackson's election symbolized the new power of common citizens. For many Americans, social or religious reform was a goal. Some wanted to end slavery. Others wanted to expand education or women's rights. Throughout this period, sectional rivalries grew more bitter.

The election of Andrew Jackson ushered in a new era of American politics. The American political system became more democratic during the Jacksonian era:

- Nominating convention replaced caucus system of choosing presidential candidates.
- Voting rights were expanded for white males.
- Andrew Jackson's spoils system favored common people.

The United States underwent dramatic social and cultural changes during the early and mid-1800s. Spurred on by a revival of religion and a heightened belief in the power of individuals, Americans engaged in reform efforts that sought to change American society, but in ways that upheld American ideals and values. Despite the reform movements, little changed for some groups:

- Women's movement gained attention but accomplished little else.
- Native Americans were driven out of the South.
- Nativism led to discrimination against immigrants.

The Second Great Awakening in the early 1800s increased support for many religious groups in the United States and inspired reform in the country:

- Commitment to religion swelled church congregations.
- New religions were established.
- American literature blossomed; romanticism and transcendentalism influenced art.
- Prison reform movement resulted in better facilities.
- Access to education was expanded.
- Abolitionist and temperance movements grew steadily.

In the midst of the nation's reform movement, a number of citizens embarked on a crusade known as abolitionism to end slavery in the United States. Abolitionist reformers challenged the morality and legality of slavery in the United States. Reform efforts further divided the country:

- Members of newly established religions were persecuted.
- Many Northerners opposed slavery but saw abolition as a threat to the existing social system.
- Some publishers of abolitionist literature were attacked.
- Southerners defended slavery as an economic necessity.
- The House of Representatives was pressured to impose a gag rule limiting debate on abolitionist petitions.

Manifest Destiny

During this period, from 1835 to 1848, Americans strove to expand the nation's boundaries. Many believed they had a "manifest destiny" to spread democratic ideals. Others simply wanted to go west to find a new and better life. In Texas settlers came into conflict with Mexico, while those going west along the Oregon Trail came into conflict with Native Americans.

In the 1840s, Americans headed west to the frontier states of the Midwest and the rich lands of California and Oregon. Latecomers to the Midwest set their sights on California and Oregon. Oregon was divided. Great Britain and the United States claimed parts of Oregon, but the two countries divided the territory without conflict. The area was almost completely British until American missionaries arrived in the 1830s. Large numbers of Americans sought farmland in southern Oregon in 1840.

In 1821, after a bloody struggle, Mexico gained its independence from Spain, and their new nation included California. So, the territory was part of Mexico, although Americans still settled there. The local California government invited foreign settlers but was suspicious of them. The United States tried to purchase California from Mexico, but Mexico refused. An uprising overthrew the California government, and troops secured the territory during the war with Mexico.

The Midwest was also settled. In the early 1800s, squatters settled land that they did not own in Ohio, Indiana, Illinois, Michigan, and Wisconsin. The Preemption Act allowed squatters to buy up to 160 acres of land each.

Settlers emigrated from the United States to Texas and fought Mexico to gain independence. Mexico invited Americans and others to populate Texas. Mexico passed strict laws against American immigrants, which led to Texas's war for independence. Congress voted to annex Texas in 1845, and Texas also voted for annexation. Boundary disputes in Texas, along with the American attempt to purchase the California territory, led to the start of the war with Mexico. The United States won the war and gained Texas, California, and much of the territory that is now the West and Southwest.

Civil War Era

The growing sectional crisis in the 1800s led to the Civil War, the most wrenching war in American history, with over 600,000 American casualties—the most of any conflict involving the United States. The peace that was forged after four years of internal conflict reunited the nation and ended slavery. It did not, however, end the problems of racial inequality. When the nation gained new territory, the slavery controversy intensified. Would new states be slave or free? Who would decide? States that allowed slavery were determined to prevent the states from gaining a majority in the Senate. Political compromise broke down by 1860, and when Abraham Lincoln was elected president, many Southern states decided to secede.

Important Events Leading to the Civil War

Key events of the 1850s led to the Civil War:

- California entered the Union as a free state, giving free states a Senate majority.
- Fugitive Slave Act passed to help Southerners recover enslaved people who escaped to the North; act caused outrage in North.
- *Uncle Tom's Cabin* was published, angering many Southerners.

The passing of the Kansas-Nebraska Act heightened tensions:

- Angered Northerners by repealing the Missouri Compromise.
- Popular sovereignty regarding the slavery issue led to violence in "Bleeding Kansas."
- Republican Party was formed by former Whigs and member of Free-Soil Party.
- *Dred Scott* decision by Southern-dominated Supreme Court angered Northerners.
- Debates in Senate over Kansas led to caning of Charles Sumner.
- Events in Kansas angered John Brown, who then raided Harpers Ferry.

The election of 1860 added to the tension:

- Democratic Party split between North and South.
- Republicans nominated eventual winner Abraham Lincoln.
- Southern states established Confederacy in February 1861.
- Fort Sumter fired upon in April 1861, starting the Civil War.

Military Campaigns

The Civil War was a milestone in American history. The four-year-long struggle determined the nation's future. With the North's victory, slavery was abolished. During the war, the Northern economy grew stronger, while the Southern economy stagnated. Military innovations, including the expanded use of railroads and the telegraph, coupled with a general conscription, made the Civil War the first "modern" war.

The major military campaigns during the Civil War included:

1861

July: The Battle of Bull Run (Manassas) demonstrated that the war would not be over quickly.

September: Ulysses S. Grant, commander in chief of the Union army, led troops into Kentucky and Missouri.

1862

March: Two ironclad ships, the *Monitor* and the *Virginia,* battled to a draw.

April: The Battle of Shiloh made General Grant well known.

May: Union forces captured New Orleans.

September: The Battle of Antietam marked the bloodiest one-day battle in U.S. history.

1863

July: The Battle of Gettysburg turned the tide of war in favor of the Union.

1864

May: Grant and Robert E. Lee, commander in chief of the Confederate army, met in the Battle in the Wilderness and at Spotsylvania.

June: Grant and Lee battled at Cold Harbor.

September: Atlanta fell.

November: Union general William Sherman began his destructive March to the Sea.

1865

April 11: Lee surrendered to Grant at Appomattox Courthouse.

Domestic and Foreign Affairs

The Civil War brought great changes to the lives of soldiers and civilians alike. Many changes took place on the domestic front as well as with foreign affairs. Although the Civil War strengthened the federal government and ended slavery, it left the South socially and economically weakened. Despite the fact that the country was independent, there were still tensions between Great Britain and United States.

The major domestic and foreign affairs during the Civil War included:

1861

April: Elizabeth Blackwell started the nation's first training program for nurses.

President Lincoln ordered a blockade of all Confederate ports.

November: The *Trent* Affair increased tension between Great Britain and the United States.

1862

April: The South introduced conscription for military service.

1863

January: Lincoln's Emancipation Proclamation went into effect.

April: Food shortages in the South led to rioting.

November: Lincoln delivered the Gettysburg Address.

1864

March: Lincoln promoted Ulysses S. Grant to general-in-chief of the Union army.

November: Lincoln was reelected president.

1865

January: The thirteenth Amendment to the Constitution, banning slavery in the United States, passed the House of Representatives.

April 14: John Wilkes Booth assassinated Lincoln.

Following the turmoil of the Civil War and the subsequent Reconstruction, the United States began its transformation from a rural nation to an industrial, urban nation. This change spurred the growth of cities, the development of big business, and the rise of new technologies such as the railroads. New social pressures, including increased immigration, unionization movements, and the Populist movements in politics, characterized the period from 1865 to 1900 as well.

Emergence of the Modern United States

After the Civil War, a dynamic period in American history began with the settlement of the West. The lives of western miners, farmers, and ranchers were often filled with great hardships, but the wave of American settlers continued. Railroads hastened this migration west. During this period, many Native Americans lost their homelands and their way of life.

Miners and ranchers settled large areas of the West. People migrated to the West in search of economic opportunity. The discovery of gold, silver, and copper attracted settlers to Colorado, the Dakota Territory, Nevada, and Montana. Growth of cattle and sheep ranching attracted settlers to Texas, Montana, Wyoming, and other western areas. Railroads provided an easy way to ship sheep and cattle to Eastern markets.

After 1865, settlers staked out homesteads and began farming the Great Plains. The need for new farming techniques led to several technological innovations. Cheap land available through the Homestead Act encouraged settlement. Farming technology and climate moderation made the Great Plains into the Wheat Belt. Railroads brought scarce timber and coal to the Great Plains.

The settlement of the West dramatically changed the way of life of the Plains Indians. Some Native American groups fought the federal government in an attempt to keep their ancestral homelands. The federal government forced Plains Indians off their lands with the promise of receiving new land. White settlers moved onto lands promised to Native Americans. The widespread slaughter of buffalo by white men destroyed a major part of Native American way of life. Railroads helped displace Native Americans by moving settlers west, taking lands, and promoting buffalo slaughter.

Industrialization

American industry grew after the Civil War, bringing revolutionary changes to American society. Several factors were behind the industrialization: abundant natural resources, cheap immigrant labor force, high tariffs that reduced foreign goods, and national communication and transportation networks.

After the Civil War, big business assumed a more prominent role in American life. Large national corporations formed in the United States in the mid-1800s and contributed to greater production. At this time, there was little or no government intervention; there was a development of pools, trusts, holding companies, and monopolies; small businesses could not compete with economies-of-scale of large businesses; and the practices of some big businesses sometimes limited competition.

In an attempt to improve their working conditions, industrial workers came together to form unions in the late 1800s. People tried to balance the power of corporations with the needs of workers. The workplace was changing. Rural migration and immigration created a large, concentrated workforce. In large-scale industries, low wages, long hours, and dangerous working conditions were common. During this time, the first large unions were formed, but they had little bargaining power against large companies.

European and Asian immigrants arrived in the United States in great numbers during the late 1800s. Providing cheap labor, they made rapid industrial growth possible. They also helped populate the growing cities. The immigrants' presence affected both urban politics and labor unions. Reactions to immigrants and to an urban society were reflected in new political organizations and in literature and philosophy.

Political Parties

During the late 1800s, political parties often focused on party competition rather than on important issues. Rural Americans were suffering economically, and they began to organize to obtain relief. Many states passed laws segregating African Americans and limiting their voting rights.

The Republican Party, which appealed to rural and small-town voters, was popular in the North and the Midwest. The party was split over civil service reform. It favored higher tariffs and the gold standard.

The Democratic Party was strongly supported by Southerners, immigrants, and urban workers. It supported civil service reform, cutting tariffs, and regulating interstate commerce. The party was split over silver coinage.

In the late 1890s an independent political movement called populism emerged to challenge the two major parties. Currency and credit problems led to the rise of the Populist movement. Populists sought government control over business to protect farmers. They supported national control of railroads, increased money supply, and direct election of U.S. senators. Support of the party declined when the gold crisis was resolved. The Populist Party lost presidential elections but inspired reforms that were later adopted.

Progressive Era and World War I Through the New Deal

As the United States entered the twentieth century, it grew to become a world power. While the nation was expanding its territory into other parts of the world, conditions at home gave rise to a widespread Progressive movement. This movement worked for various reforms in government, business, and society. While Americans focused on their own country, Europe slid into a devastating world war that eventually involved the United States as well.

During the late 1800s and early 1900s, economic and military competition from world powers convinced the United States it must become a world power. The United States became an empire when it acquired the Philippines and territory in the Caribbean. American influence in Central and South America grew as the United States took a more active role in Latin American affairs.

U.S. actions in the Pacific included the following:

- Expanded Chinese and Japanese markets.
- Annexed the Midway Islands as refueling depots for expanded navy.
- Built coaling stations on Samoan Islands.
- American business leaders led successful campaign for Hawaiian annexation.
- Victory over Spain gave U.S. control over Guam and the Philippines.

U.S. actions in Latin America included the following:

- At Pan-American Conference, invited Latin American countries to trade with the U.S.
- Supported Cuba's rebellion against Spain, leading to Spanish-American War; victory over Spain gave U.S. control over Cuba and Puerto Rico.
- Built the Panama Canal.
- Issued the Roosevelt Corollary, stating that the U.S. would intervene in Latin America to maintain stability.

Progressivism

Industrialization changed American society. Cities were crowded with new immigrants, working conditions were often bad, and the old political system was breaking down. These conditions gave rise to the Progressive movement. Progressives campaigned for both political and social reforms for more than two decades and enjoyed significant successes at the local, state, and national levels.

Progressives shared some basic beliefs:

- People could improve society by relying on science and knowledge.
- Industrialism and urbanization caused problems.
- Government should fix problems.
- To achieve reform, the government itself had to be reformed.

Government reform included:

- Commission and city-manager forms of government were adopted.
- Direct primary system let citizens choose office candidates.
- Initiative, referendum, and recall were adopted.
- The Seventeenth Amendment gave voters the right to elect senators directly.
- The Nineteenth Amendment gave women the right to vote.

Business regulation included:

- Interstate Commerce Commission was strengthened.
- Consumer protection laws were passed.
- Federal Trade Commission was set up to regulate business.
- Federal Reserve system was set up to control money supply.

Social reforms included:

- Zoning laws and building codes improved urban housing.
- Child labor laws were passed.
- Worker's compensation laws were passed.
- The temperance movement worked to ban alcohol.

World War I

The United States reluctantly entered World War I in 1917 after German submarines violated American neutrality. After the war ended, President Wilson supported the Treaty of Versailles, believing its terms would prevent another war. The U.S. Senate, however, rejected the treaty. It did not want the country to be tied to European obligations. Instead, Americans turned their attention to the difficult adjustment to peacetime.

Mobilizing for the war affected the Armed Forces and the domestic front, both of which led to postwar problems. When the United States declared war against Germany in April 1917, the army and National Guard together had slightly more than 300,000 troops, so Congress passed Selective Service Act, which required young men between the ages of 21 to 30 to register for the draft. World War I was also the first war that employed women, although only in noncombat roles.

To successfully fight the war, the United States had to mobilize the entire nation. The federal government created new agencies to mobilize the economy, draft soldiers, and build public support. The War Industries Board controlled war materials and production. The Committee on Public Information created war propaganda. The government worked with employers and labor to ensure production. Congress passed the Espionage and Sedition Acts to limit opposition to the war, and increased taxes and sold Liberty Bonds to pay for it.

As American society moved from war to peace, turmoil in the economy and the fear of communism caused a series of domestic upheavals. The postwar period proved a difficult readjustment period for the United States. The cost of living greatly increased. Economic problems led to racial violence and widespread strikes. The fear of communism led to the Red Scare and Palmer raids.

Postwar and New Deal

The 1920s was an era of rapid change and clashing values. Many Americans believed society was losing its traditional values, and they took action to preserve these values. Other Americans embraced new values associated with a freer lifestyle and the pursuit of individual goals. Writers and artists pursued distinctively American themes, and the Harlem Renaissance gave African Americans new pride.

Prosperity was the theme of the 1920s, and national policy favored business. Although farmers were going through an economic depression, most people remained optimistic about the economy. The middle class bought on credit the many new convenience products available. One of the most popular purchases of the day was the automobile, which had a major impact on how Americans lived.

Prosperity in the United States seemed limitless until the Great Depression, which began in 1929 and lasted through most of the 1930s. Overproduction and agricultural problems contributed to the economic catastrophe. President Hoover looked to voluntary business action and to limit government relief as solutions, but these efforts failed. Meanwhile, millions of Americans lost their jobs and life savings. Artists and writers depicted this suffering, and many people turned to lighthearted films to escape their difficult lives.

Unlike Herbert Hoover, Franklin Delano Roosevelt was willing to employ deficit spending and greater federal regulation to revive the depressed economy. In response to his request, Congress passed a host of new programs. Millions of people received relief to alleviate their suffering, but the New Deal (the name given to Roosevelt's policies for ending the Depression) did not really end the Depression. It did, however, permanently expand the federal government's role in providing basic security for citizens.

Several programs emerged from the New Deal. These programs involved finances and debt, agriculture and industry, work and relief, and social issues. In the area of finances and debt, the Emergency Banking Relief Act regulated banks, the Federal Deposit Insurance Corporation insured bank deposits, the Farm Credit Administration refinanced farm mortgages, and the Home Owners' Loan Corporation financed homeowners' mortgages. In agriculture and industry, the Agricultural Adjustment Administration paid farmers to limit surplus production, the National Industrial Recovery Act limited industrial production and set prices, the National Labor Relations Act gave workers the right to organize unions and bargain collectively, and the Tennessee Valley Authority financed rural electrification and helped develop the economy of a seven-state region. In work and relief issues, the Civilian Conservation Corps created forestry jobs for young men, the Federal Emergency Relief Administration funded city and state relief programs, and the Public Works Administration created work programs to build public projects, such as roads, bridges, and schools. A social "safety net" was also established with the Social Security Act, which provided income for the elderly, handicapped, and unemployed, and monthly retirement benefits for people over 65.

World War II

The rise of dictatorships in the 1930s led to World War II, the most destructive war in the history of the world. After the war, the fragile alliance between the United States and the Soviet Union collapsed into the Cold War—a period of intense political, economic, and military competition.

After World War I, Europe was unstable. Fascists led by Benito Mussolini seized power in Italy, and Adolf Hitler and the Nazis took control of Germany. Meanwhile, Japan expanded its territory in Asia. As the Nazis gained power, they began a campaign of violence against Jews. When Germany attacked Poland, World War II began. The United States clung to a position of neutrality until Japan attacked Pearl Harbor.

Axis Powers

The Axis powers were comprised of Italy, Germany, and Japan. In Italy, Mussolini's Fascist Party believed in supreme power of the state. Italy cooperated with Germany from 1936 onward. In Germany, Hitler's Nazi Party believed in all-powerful state, territorial expansion, and ethnic purity. They invaded Poland in 1939, France in 1940, and the Soviet Union in 1941. In Japan, military leaders pushed for territorial expansion. Japan attacked Manchuria in 1931, invaded China in 1937, and attacked Pearl Harbor in 1941.

Allied Powers

The Allies were the United States, Great Britain, and France. The United States passed Neutrality Acts in 1935, 1937, and 1939. It gave lend-lease aid to Britain, China, and the Soviet Union. The United States declared war on Japan in 1941. Great Britain tried to appease Hitler by allowing territorial growth. It declared war on Germany in 1939 and resisted German attack in 1940. Great Britain received U.S. aid through the lend-lease program and cash-and-carry provision. Like Great Britain, France tried to appease Hitler. It declared war on Germany in 1939 after Poland was invaded. France was occupied by Nazis in 1940.

Initially, the Soviet Union was part of neither the Axis powers or the Allied powers, but it played a significant part in the world war. Communists, led by harsh dictator Joseph Stalin, created industrial power. They signed a nonaggression pact with Germany in 1939. The Soviet Union received U.S. aid and eventually fought with the Allies to defeat Germany.

United States Joins the War

The United States entered World War II unwillingly and largely unprepared. The American people, however, quickly banded together to transform the American economy into the most productive and efficient war-making machine in the world. American forces turned the tide in Europe and the Pacific, and they played a crucial role in the defeat of Germany, Italy, and Japan.

Significant events in the Pacific led to the Allies' victory, lending to the transformation of the United States:

> **1941:** Japan attacked Pearl Harbor on December 7.
>
> **1942:** The United States defeated Japan in the Battles of the Coral Sea and Midway.
>
> **1943:** The United States launched its island-hopping campaign.
>
> **1944:** The United States retook the Philippines.
>
> **1945:** The United States dropped the atomic bombs; Japan surrendered on August 15.

The Allies' invasions and victories in North Africa and Europe were of utmost significance in the overall victory in World War II:

> **1942:** The Allies turned the tide in the Battle of the Atlantic.
>
> **1943:** The Allies invaded Italy; Germans surrendered at Stalingrad.
>
> **1944:** The Allies invaded Normandy on June 6.
>
> **1945:** Germany surrendered unconditionally on May 7.

While battles were ensuing overseas, several changes occurred on the home front:

1941: President Roosevelt forbade race discrimination in defense industries.

1942: WAAC (Women's Army Auxiliary Corps) was established; Japanese American relocation was ordered.

1943: OWM (Office of War Mobilization) was established; Detroit and Zoot Suit riots occurred.

1944: The case of *Korematsu v. United States* was decided.

1945: The UN charter was signed.

Post-World War II Period

After World War II, an intense rivalry developed between the United States and the Soviet Union—two superpowers with very different political and economic systems. This rivalry, known as the Cold War, led to a massive buildup of military weapons on both sides. The determination of American leaders to contain communism also led to the Korean War, from 1950 to 1953, in which over 36,500 Americans died.

The Soviet Union had two general goals in the years after World War II: to create a protective sphere of communist countries along the European border, and to promote the spread of communism. During this time, the Western Allies' goals were to contain the spread of communism by supporting capitalist democratic governments.

During the Cold War, the Soviet Union tried to obtain its goals while the Western Allies tried to hold back the spread of communism. In Europe, the Soviet Union occupied eastern European nations and saw that communist governments were established; the Western Allies expected free elections to occur in Soviet-controlled eastern Europe. In the Middle East, the Soviet Union sought access to oil in Iran, aided communists in Greece, and pressured Turkey for access to the Mediterranean; the Western Allies forced Soviet withdrawal from Iran and pledged aid to halt Soviet threats to Turkey and Greece. The Soviet Union had significant involvement in Asia: Communists seized power in China in 1949 and China and the Soviet Union signed a treaty of friendship and alliance. Communist North Korea invaded South Korea to start the Korean War, and the Chinese troops fought for North Korea. The Western Allies were also involved with Asia. They aided China's Nationalist government, and dedicated money and troops to establish a democratic stronghold in Japan. The United States' troops were sent to fight for South Korea in the Korean War. At home, the Soviet Union promoted development of high-technology weapons and surveillance while the Western Allies focused on the development of advanced technology weapons.

After World War II, the United States enjoyed a period of economic prosperity. Many more Americans could now aspire to a middle-class lifestyle, with a house in the suburbs and more leisure time. Television became a favorite form of entertainment. This general prosperity, however, did not extend to many Hispanics, African Americans, Native Americans, or people living in Appalachian Mountains.

More Recent Developments

From a presidential assassination to massive governmental programs, from the Vietnam War to the civil rights movement, the post-World War II decades immensely affected the lives of Americans. The nation struggled to put its social and political ideals into practice while fighting military wars overseas and social wars at home.

President John F. Kennedy urged Americans to work for progress and to stand firm against the Soviets. Cold War tensions and the threat of nuclear war peaked during the Cuban missile crisis in 1962. Kennedy's assassination in 1963 changed the nation's mood, but his successor, Lyndon Johnson, embraced ambitious goals, including working toward the passage of major civil rights legislation and eradicating poverty.

The New Frontier and the Great Society

John F. Kennedy encountered both success and setbacks on the domestic front. Some significant policies went into effect during this time period:

- Office of Economic Opportunity fought illiteracy, unemployment, and disease.
- Civil Rights Act of 1964 prohibited race discrimination and social segregation. (Even though this act was passed after his assassination, John F. Kennedy was instrumental in establishing it.)
- Voting Rights Act protected the right to vote.
- Medicare and Medicaid Acts provided federal medical aid to the elderly and the poor.
- Elementary and Secondary Education Act increased aid for public schools.

As president, John F. Kennedy had to confront the challenges and fears of the Cold War. At this time, the nation devoted much of its scientific and technological resources to competing with the Soviet Union. The United States was involved in a number of ways with its foreign policy:

- "Flexible response" policy maintained opposition to communism.
- U.S. pledged aid to struggling Latin American nations.
- Peace Corps offered humanitarian aid in poor countries.
- Nuclear Test Ban Treaty with the Soviet Union eased Cold War tensions.

Several Supreme Court rulings added to the New Frontier—President Kennedy's efforts to implement a legislative agenda to increase aid to education, provide health insurance to the elderly, create a Department of Urban Affairs, and help migrant workers. More rulings added to the Great Society—President Johnson's vision of the more perfect and equitable society the United States could and should become. The following court rulings were significant to these efforts:

- *Reynolds v. Sims* boosted voting power of urban dwellers, including many minorities.
- Extension of due process gave more protection to people accused of crimes.
- Supreme Court ruled that states could not require prayer and Bible readings in public schools.

Major Events in the Civil Rights Movement

In the 1950s, African Americans and other supporters of civil rights challenged segregation in the United States, so they began a movement to win greater social equality. African American citizens and white supporters created organizations that directed protests, targeted specific inequalities, and attracted the attention of the mass media and the government. Because of national television coverage, the civil rights movement gained momentum in the early 1960s. In the mid-1960s, civil rights leaders began to understand that merely winning political rights for African Americans would not address the problem of African American's economic status, so the civil rights movement tried to address the persistent economic inequality of African Americans.

The following timeline presents significant events in the civil rights movement:

1954: *Brown v. Board of Education* attacked school segregation; separate-but-equal doctrine was ruled unconstitutional.

1955: Rosa Parks inspired Montgomery bus boycott.

1957: Southern Christian Leadership Conference (SCLC) was formed to fight segregation and encourage African Americans to vote.

1960: Sit-ins began and spread to over 100 U.S. cities.

1961: Freedom Rides began.

1963: Birmingham demonstrations and the March on Washington helped build support for the civil rights movement.

1964: Twenty-fourth Amendment abolished poll tax; Civil Rights Act of 1964 outlawed discrimination based on race, gender, religion, or national origin, and gave equal access to public facilities.

1965: Voting Rights Act ensured African Americans of the right to vote; Watts riot sparked a five-year period of urban racial violence; splinter groups within the civil rights movement advocated more aggressive means of gaining racial equality.

1968: Dr. Martin Luther King, Jr. was assassinated; Civil Rights Act of 1968 outlawed discrimination in the sale and rental of housing.

The Vietnam War

From 1964 to 1969, American efforts to stop the spread of communism led to U.S. involvement in the affairs of Vietnam; it was a reflection of the Cold War strategy. After providing South Vietnam with much aid and support, the United States finally sent in troops to fight as well. American military procedures differed significantly from those of the Vietcong troops. The Vietnam War created bitter divisions among Americans. Supporters argued that patriotism demanded that communism be halted. Opponents argued that intervening in Vietnam was immoral. Many young people protested or resisted the draft. Victory was not achieved, although more than 58,000 American soldiers died. After the Vietnam War, the United States had many wounds to heal. Many Americans became more wary of their leaders and more reluctant to intervene in the affairs of other nations.

The Protests of the 1960s

Protest, sparked largely by the Vietnam War, characterized the 1960s. Young people often led the civil rights and antiwar movements. Some of them wanted to change the entire society and urged more communal, less materialistic values. Young people were not the only protesters, however. Using the civil rights movement as a model, women, Hispanic Americans, and Native American also organized to gain greater recognition and equality.

During the 1960s, many of the country's young people raised their voices in protest against numerous aspects of American society. While the protest movements challenged the opinions and values of many Americans, the courts protected the protesters' rights of self-expression under the Constitution. During the 1960s and 1970s, a large number of American women organized to push for greater rights and opportunities in society. Women organized to claim their rights and responsibilities as citizens and employees. Throughout the 1960s and 1970s, minority groups developed new ways to improve their status in the United States. African Americans, Hispanics, and Native Americans organized to fight discrimination and to gain access to better education and jobs. Environmental issues also became a significant concern for many Americans, inspiring a grassroots campaign to protect nature.

Societal Changes (1968-Present)

A reassessment of postwar developments marked the last three decades of the twentieth century. The Cold War ended and political boundaries were redrawn. The Unites States remained a global force, but the role of the federal government was diminished in the wake of scandal and a renewed conservatism. As the United States entered a new century, the nation continued to redefine itself. The country's social diversity posed new challenges and provided new strength to the nation.

The protests of the 1960s were passionate and sometimes violent. In 1968, the nation elected Richard Nixon president, largely on his promise to uphold the values of what he called "Middle America." In foreign policy, Nixon charted a new path with a historic visit to China. At home he introduced "New Federalism." In 1974 the Watergate scandal forced Nixon to resign. Presidents Gerald Ford and Jimmy Carter faced an economic downturn and a major energy crisis, respectively.

The 1980s saw the rise of a new conservatism. President Ronald Reagan, standing for traditional values and smaller government, symbolized this movement. While tax cuts and new technologies fueled an economic boom, Reagan embarked on a massive military buildup and expanded efforts to contain communism. During President George Bush's term, the United States fought the Persian Gulf War, and the Cold War came to a dramatic end with the fall of the Soviet Union.

During the 1990s, a technological revolution transformed society. Personal computers grew faster and more powerful; communications deregulation expanded cellular phone usage; the Internet provided a worldwide network of information; and biotechnology research increased knowledge of human genetics. During Bill Clinton's presidency, a new global economy emerged based on regional trade blocs; the ozone layer and global warming become major environmental issues; Clinton and Congress cut spending and reformed welfare and health care; the U.S. economy grew rapidly and the federal budget was balanced; and the U.S. tried to end violence in Haiti, the Middle East, and the Balkans. Despite the progress Clinton made, scandal and impeachment tarnished his administration. In 2000, after election results were disputed in Florida, the Supreme Court resolved the dispute, and George W. Bush won the presidency. He focused on cutting taxes, reforming education, and working on energy problems. On September 11, 2001, terrorists destroyed the World Trade Center and attacked the Pentagon, killing thousands of people. In response to those attacks, Bush organized a global coalition and launched a new war on terrorism. The War in Iraq ended the regime of Saddam Hussein.

Government/Political Science/Civics

The following topics are covered in the Government/Political Science/Civics portion of the test:

- Political theory
- United States government and politics
- Comparative government and politics
- International relations

Political Theory

The purpose of government is to maintain social order, provide public services, provide national security and a common defense, and provide for and control the economic system. In so doing, governments make decisions that are binding on all citizens, and government has the authority to require all individuals to obey the decisions and the power to punish those who do not obey them.

- **Maintain social order:** English philosopher John Locke (1632-1704) explained the social contract theory in 1690 in *Two Treatises of Government*. According to this theory, people need government to maintain social order because they have not yet discovered a way to live in groups without conflict. Governments provide ways of resolving conflicts among group members, helping to maintain social order because they have the power to make and enforce laws.

- **Provide public services:** Abraham Lincoln identified this purpose of government in 1854 by saying that government should do for a community whatever they need to have done to promote the general welfare, that individuals could not or would not do on their own.

- **Provide national security:** Government should protect the people against attack by other states or from threats such as terrorism. The government also handles normal relations with other nations.

- **Make economic decisions:** Governments use their power to reduce conflicts such as material scarcity. Governments intervene not only in domestic affairs but also in economic affairs of another nation. Governments pass the laws that shape the economic environment of the nation. They also may make choices that distribute benefits and public services among citizens.

Major Political Theorists

Many scholars have constructed theories that attempt to explain the origin of the state:

- **Evolutionary Theory:** Some scholars believe that the state evolved from the family. The head of the primitive family was the authority that served as a government.

- **Force Theory:** This theory states that government emerged when all the people of an area were brought under the authority of one person or group.

- **Divine Right Theory:** This theory presents the notion that a god or gods have chosen certain people to rule by divine right. People believed that the state was created by God, and those who were born to royalty were chosen by God to govern.

- **Social Contract Theory:** English philosopher Thomas Hobbes (1588-1679) was one of the first to theorize on the social contract. He wrote that in a natural state, no government existed. By contract, people surrendered to the state the power needed to maintain order. The state then agreed to protect its citizens. Hobbes believed that people did not have the right to break this agreement. John Locke took the social contract a step further. He wrote that people were naturally endowed with the right to life, liberty, and property. To preserve their rights, they willingly contracted to give power to a governing authority. When government failed the preserve the rights of the people, the people had the rights to break the contract.

Economic Theories

Governments around the world provide for many kinds of economic systems. All economic systems, however, must make three major economic decisions: what and how much should be produced, how goods and services should be produced, and who gets the goods and services that are produced. Each major type of economic system in the world—capitalism, socialism, and communism—answers these questions differently.

Capitalism

Capitalism emphasizes freedom of choice and individual incentive for workers, investors, consumers, and business enterprises. Pure capitalism has five main characteristics:

1. Private ownership and control of property and economic resources
2. Free enterprise
3. Competition among businesses
4. Freedom of choice
5. The possibility of profits

Capitalism developed gradually from the economic and political changes in medieval and early modern Europe over hundreds of years. In 1776, Adam Smith, a Scottish philosopher and economist, provided a philosophy for the system of the free market (buyers and sellers were free to make unlimited economic decisions in the marketplace). In theory, a free enterprise means that economic decisions are made by buyers (consumers) and sellers (producers).

Competition plays a key role in a free-enterprise economy. Today the American economy and others like it are described by economists as mixed-market economies, which are economies in which free enterprise is combined with and supported by government decisions in the marketplace.

Socialism

In socialism, government owns the basic means of production, decides how to use resources, distributes the products and wages, and provides social services such as education, health care, and welfare. Socialism has three main goals:

1. The distribution of wealth and economic opportunity equally among people
2. Society's control, through its government, of all major decisions about production
3. Public ownership of most land, of factories, and of other means of production

The socialists who believe in peaceful changes want to work within the democratic political system to improve economic conditions, under a system called democratic socialism. Under this system the people have basic human rights and have some control over government officials through free elections and multiparty systems.

Communism

Communism emphasizes no social classes, all property is held in common, and government is not necessary. German philosopher and economist Karl Marx (1818-1883) was a thinker and writer who was a socialist advocating violent revolution. He believed that in industrialized nations the population is divided into capitalists (or the bourgeoisie who own the means of production) and workers (or the proletariat) who work to produce the goods. He studied the conditions of his time and concluded that the capitalist system would collapse, because over time smaller and smaller groups of capitalists would control all means of production, and therefore, all wealth. Marx interpreted all human history as a class struggle between the workers and the owners of the means of production. In *The Communist Manifesto,* Karl Marx wrote that economic events would lead to communism.

In communist nations, government planners decide how much to produce, what to produce, and how to distribute the goods and services produced. This system is called a command economy because decisions are made at the upper levels of government and handed down to managers.

Political Orientations

A *liberal* believes the government should actively promote health, education, and justice. Liberals are willing to curtail economic freedom to increase equality; for example, by regulating business to protect consumers. In social matters, however, liberals believe the government should not restrict most individual freedoms.

A *conservative* believes in limiting the role of government, except in supporting traditional moral values. Conservatives believe private individuals, not the government, should solve social problems. They oppose government limitations on businesses and believe free markets ensure the best economic outcomes.

Moderates fall between liberals and conservatives. For example, a moderate may want the government to regulate business and support traditional values.

Libertarians support both economic and social freedoms—free markets and unrestricted speech.

United States Government and Politics

The United States Constitution is simple and brief. It establishes the structure and powers of government but does not spell out every aspect of how government will function. The Constitution rests on the following six major principles of government:

1. **Popular sovereignty**—Rule by the people. The government is based on the consent of the governed; the authority for government flows from the people.
2. **Federalism**—Power is divided between national and state governments. Both levels have their own agencies and officials and pass laws that directly affect citizens. (see more on federalism in the following section)
3. **Separation of powers**—Each of the three branches of government (legislative, executive, judicial) has its own responsibilities:

    Legislative branch: Makes the law; Article I, Section 8, states the expressed powers of Congress.

    Executive branch: Carries out acts of Congress; Article II grants president broad but vaguely described powers.

    Judicial branch: Interprets the law; Article III establishes Supreme Court and allows Congress to set up lower courts.
4. **Checks and balances**—Each branch of government holds some control over the other two branches. Congress passes laws. The president can check Congress by vetoing its legislation. This veto power is balanced, however, by the power of Congress to override the veto by a two-thirds vote of each house. The federal courts restrain Congress by ruling on the constitutionality of laws. This power of the judicial branch is balanced by the power of the president to appoint federal judges. This presidential power is balanced, in turn, by the Constitution's requirement that the Senate approve appointments. Checks and balances created a system of shared powers.
5. **Judicial review**—Courts have power to declare laws and actions of local, state, or national governments invalid if they violate the Constitution. The Supreme Court is the final authority on the meaning and interpretation of the Constitution. Because the Constitution is the supreme law of the land, acts contrary to it must be void.
6. **Limited government**—The Constitution limits the powers of government by making explicit grants of authority. The first 10 amendments set specific limits in the areas of freedom of expression, personal security, and fair trials.

Federalism

The Constitution divided government authority by giving the national government certain specified powers, reserving all other powers to the states or to the people. Additionally, the national and state governments share some powers. The Constitution denied some powers to each level of government. Federalism is not a static relationship between different levels of government. It is a dynamic concept that affects everyday decisions at all levels. Delegated powers are powers the Constitution grants or delegates to the national government. Three types of powers make up the delegated powers:

- **Expressed:** Those powers directly expressed or stated in the Constitution by its founders. Most of these powers are found in the first three articles of the Constitution. This authority includes the power to levy and collect taxes, coin money, make war, raise an army and navy, and regulate commerce among the states.

- **Implied:** Those powers that the national government requires to carry out the powers that are expressly defined in the Constitution. Implied powers are not specifically listed, but they depend on the expressed powers. These powers have helped the national government strengthen and expand its authority to meet many problems the founders did not foresee.

- **Inherent:** Those powers that the national government may exercise simply because it is a government.

The expressed, implied, and inherent powers of the national government are to regulate foreign and interstate commerce, coin money, provide an army and navy, declare war, establish federal courts below the Supreme Court, conduct foreign relations, and exercise powers implied from the expressed powers. Concurrent powers of the national and state governments are to levy taxes, borrow money, spend for general welfare, establish courts, and enact and enforce laws. Reserved powers for state governments are to regulate intrastate commerce, establish local government systems, administer elections, and protect the public's healthy, welfare, and morals.

Developing Federalism

Federalism has continued to define the roles of state and national governments. Throughout American history, there have been two different views of how federalism should operate. One view—the states' rights position—favors state and local action in dealing with problems. The other view—the nationalist position—favors national action in dealing with these matters.

The growth in the size and power of the national government has shaped the development of American federalism. The Constitution's flexibility has allowed the Supreme Court, Congress, and the president to stretch the government's powers to meet the needs of a modern industrial nation. The expansion of the national government's powers has been based on three major constitutional provisions: the war powers, the power to regulate interstate commerce, and the power to tax and spend. As the national government has grown and enlarged its powers, Congress has developed two major ways to influence the policies of state and local governments by providing money through various federal grants and by imposing mandates that preempt the ability of state and local governments to make their own policies. Today, as federal government loosens regulations, states are gaining responsibility.

Federalism, Public Policy, and Politics

Federalism determines whether public policy originates at the local, state, or national level, and it affects public policy making in two ways: it affects how and where new policies are made in the United States, and it introduces limits on government policy making.

Federalism is also involved with politics. Federalism lessens the risk of one political party monopolizing power, as each party has a chance to win some elections somewhere in the system. It increases opportunities for citizens of the United States to participate in politics at the local, state, and national levels. It also increases the possibility that a person's participation will have some practical effect at any one of these levels.

Civil Liberties and Civil Rights, Political Beliefs and Behaviors

Because critics attacked the proposed Constitution for not protecting the rights of the people, the founders promised to add a list of such rights. The first Congress quickly proposed 12 amendments and sent them to the states for ratification. In 1791, the states ratified 10 of the amendments, which became known as the Bill of Rights.

The First Amendment Freedom of:

> *Religion:* The *establishment clause* prevents Congress from creating a state-sponsored religion. The *free exercise clause* prevents the government from impeding the religious beliefs of Americans—but not necessarily the way those beliefs are practiced.

> *Speech:* Pure speech and symbolic speech (in most cases) are protected. Seditious speech (treasonous speech), defamatory speech (slander and libel), and "fighting words" are not protected.

Press: A free press is invaluable in a democracy to ensure that its citizens remain well informed of government actions. In general, the press is regulated when reporting on matters of national security or to ensure a fair trial.

Assembly: The right of assembly is closely related to the right of free speech. However, assembly in public areas must usually be cleared with a permit to ensure public safety.

Citizenship

Citizens are members of a political society—a nation. As such, citizens of the United States have certain rights, duties, and responsibilities. The U.S. government, then, draws its power from the people and exists to secure their fundamental rights and equality under the law. Duties of citizens include obeying the law, paying taxes, and being loyal to the American government and its basic principles. As participants in government, citizens have the responsibility to be informed, vote, respect the rights and property of others, and respect different opinions and ways of life. Concerned citizens must be willing to exercise both their rights and their responsibilities. A person who is born on American soil, born to a parent who is an American citizen, or naturalized, is a U.S. citizen. A person can lose citizenship through expatriation, by being convicted of certain crimes, or through denaturalization. Responsibilities of citizens include knowing about rights and laws, participating in political life, and voting.

Rights of the Accused

A major challenge for democratic political systems is dealing with crime and criminals. A crime is an act against a law of the state. It may also harm an individual or a person's property. On the one hand, society must protect itself against criminals. At the same time, individual rights must be preserved. Justice in a democracy means protecting the innocent from government police power as well as punishing the guilty. The Fourth Amendment protects people from unreasonable searches and seizures. The Fifth Amendment protects people from self-incrimination and from double jeopardy (being tried twice for the same crime). The Sixth Amendment guarantees the right to legal counsel. The Eighth Amendment prohibits cruel and unusual punishment.

Equal Protection of the Law

Many forms of discrimination are illegal. The Declaration of Independence affirmed an ideal of American democracy when it stated "all men are created equal." This statement does not mean that everyone is born with the same characteristics or will remain equal. Rather, the democratic ideals of equality means all people are entitled to equal rights and treatment before the law. The Supreme Court uses three tests—rational basis, suspect classifications, and fundamental rights—to determine violations of equal protection. *Brown v. Board of Education of Topeka* (1954) overruled the separate-but-equal doctrine. Civil rights movements throughout the 1960s and 1970s sought to end segregation and discrimination.

Challenges for Civil Liberties

Changing ideas, social conditions, and technology will always create new issues for civil liberties. Key issues today involve affirmative action, discrimination against women, the right to know about government actions, privacy, and the fight against terrorism. The affirmative action debate continues over whether minorities should be compensated for past injustices. Efforts to stop discrimination against women in employment, housing, and credit policies continue. Citizens' right to know and right to privacy sometimes clash with government's need for security and the need to protect society.

Political Parties

Political parties play a large role in the decisions made by government. In one-party systems, the party is the government. The decisions of party leaders set government policy. Two-party systems have two parties competing for power. Multiparty systems allow more than one political party. Several parties often combine forces to obtain a majority and form a coalition government.

In the United States in the late 1700s, two political parties—Federalists and Democratic-Republicans—formed, despite George Washington's warnings. Before the Civil War, there were conflicts over issues such as slavery, which caused divisions within nation's political parties; the Democratic-Republicans split into Democrats and Whigs. After the Civil War, Republicans and Democrats emerged as the two dominant parties. Today, third parties continue to impact the political scene, despite obstacles presented by the two-party tradition.

Political parties are organized at the local, state, and national levels. Functions of political parties include recruiting candidates for public office, educating the public about issues, running and staffing the government, rewarding party loyalists with favors, watching over the party in power, and encouraging compromise and moderate government policies.

Party nominations are often hard-fought contests. Historically, individuals have sought nomination for public office in one of four ways: caucus, nominating convention, primary election, or petition. Though election laws vary greatly from state to state, all candidates have reached the ballot through one or more of these methods. *Caucuses* are a private meeting of party leaders, used early in our nation's history and in some states today. *Nominating conventions* require an official public meeting of a party to choose candidates for office. *Primary elections* occur when party members select people to run in the general election; this method is most commonly used today. With *petitions,* the candidate is placed on the ballot if a certain number of voters signs a petition.

Interest Groups

An interest group is a group of people who share common goals and organize to influence government. Major categories of interest groups include business and labor groups, agricultural groups, environmental groups, public-interest groups, government groups, and professional associations. Most groups try to influence government policy by lobbying lawmakers, running publicity campaigns, and providing funds for candidates' election campaigns.

Public Opinion

Every elected official wants to know what the public is thinking. Public opinion is considered the ideas and attitudes that a significant number of Americans hold about government and politics; factors such as family, schools, peer groups, economic and social status, the mass media, and government leaders shape one's political beliefs. In America, most people fall into the categories of liberal, conservative, or moderate, depending on their basic beliefs about government and society. These categories affect citizens' opinions on various issues. Officials measure public opinion by meeting with leaders of interest groups and talking with voters, as well as through scientific polling methods.

Mass Media

The mass media include all the means for communicating information to the general public. Traditionally there have been two types of mass media: print media such as daily newspapers and popular magazines, and the broadcast media for transmitting words, sounds, and images. The relationship between the media and U.S. government officials is complex. They need to work together, but their jobs often place them in adversarial positions. Politicians want to use the mass media to help them reach their goals, such as convincing the public that their policies are worthwhile and getting re-elected. Politicians also want the media to pass on their messages just as the politicians present them. The president interacts with media through news releases and briefings, press conferences, background stories, leaks, and media events. For Congress, media coverage focuses on confirmation hearings, oversight activities, and the personal business of members. The Supreme Court receives less media attention due to the remoteness of judges and the technical nature of their work. The Internet helps citizens to gather information about political issues and government services and to communicate with legislators and government leaders.

Despite the limitations on radio pirates, the mass media in the United States have more freedom than anywhere else in the world. Such freedom has given rise to many diverse avenues of expression. Internet communications and cable television are among the fastest-growing forums. Government regulations are aimed at providing order, fairness, and access to media. The First Amendment protects freedom of the press. The Federal Communications Commission (FCC) regulates media content and ownership. The Telecommunications Act of 1996 updated regulations on cost, competition, and program content. Debates continue over regulation of Internet content and e-commerce taxation.

Comparative Government and Politics

There are more than 190 countries in the world, and each country's history, culture, economic needs, natural resources, and geography shape its government. There are three basic types of government: long-standing democracies, nations in transition to democracy, and authoritarian governments. Democratic governments take several forms. One of the most widespread is parliamentary government. In this form of government, executive and legislative functions both reside in the elected assembly, or parliament. Often the parliament selects the leaders of the executive branch of government, who are known as the Cabinet. In presidential governments, the executive branch is separate from the legislative and judicial branches. In authoritarian governments, citizens lack most civil rights, human rights abuses occur, and government criticism is restricted.

Major Regime Types

Governments can be classified in many ways. The most time-honored systems come from the ideas of the ancient Greek philosopher Aristotle. It is based on a key question: Who governs the state? Under this system of classification, all governments belong to one of the following three major groups:

- **Autocracy:** A system of government in which the power and authority to rule are in the hands of a single individual. This is the oldest and one of the most common forms of government. Several forms of autocracy exist. One form is totalitarian dictatorship, in which the ideas of a single leader are glorified. The government seeks to control all aspects of social and economic life. Another form is a monarchy, in which a king, queen, or emperor exercises the supreme powers of government. Absolute monarchs have complete and unlimited power to rule their people. Today some countries have constitutional monarchs who share governmental powers with elected legislatures or serve mainly as the ceremonial leaders of their governments.

- **Oligarchy:** A system of government in which a small group holds power. The group derives its power from wealth, military power, social position, or a combination of these elements. Sometimes oligarchies claim they rule for the people, and they may have some type of legislature or national assembly elected by or representing the people. These legislatures, however, approve only policies and decisions already made by the leaders.

- **Democracy:** A system of government in which rule is by the people. The key idea is that the people hold sovereign power. Democracy may take one of two forms. One form is a direct democracy, in which the people govern themselves by voting on issues individually as citizens. Another form is a representative democracy, in which people elect representatives and give them the responsibility and power to make laws and conduct government. In a republic, voters are the source of the government's authority.

Foreign Policy

Foreign policy consists of the strategies and goals that guide a nation's relations with other countries and groups in the world. The specific strategies that make up U.S. foreign policy from year to year and even decade to decade change in response to changes in the international environment, such as the collapse of communism. However, the long-term goals of that policy remain constant, reflecting both the nation's ideals and its self-interest.

Until the late 1800s, the United States practiced isolationism, avoiding involvement in world affairs. With the outbreak of two world wars in the mid-1900s, the United States practiced internationalism, becoming more involved in world affairs. Today, the country practices interdependence, in which key foreign policy issues include global economy and global terrorism.

The powers of foreign policy lie in the hands of only a few people. The president serves as the head of state and the commander in chief of the armed forces. People such as the secretaries of state and defense and the national security adviser influence the president's foreign policy. Congress has the power to declare war and appropriate money; Senate ratifies treaties and confirms diplomatic appointments. It is the duty of the president and Congress to make American foreign policy. Appointed officials in the executive branch, however, carry out foreign policy on a day-to-day basis. Two departments in the executive branch are primarily responsible for foreign policy and for national security. The Department of State, one of the smallest Cabinet-level departments in terms of employees, carries out foreign policy. The State Department keeps the president informed of international issues, maintains diplomatic relations and negotiates treaties with foreign governments, and protects the interests of Americans traveling abroad. The Department of Defense is the largest of all the executive departments both in terms of money spent and people employed. It looks after the national security of the United States by supervising the armed forces and assisting the president in carrying out the duties of commander in chief.

International Relations

International organizations play a key role in world politics. There are two types of such organizations:

- **Nongovernmental organizations (NGOs)** are made up of individuals and groups outside the scope of government. The International Red Cross is an example of an NGO. NGOs are funded largely by donations from private individuals and charitable foundations.

- **Intergovernmental organizations (IGOs)** are composed of members of national governments. The United Nations (UN) is the most significant example of an IGO with a global membership and mission. IGOs are created through agreements, usually treaties, negotiated by the member states. The powers of an IGO are established and limited by its members.

In today's interdependent world, citizens, national leaders, and officials in international organizations must increasingly band together to deal with global issues that affect a large part of the world's population and that cannot be solved by the actions of any single nation. Important global issues today include defeating terrorism, limiting the spread of nuclear weapons, promoting human rights, and protecting the environment.

Geography

The following topics are covered in the Geography portion of the test:

- The world in spatial terms
- Places and regions
- Physical systems
- Earth-sun relationships and climate
- Human systems
- Environment and society
- The uses of geography

The World In Spatial Terms

Geographers use a wide array of tools and technologies—from basic globes to high-tech global positioning systems—to understand the earth. These help them collect and analyze a great deal of information. However, the study of geography is more than knowing a lot of facts about places. Rather, it has more to do with asking questions about the earth, pursuing answers, and solving problems.

Latitude, Longitude, and Location

Lines on globes and maps provide information that can help you locate places. These lines cross one another, forming a pattern called a grid system.

Lines of latitude, or parallels, circle the earth parallel to the equator and measure the distance north or south of the equator in degrees. The equator is measured at 0 degrees latitude, while the Poles lie at latitudes 90 degrees N (north) and 90 degrees S (south). Parallels north of the equator are called *north latitude,* and parallels south of the equator are called *south latitude*.

Lines of longitude, or meridians, circle the earth from Pole to Pole. These lines measure distances east or west of the starting line, which lies at 0 degrees longitude and is called the *prime meridian*. By international agreement, the prime meridian is the line of longitude that runs through the Royal Observatory in Greenwich, England. Places east of the prime meridian are known as *east longitude,* and places west of the prime meridian are known as *west longitude*.

Every place has a global address, also called its absolute location. You can identify the absolute location of a place by naming the longitude and latitude lines that cross exactly at that place. For example, the city of Tokyo, Japan, is located at 36 degrees N latitude and 140 degrees E longitude. For more precise readings, each degree of latitude and longitude is subdivided into 60 units called minutes.

A *globe* is a scale model of the earth. Because the earth is round, a globe presents the most accurate depiction of geographic information such as area, distance, and direction. However, globes show little close-up detail. A printed map is a symbolic representation of all or part of the planet on a flat piece of paper. Unlike globes, maps can show small areas in great detail.

To create maps that are not interrupted, mapmakers, or *cartographers,* use mathematical formulas to transfer information from the three-dimensional globe to a two-dimensional map. However, when the curves of a globe become straight lines on a map, distortion of size, shape, distance, or area occurs. The purpose of the map usually dictates with projection is used. The curved surface of the earth cannot be shown accurately on a flat map. Every map projection stretches or breaks the curved surface of the planet in some way as it is flattened. Distance, direction, shape, or area may be distorted. Cartographers have developed many map projections, each with some advantages and some degree of inaccuracy. Four of the most popular map projections, named for the cartographers who developed them, are shown in the following pages.

Winkel Tripel Projection

Most general reference world maps use the Winkel Tripel projection. Adopted by the National Geography Society in 1998 for use in most maps, the Winkel Tripel projection provides a good balance between the size and shape of land areas as they are shown on the map. Even the polar areas are depicted with little distortion of size and shape.

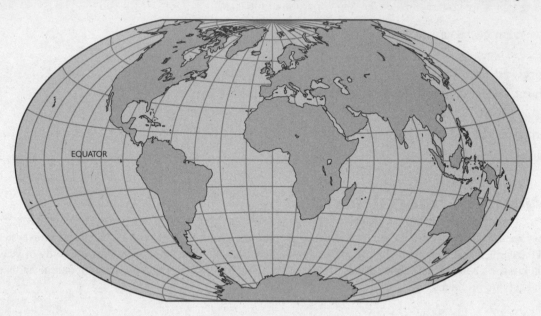

Winkel Tripel projection.

Robinson Projection

The Robinson projection has minor distortions. The sizes and shapes near the eastern and western edges of the map are accurate, and the outlines of the continents appear much as they do on the globe. However, the shapes of the polar areas appear somewhat distorted.

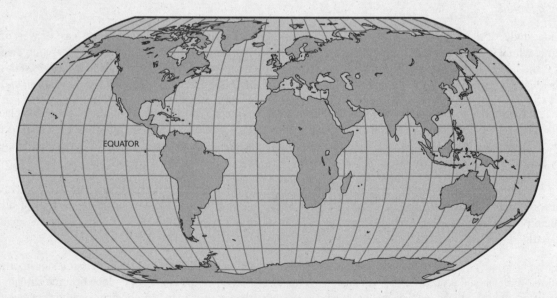

Robinson projection.

Goode's Interrupted Equal-Area Projection

And interrupted projection map looks something like a globe that has been cut apart and laid flat. Goode's Interrupted Equal-Area projection shows the true size and shape of the earth's landmasses, but distances are generally distorted.

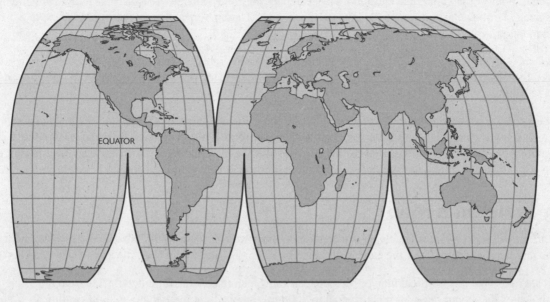

Goode's Interrupted Equal-Area projection.

Mercator Projection

The Mercator projection, once the most commonly used projections, increasingly distorts size and distance as it moves away from the equator. This makes areas such as Greenland and Antarctica look much larger than they would appear on a globe. However, Mercator projections do accurately show true directions and the shapes of landmasses, making these maps useful for sea travel.

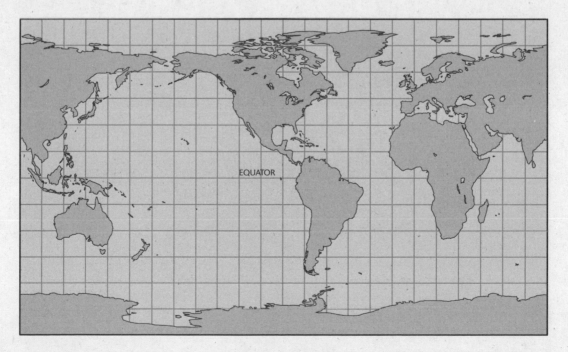

Mercator projection.

Types of Maps

A *physical map* shows the location and the topography, or shape, of the earth's physical features. Physical maps use colors or patterns to indicate relief—the differences in elevation, or height, of landforms. Some physical maps have contour lines that connect all points of land of equal elevation. Physical maps may show mountains as barriers to transportation. Rivers and streams may be shown as routes into the interior of a country. These physical features often help to explain the historical development of a country.

A *political map* shows the boundaries between countries. Smaller internal divisions, such as states or counties, may also be indicated by different symbols. Political maps often show human-made features such as capitals, cities, roads, highways, and railroads.

Maps that emphasize a single idea or a particular kind of information about an area are called *special-purpose maps*. There are many kinds of special-purpose maps, each designed to serve a different need. Some special-purpose maps such as economic activity maps and natural resource maps show the distribution of particular activities, resources, or products in a given area. Colors and symbols represent the location or distribution of activities and resources.

Using Scale on a Map

All maps are drawn to a certain scale. Scale is a consistent, proportional relationship between the measurement shown on the map and the measurement of the earth's surface. The scale of a map varies with the size of the area shown.

A small-scale map, like this political map of Mexico, can show a large area but little detail. Note that the scale bar for this map indicates that about one-half inch is equal to 300 miles, and a little more than one-half centimeter is equal to 300 kilometers.

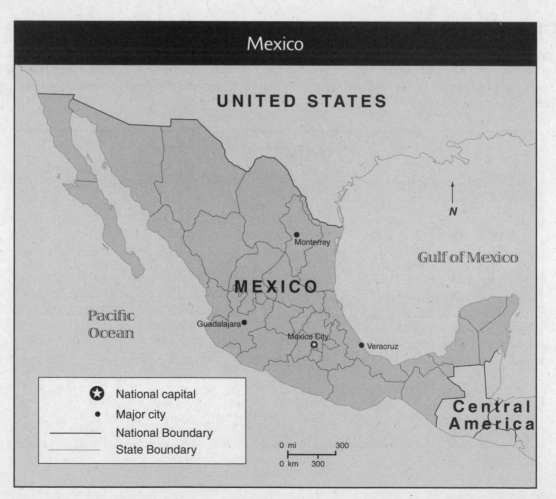

A large-scale map, like this map of Mexico City, can show a small area on the earth's surface with a great amount of detail. Study the scale bar. Note that the map measurements correspond to much smaller distances than on a small-scale map.

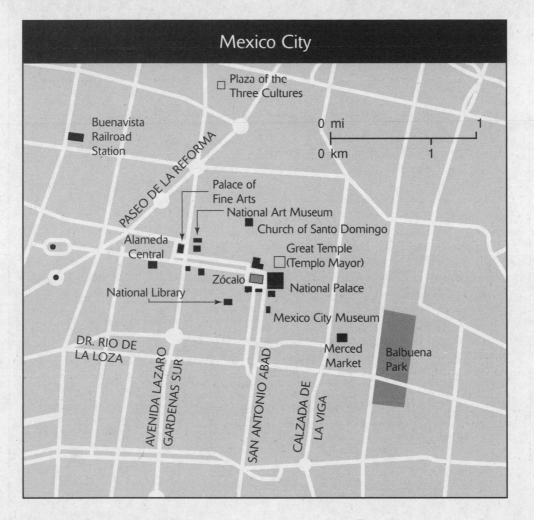

Places and Regions

Geographers study how the earth's features influence human life, and how humans affect the earth, by looking at population, culture, and political/economic systems, along with resources, trade, and the environment. Global population is growing rapidly, placing more demands on food production, but the rate of population growth varies from place to place.

A society's culture is made up of many elements, including language, religion, and government and economic activities. Cultures may change due to internal factors such as new ideas and inventions, or because of spatial interaction such as trade, migration, or war. Today cultural diffusion has increased rapidly due to industrialization and the Information Revolution. The governments of the world's nearly 200 independent countries manage their individual territories, their populations, and their global relationships. Different countries' economic activities depend on the resources available. Economic activities have led to increased pollution of the air, land, and water, causing damage to ecosystems.

Following are maps of major places and regions in the world.

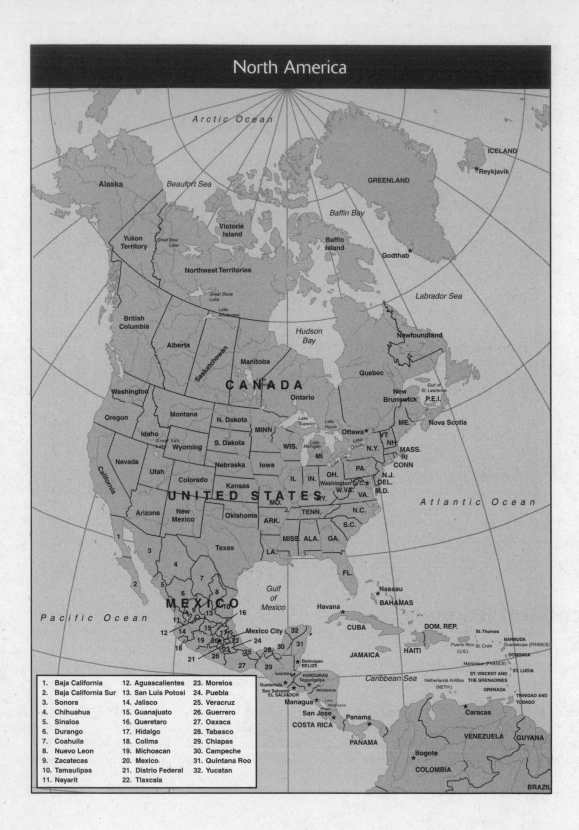

North America

1. Baja California
2. Baja California Sur
3. Sonora
4. Chihuahua
5. Sinaloa
6. Durango
7. Coahuila
8. Nuevo Leon
9. Zacatecas
10. Tamaulipas
11. Nayarit
12. Aguascalientes
13. San Luis Potosi
14. Jalisco
15. Guanajuato
16. Queretaro
17. Hidalgo
18. Colima
19. Michoacan
20. Mexico
21. Distrio Federal
22. Tlaxcala
23. Morelos
24. Puebla
25. Veracruz
26. Guerrero
27. Oaxaca
28. Tabasco
29. Chiapas
30. Campeche
31. Quintana Roo
32. Yucatan

South America

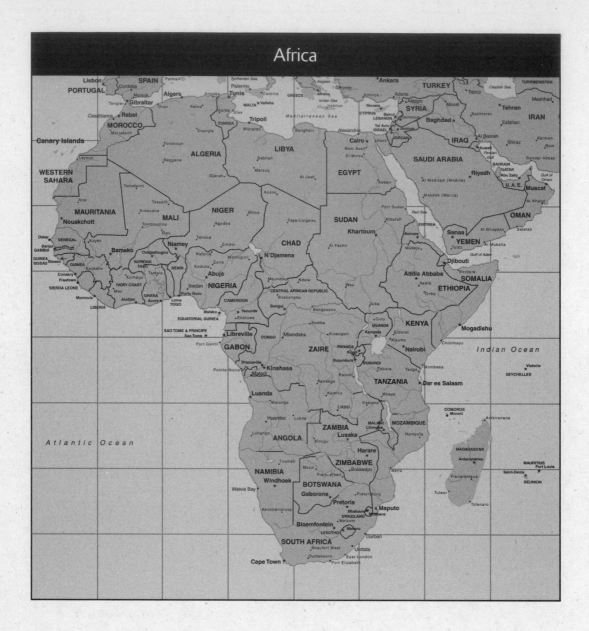

Europe

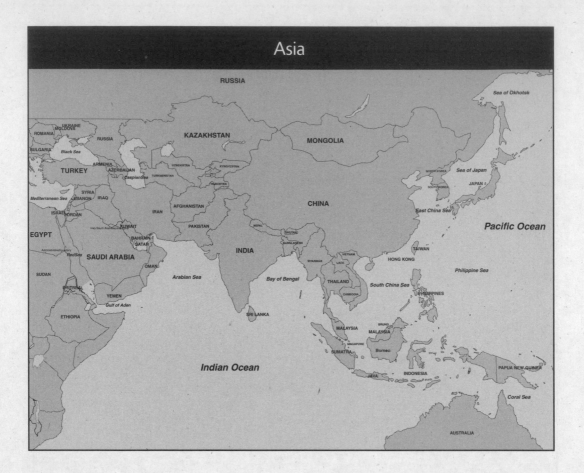

- **World population:** Population growth rates vary, posing different problems for different countries. The world's population is unevenly distributed. Large numbers of people migrate from rural villages to cities. People emigrate because of wars, food shortages, persecution, lack of jobs, or other issues.

- **Global cultures:** Language, religion, social groups, government, and economic activities define cultures. Geographers divide the earth into specific cultural regions. Trade, migration, and war change cultures. The world's first civilizations arose in culture hearths—early centers of civilization whose ideas and practices spread to surrounding areas..

- **Political and economic systems:** A country's different levels of government may be organized as a unitary system, a federal system, or a confederation. An autocracy, an oligarchy, and a democracy differ in the way they exercise authority. The three major economic systems are traditional economy, market economy, and command economy.

- **Resources, trade, and the environment:** Peoples are increasingly interdependent. Because natural resources are not evenly distributed, countries must trade. Governments can create or eliminate trade barriers. Human economic activities have led to pollution.

Physical Systems

In their work geographers analyze how certain natural phenomena, such as volcanoes, hurricanes, and floods, shape the earth's surface. The earth's systems are endlessly fascinating. Geographers look at how physical features interact with plant and animal life to create, support, or change ecosystems. An *ecosystem* is a community of plants and animals that depend upon one another, and their surroundings, for survival.

The earth is composed of three layers: the core, the mantle, and the crust. The crust is broken into more than a dozen great slabs of rock called plates that rest—or more accurately, float—on a partially melted layer in the upper mantle. The plates carry the earth's oceans and continents. Many scientists theorize that plates moving slowly around the globe have produced earth's largest features—not only continents, but also oceans and mountain ranges. Scientists use the term *plate tectonics* to refer to all of these activities (pushing up mountains, creating volcanoes, producing earthquakes), which may create many of the earth's physical features.

Internal forces cause rising of landforms and can be dramatic and sudden. Scientists believe that some of these changes in the earth's surface come from internal forces associated with plate tectonics. One of these internal forces relates to the slow movement of magma within the earth. Other internal forces involve movements that can fold, lift, bend, or break the rock along the earth's crust. Mountains are formed in areas where giant continental plates collide. They are also created when a sea plate collides with a continental plate. In a process called *subduction,* the heavier sea plate dives beneath the lighter continental plate. Plunging into the earth's interior, the sea plate becomes molten material. Then, as magma, it bursts through the crust to form volcanic mountains. In other cases where continental and sea plates meet, a different process, known as *accretion,* occurs. During accretion pieces of the earth's crust come together slowly as the sea plate slides under the continental plate. This plate movement levels off seamounts, underwater mountains with steep sides and sharp peaks, and piles up the resulting debris in trenches.

New land is also created where two sea plates converge. In this process one plate moves under the other, often forming an island chain at the boundary. Sea plates can also pull apart in a process known as *spreading*.

External forces, such as weathering and wind, glacial, and water erosion, also shape the surface of the earth. External forces usually wear away landforms and are usually slow.

Earth-Sun Relationships and Climate

The earth's position in relation to the sun affects temperatures on the earth. The rotation of the earth causes day and night. The earth's revolution and its tilt in relation to the sun produce the seasons. Global temperatures may be increasing as a result of human activity.

Latitude and elevation affect climate. Wind patterns and ocean current also play a key role in the earth's climates. Climate is affected by recurring phenomena such as El Niño, because of the trade winds and the westerly breezes. Landforms shape and are shaped by climate patterns. Large bodies of water bring cool or warm currents that cool or warm land; mountains cause rain shadows with heavy precipitation on the windward side and arid climates on the leeward side. Geographers divide the world into major climate regions. Each climate region has its own characteristic natural vegetation. Climate patterns change over time as a result of both natural processes and human activity.

Human Systems

Geographers also examine how people shape the world—how they settle the earth, form societies, and create permanent features. A recurring theme in geography is the ongoing movement of people, goods, and ideas. For example, migrants entering a long-established society usually bring different ideas and practices that may transform that society's traditional culture. In studying human systems, geographers also look at how people compete or cooperate to change or control aspects of the earth to meet their needs.

United States and Canada

Both Canada and the United States are home to various groups of native peoples and descendants of immigrants. Physical geography impacts the distribution and density of population in the United States and Canada. North America's settlements and its largest cities developed along waterways.

Native Americans were North America's earliest peoples. Europeans set up colonies in North America for trading, conquest, and religious freedom. The 13 British colonies won their independence from Britain in 1776 and formed their own republic, the United States of America. In 1867 the eastern provinces combined to form the Dominion of Canada. Canada today encompasses 10 provinces and 3 territories; it became an independent country in 1931. Industrialization and technology enable westward expansion and spurred social change.

The immigrant roots of the United States and Canada make these two countries diverse. Both countries have a heritage of religious freedom. Musical and artistic expression began with immigrants and gradually become uniquely North American. Health care is supported by the governments of both countries but in different ways. Both countries in the region have high standards of living.

The region's economy has shifted from reliance on agriculture and traditional manufacturing to emphasis on service and high-tech industries. Agriculture is a key economic activity of the region, although it employs only a small percentage of the workforce. Technology and improved agricultural methods have helped farmers overcome the limitations of physical geography and climate. Dependable transportation and advanced communications systems have helped make the region an economic leader. The United States and Canada are among the world's leading exporters. The region's two countries are each other's largest trade partners. The region also trades with countries and trade blocs around the world.

The United States and Canada are working to manage their rich natural resources responsibly. Acid rain, smog, and water pollution, among other issues, cause damage to the region's environment and affect human health. Cooperative efforts to address environmental concerns are making a difference in the region.

Latin America

Latin America's people descended from indigenous peoples: Europeans, Africans, and Asians. Latin Americans speak Spanish, Portuguese, other European languages, indigenous languages, and mixed dialects or patois. Latin America's population is mostly concentrated in coastal areas. Urbanization has created an imbalance in Latin America's population density. The region has some of the world's largest cities.

The Maya, the Aztec, and the Inca developed complex civilizations before Europeans arrived. Spanish and Portuguese colonization had a lasting effect of Latin America's culture. Most Latin American countries achieved independence during the 1800s and developed democratic self-rule in the twentieth century. The political, economic, and cultural legacy of colonialism still challenges Latin America.

Religion plays an important role in Latin American life. Educational quality varies throughout the region. As each country improves its economy, nutrition, and sanitation, people's health improves. Latin American traditional arts, music, and literature reflect the region's cultural diversity. Deep divisions between economic and social classes still characterize Latin American life. Latin Americans value family activities, sports such as futbol and jai alai, and holidays and festivals.

Latin America's economy is based on the export of agricultural products. A small group of wealthy families or businesses owns a large percentage of the agricultural land in Latin America. The economy of many Latin American countries is linked to one or two cash crops. The maquiladora system, trade agreements, and the international borrowing are attempts to speed the industrialization of many Latin American countries. Geographic and economic realities have presented obstacles to developing transportation and communications in the region.

A key challenge for the Latin America region is sustainable development. Damage to the Amazon rain forest has both local and global consequences. Slash-and-burn cultivation contributes to Latin America' environmental challenges. Latin America' urban environmental problems are a result of rapid urbanization. Solutions to the region's environmental concerns will come through cooperation among local, national, regional, and international governments and organizations.

Europe

Europe's cultures and ethnic groups are diverse. Physical features, climate, and resources have affected the region's population density and distribution. Industrialization, urbanization, and patterns of migration have helped define Europe as a region.

The contributions of Greek and Roman civilizations have influenced much of European history. During the Middle Ages, Christianity played a major role in shaping European societies. Trade, colonization, and immigration spread European cultures to other continents. After World War II, the Cold War divided communist-controlled eastern Europe from noncommunist western Europe. The European Union was formed to promote economic and political unity and stability among European countries. After years of communist rule, countries in eastern Europe face a difficult transition to market economies. Europe's economic activities include manufacturing, service and technology industries, and agriculture. Much of Europe has well-developed communications and transportation systems.

Most of Europe's various languages belong to one language family. Religion has influenced European values and has sometimes contributed to conflicts. Because of colonialism, European art and culture have profoundly influenced the Western world. Eastern and western European countries have differences in standards of living. Some European governments provide comprehensive social services to their citizens.

Acid rain is damaging Europe's forests, waterways, wildlife, and buildings. Air pollution from Europe's factories endangers public health and the environment. Greenhouse gases contribute to global warming. Pollution threatens the water quality and wildlife in the Mediterranean Sea and eastern Europe. European countries are taking steps to reduce pollution and clean up the environment.

Russia

More than 80 percent of Russia's population is ethnic Russian, and the remainder comprises about 100 different ethnic groups. Although more than 100 different languages are spoken in Russia, Russian is the official language. Russia is experiencing a population crisis, largely the result of health care problems. Russia's population is unevenly distributed, with 75 percent of Russians living west of the Urals.

Kievan Rus, an early Slavic state, grew out of settlements of Slavs and Varangians. Under the czars Russia expanded its territory and became an enormous empire. In 1917 a revolution overthrew Czar Nicolas II. Later that year, the Bolsheviks, under Lenin, seized power. In 1922 the communists formed the Union of Soviet Socialist Republics, or Soviet Union. In December 1991 the Soviet Union collapsed and was replaced by Russia and other independent republics.

Since the Soviet Union's collapse, many Russians have resumed their religious practices. Post-Soviet Russian schools are more open to new ideas and methods, but they face low budgets, overcrowding, and disrepair. Russia's artistic golden age began in the 1800s. After 1917, the Soviet government severely restricted certain kinds of artistic expression. Today Russians' respect for culture, traditions, and the arts has increased as a result of their new freedoms.

The Soviet economy was a command economy controlled by government agencies. Since the 1980s the Russians have been making the difficult transition from the Soviet command economy to a market economy. After the breakup of the Soviet Union, Boris Yeltsin encouraged privatization of state-owned farms and businesses. Transportation and communications systems must improve in order to support a strong market economy. To take its place as a full partner in the global community, Russia needs good international trade and strong political and economic relations.

Soviet leaders' drive for an industrial-based economy caused major and lasting damage to Russia's water, soil, and air. Russia needs to manage its use of natural resources properly in order to avoid more environmental damage. Radioactivity from nuclear waste, nuclear accidents, and nuclear weapons poses a grave danger to Russia's environment and its people's health.

North Africa, Southwest Asia, and Central Asia

Movement and interaction of people have created this region's ethnic diversity. The largest concentrations of population are in coastal and river valley areas where water is readily available. Urbanization has caused increased pollution and overcrowding, challenges that city and regional governments are addressing in many ways.

Early peoples in the region were among the first to domesticate plants and animals. Two of the world's earliest civilizations arose in Mesopotamia and the Nile River valley. Three of the world's major religions—Judaism, Christianity, and Islam—trace their origins to Southwest Asia. After centuries of foreign rule, independent states arose in North Africa, Southwest Asia, and Central Asia during the 1900s.

Islam and the Arabic language have been unifying forces in much of North Africa, Southwest Asia, and Central Asia. Many people in the region speak Arabic. Other major languages in the region include Hebrew, Berber, Greek Fasi, Pushtu, Kurdish, and various Turkic languages. The peoples of North Africa, Southwest Asia, and Central Asia have expressed themselves from the earliest times through the arts and architecture. Tradition, especially religious observance, plays an important role in everyday life in the region.

Although North Africa, Southwest Asia, and Central Asia have limited arable land, a relatively large percentage of the region's people work in agriculture. The oil-producing countries in North Africa, Southwest Asia, and Central Asia have experienced greater economic growth than other countries in the region. Expanded and more advanced transportation and communications systems are helping connect the region's urban and economic centers with one another and with the world. Interdependence is increasing among the countries of the region, especially in controlling oil production and prices.

Countries in the region have modified their environments to meet people's needs for water for drinking and irrigation. New technologies and destructive wars have subjected the region's environment to stress. People are working to revive areas damaged by past events.

Africa South of the Sahara

The uneven distribution of the 711 million people in Africa south of the Sahara is linked to the region's physical geography. The spread of AIDS has significantly impacted health and economic development in the region. Africa south of the Sahara is urbanizing faster than any other region in the world. Thousands of ethnic groups make up the population of Africa south of the Sahara.

The movement of different groups, including the migrations of Bantu peoples, helped shape the history of Africa south of the Sahara. From the 700s to the 1600s, powerful trading empires arose and prospered in West Africa. European colonization cut across traditional ethnic territories. Most of the countries in Africa south of the Sahara won independence in the second half of the 1900s.

The many languages of Africans south of the Sahara contribute to the diversity of the region. The peoples of the region are followers of Christianity, Islam, or traditional African religions. The various art forms created by Africans south of the Sahara have influenced cultures around the world. Although they have diverse lifestyles, most peoples in the region value family ties, and many live in extended families.

Most people in Africa south of the Sahara engage in subsistence farming, and most countries in the region depend on the export of one or two cash crops. Mineral resources are not evenly distributed across Africa south of the Sahara, casing economic imbalances among the region's countries. Africa south of the Sahara has taken actions to break its dependence on old trading patterns, and manufacturing is gaining strength in the economies of some countries in the region. New transportation networks and new forms of communication are changing the lives of Africans south of the Sahara.

Desertification, drought, and conflict have contributed to hunger in Africa south of the Sahara. Deforestation, hunting, tourism, and meeting the basic needs of people are all issues in the debate over land use in the regions. Africans south of the Sahara are working toward political stability and economic independence in the twenty-first century.

South Asia

The population of South Asia reflects a rich and complex mix of religions, languages, and social groupings. The diverse cultures of South Asia have made rich contributions to the arts. South Asia has a high overall population density, but population distribution varies from region to region according to climate and terrain. There is a sharp contrast between urban and rural life in South Asia. South Asia faces the challenge of improving the quality of life for much of its population. Even with the challenges it faces, South Asia benefits from its cultural diversity.

One of the world's first civilizations developed in the Indus River valley. South Asia gave birth to two of the world's major religions, Hinduism and Buddhism. South Asia was shaped by a series of invasions and conquests, including the expansion of the British Empire into the region. South Asian countries today face the challenges of independence and establishing new governments. Several South Asian countries have had female leaders after becoming independent.

Agriculture provides a living for most of South Asia's people, and it also provides cash crops for export. South Asia's mines and fisheries contribute to its exports. The region is experiencing rapid growth in the high-tech sector and continues to develop light and heavy industries. Tourism offers both benefits and challenges to the South Asian economy.

South Asia faces the complex task of managing its rich and varied natural resources. South Asia is seeking scientific solutions to its environmental challenges. Conflict in South Asia stems from issues of nationalism, religion, and ethnicity.

East Asia

East Asia's 1.5 billion people are made up of many different ethnic groups with a variety of religions, languages, and cultures. Population in East Asia is unevenly distributed. It is concentrated in urban areas, in river valleys, and on coastal plains. Japan, Taiwan, and South Korea are highly urbanized countries. Mongolia is predominantly rural. In China most people live in rural areas. Massive migration from rural to urban areas has caused farm labor shortages in parts of East Asia.

Confucianism and Daoism developed in China in 500 B.C.E. Buddhism spread from India throughout East Asia. China was ruled by a succession of dynasties until the early 1900s. Contact with the West forced East Asians to modernize. Revolutions and wars transformed East Asia in the 1900s. By the end of the 1900s, East Asian countries had important roles in the global economy.

Sino-Tibetan languages and Korean and Japanese are the region's main languages. East Asians often adopt practices from more than one religious tradition. Rising standards of living since 1945 have brought dramatic improvements in education and health care for some countries. East Asians have a long history of traditional arts and activities.

East Asian economies include market and command systems, as well as a mix of both. East Asia was once mainly agricultural, but trade and industry have brought prosperity and economic growth to most of its countries. Most Chinese work in agriculture, although industry and commerce are thriving in certain areas as a result of government-sponsored economic reforms. Japan is East Asia's leading industrial country, followed by Taiwan and South Korea. Trade and business investments bring together capitalist and communist countries in East Asia.

Rapid industrial growth in East Asia has caused environmental challenges that were ignored for decades. Japan, with its strict anti-pollution laws, has become a global leader in protecting and cleaning up the environment. China's economic development and the needs of its large population have a decisive impact on the environment. East Asia is subject to natural disasters such as flooding, earthquakes, tsunamis, and typhoons. Human activities in East Asia such as clear-cutting forests, farming, and mining have caused environmental disasters such as erosion, desertification, and flooding.

Southeast Asia

Southeast Asia has a diversity of ethnic and cultural groups. Most Southeast Asians live either in river valley lowlands or on coastal plains. Southeast Asian cities are growing rapidly as a result of migration from rural to urban areas. Since the 1970s, large numbers of Southeast Asians have migrated to escape political oppression and economic distress.

Southeast Asia's early empires and kingdoms controlled shipping and trade that linked East Asia, South Asia, and Southwest Asia. European countries colonized all of Southeast Asia except Thailand (Siam). All of the region's countries are now independent. During the late 1900s, political conflict between communist and noncommunist forces divided much of Southeast Asia.

Southeast Asian culture reflects the ways of life of peoples who migrated from other regions as well as those of indigenous peoples. Buddhism, Hinduism, and Islam greatly influenced Southeast Asian art, architecture, drama, and celebrations. In spite of rapid population growth, Southeast Asia's economic development has led to many improvements in the region's quality of life.

Agriculture is the leading economic activity in Southeast Asia. The countries of the region are industrializing at different rates, which causes great variation in economies, occupations, transportation, and communications. Through the Association of Southeast Asian Nations (ASEAN) and other organizations that were formed to promote regional development and trade, the countries of Southeast Asia are becoming more interdependent.

Volcanic eruptions, flash floods, and typhoons have serious effects on Southeast Asians' lives. Industrialization and economic development in Southeast Asia often result in the pollution of air, land, and water. The region's countries are taking steps to protect the environment.

Australia, Oceania, and Antarctica

Many different peoples settled in the South Pacific, resulting in diverse cultures and lifestyles. The population of the South Pacific is unevenly distributed because both the physical geography and the climate differ dramatically from place to place and because many areas cannot support life. Migration between and within South Pacific countries has influenced population patterns and caused a blending of cultures.

Many of the area's earliest inhabitants came from Southeast Asia and survived by hunting, gathering, and, in some cases, farming. European countries were attracted to the area by its plentiful raw materials, rich fishing areas, and fertile coastal land. During the late 1800s and early 1900s, European countries, Japan, and the United States sought possessions in the region. Australia, New Zealand, and a number of Pacific islands are independent; a few island groups are still under foreign rule.

The culture of the South Pacific is a mixture of Western and indigenous lifestyles. Some people in the area still live in traditional villages; others live in modern urban areas. Modern technology helps provide services to people in some remote areas.

Agriculture is the most important economic activity in the region, although mining is done in Australia and some island countries. Manufacturing in Australia and New Zealand centers on food processing, and the rest of the region engages in small-scale production of clothing and crafts. The importance of service industries, particularly tourism, is increasing in the economies of the region. Transportation and communications technologies, such as air travel, satellite communications, and the Internet, are helping people in the region to overcome geographic obstacles.

Australia, Oceania, and Antarctica have many natural resources, but the region's environment is threatened by human activity. Governments and individuals in the region are focusing on balanced management of water resources, forest, land, and wildlife. Nuclear testing conducted in Oceania during the 1940s and 1950s has had a lasting impact on its people and the environment. Scientists are studying global warming and the thinning ozone layer to prevent potential risks.

Environment and Society

Human-environment interaction, or the study of the interrelationship between people and their physical environment, is another theme of geography. Geographers examine the ways people use their environment, how and why they have changed it, and what consequences result from these changes. In some cases the physical environment affects human activities. For example, mountains and deserts often pose barriers to human movement. In other instances human activities, such as building a dam, cause changes in the physical environment. By understanding how the earth's physical features and processes shape and are shaped by human activity, geographers help societies make informed decisions.

United States and Canada

Canada and the continental United States have similar landforms, shaped by similar geologic processes. Both have high, sharp mountains and dry plateaus in the west; rolling, grassy plains in the center; and lower, older mountains in the coastal lowlands in the east. The region's waterways, including rivers, lakes, coastal waters, and intracoastal channels, played a vital role in settling the land and continue to serve as commercial highways. The Continental Divide splits the region into two large drainage areas. To the east of the Divide, waters flow to the Arctic Ocean, to the Hudson Bay, to the Atlantic Ocean, or to the Gulf of Mexico. To the west, the waters flow into the Pacific Ocean. Glacial movement shaped much of the North American landscape. The geologic factors that shaped the United States and Canada also provided the region with a wealth of natural resources.

The region encompassing the United States and Canada experiences a great variety of climates. Some climate regions of the United States and Canada are influenced primarily by latitude. Wind, ocean currents, rainfall patterns, and elevation moderate the effects of latitude in other climate zones of the United States and Canada. Climatic factors cause hazardous seasonal weather patterns in the region, including spring and summer tornadoes, summer and fall hurricanes, and winter blizzards. The region's natural vegetation reflects its climatic variety, but human interaction with the environment has greatly altered natural vegetation.

Latin America

Latin America includes Middle America, the Caribbean, and South America. Latin America's physical features include high mountain ranges, less rugged highlands, vast central plains, and volcanic islands. The water systems of Latin America, especially the mighty rivers of South America, are key to human activity in the region. Although the region is rich in natural resources, geographic, political, and economic obstacles have kept resources from being developed fully or shared equally.

Much of Latin America lies in the Tropics; however, landforms and wind patterns give the region great climatic diversity. Tropical climates such as the tropical forest and tropical savanna are the most common climates in Latin America. The natural vegetation of Latin America consists mainly of rain forests and grasslands. The tropical highlands in Latin America include three vertical climate zones that are based on latitude and elevation.

Europe

Europe is a huge peninsula extending westward from the Eurasian landmass. Europe has a long coastline with many peninsulas and islands. Europe has a large plains region in its northern areas; mountains are found along the continent's eastern and southern boundaries. Rivers provide important transportation in Europe, linking the interior of the continent with coastal ports. Europe has important deposits of minerals, oil, and natural gas.

Warm ocean currents give much of Europe a milder climate than other areas at similar latitudes. Areas of western Europe with a marine west coast climate have generally moderate temperatures. Much of southern Europe has a Mediterranean climate, with mild, rainy winters and warm, dry summers. Europe's interior has more extreme seasonal temperatures than do areas nearer the sea. Both climate and human activity affect the natural vegetation of Europe.

Russia

Russia is the largest country in the world, spanning Europe and Asia. Russia's land consists of interconnected plains and plateaus and is bordered on the south and east by mountain ranges. Most rivers in Russia flow northward and are frozen for much of the year. Russia is rich in resources such as petroleum, coal, minerals and gems, and timber.

Most of Russia has a harsh climate with wide extremes of temperatures, which creates challenges in all aspects of Russian life. Russian winters are long and cold, and its summers are short and relatively cool. Permanently frozen subsoil, or permafrost, lies beneath much of Siberia. The vegetation in Russia is varied, with treeless tundra in the far north, densely wooded taiga in the north and central areas, and temperate steppe grasslands in the southwest.

North Africa, Southwest Asia, and Central Asia

North Africa, Southwest Asia, and Central Asia are located at the crossroads of Asia, Africa, and Europe. The region is a jigsaw puzzle of peninsulas and seas. Rivers feed the inland seas and supply irrigation to parched lands; their alluvial soil deposits enrich the land, especially in the Nile River valley and delta. The movement of tectonic plates forms mountains, moves landforms, and causes earthquakes in the region. The region contains much of the world's oil and natural gas reserves.

Rainfall in North Africa, Southwest Asia, and Central Asia varies widely. Most of the region contains arid areas. The four climate regions in North Africa, Southwest Asia, and Central Asia are desert, steppe, Mediterranean, and highlands. Natural vegetation in the region varies widely and is closely related to rainfall and irrigation patterns.

Africa South of the Sahara

Africa south of the Sahara is a series of step-like plateaus, rising in a few places to mountains and slashed in the east by a rift valley. High elevations and narrow coastal plains characterized by escarpments have made traveling to Africa's interior very difficult. The region's water systems include numerous long, large, or deep lakes; spectacular waterfalls; and great rivers that drain into expansive basins. Minerals and water are the region's most abundant natural resources.

Rainfall, tropical latitudes, nearness to the equator, ocean air masses, and elevation are the main factors influencing climate variations in Africa south of the Sahara. The region can be divided into four main climate zones: tropical rain forest, savanna, steppe, and desert.

South Asia

The landforms of South Asia include mountains, plateaus, plains, and islands. South Asia has three great river systems—the Indus, Brahmaputra, and Ganges—and the world's longest alluvial plain. South Asia has few significant oil reserves, but has substantial mineral deposits, including iron ore and mica.

South Asia has highlands, tropical, and desert climates. The monsoon is a seasonal change in wind direction that brings heavy rainfall to much of South Asia from June to September. South Asia's vegetation is affected by elevation, rainfall, and human activity.

East Asia

East Asia's location at the meeting point for tectonic plates leaves the region vulnerable to earthquakes, volcanic eruptions, and tsunamis. The region of East Asia consists of China, Mongolia, and North and South Korea on the Asian continent, plus the island countries of Japan and Taiwan. East Asia's rivers provide important transportation systems and support fertile farmlands. East Asia is rich in minerals, but they are unevenly distributed. Limited farmlands, long coastlines, and large populations have made the region dependent on the sea for food.

East Asia's natural vegetation tends to parallel the region's climate zones. East Asian countries rely on the summer monsoons, which bring more than 80 percent of the region's rainfall. Ocean currents affect the climates of coastal and island regions. Powerful typhoons form in the Pacific and blow across coastal East Asia in later summer and early fall. East Asia's varied vegetation includes needle-leaved and broad-leaved evergreen trees, tropical plants, bamboo, tea, mulberry trees, and grasses as well as tropical rain forest vegetation.

Southeast Asia

Southeast Asia's mountains were formed when the Indo-Australian, Philippine, and Eurasian tectonic plates collided. Straddling the equator, Southeast Asia includes the Indochina and Malay peninsulas, as well as the islands of the Malay Archipelago. About half of Southeast Asia's 11 countries are located on the mainland. The rest are island countries, except for Malaysia, which is both a mainland and an island country. Mountains and rivers dominate the region's landscape. The island mountains are part of the Pacific Ring of Fire. Rivers on the mainland of Southeast Asia are important for agriculture, communication, and transportation. Southeast Asia contains abundant natural resources, including fossil fuels, natural steam, minerals, and gems.

Monsoons cause two main seasons in Southeast Asia, one wet and one dry. Southeast Asia's major climate is tropical rain forest, although parts of the mainland and some of the islands have other types of climate. Humid subtropical climates predominate in Laos and in northern areas of Myanmar, Thailand, and Vietnam. Highlands climates are found in the mountains of Myanmar, Borneo, and New Guinea. Southeast Asia's lush vegetation is characteristic of tropical rain forest and tropical savanna climate regions.

Australia, Oceania, and Antarctica

Australia, both a country and a continent, encompasses mountains, central lowlands, and expansive deserts. Rich mineral deposits and productive farms and ranches contribute to the Australian economy. Oceania's thousands of islands extend across the southern Pacific Ocean. The islands of Oceania were formed either directly or indirectly by volcanic activity. New Zealand's' main features are two large islands with mountain ranges, rivers, and lakes. The country boasts rich soil and timberland. Antarctica is an ice-covered continent. While Antarctica may have important mineral resources, its key resource is the information it offers to scientists.

Australia generally has a hot, dry climate. Along the edges of the vast interior desert, the steppe receives sufficient rainfall for raising livestock. Only the coastal climates provide enough rainfall for growing crops without irrigation.

Oceania enjoys a warm, moist tropical climate. Most islands have wet and dry seasons. The amount of rain during the wet season determines whether shrubs and grasses or dense rain forests will grow. New Zealand's' marine west coast climate provides year-round rainfall, with temperatures that vary without being extreme. Antarctica's extremely cold and windy climate supports primarily lichens and mosses.

The Uses of Geography

Geography can provide insight into how physical features and living things developed in the past. It can also interpret present-day trends to plan for future needs. Governments, businesses, and individuals use geographic information in planning and decision making. Data on physical features and processes can determine whether a site is suitable for human habitation or has resources worth developing. Geographic information on human activities, such as population trends, can help planners decide whether to build new schools or highways in a particular place. Geographic information helps determine where to locate fire stations and shopping malls. As geographers learn more about the relationships among people, places, and the environment, their knowledge can help us plan and build a better future.

Economics

The following topics are covered in the Economics portion of the test:

- Microeconomics I: supply and demand
- Microeconomics II: marketing
- Macroeconomics I: institutions
- Macroeconomics II: policies
- International and global economies

Microeconomics I: Supply and Demand

Microeconomics is the branch of economics that deals with the specific factors that affect an economy, such as how particular products are marketed or the behavior of individual consumers. Consumers base their decisions to buy goods and services on anticipated satisfaction, price, and their incomes. Businesses set prices according to the profit desired, the demand anticipated, and the competition expected.

Demand

Demand represents a consumer's willingness and ability to pay for products or services. The *law of demand* states that as price goes up, quantity demanded goes down; as price goes down, quantity demanded goes up. Factors explaining the inverse relationship between quantity demanded and price include the real income effect, the substitution effect, and diminishing marginal utility—or how one's additional satisfaction for a product lessens with each additional purchase of it.

The Demand Curve and Elasticity of Demand

The downward-sloping demand curve signifies that as the price falls, the quantity demanded increases. Changes in population, income, tastes and preferences, and the existence of substitutes, or complementary goods, affect demand. The price elasticity of demand is a measure of how much consumers respond to a price change. If a small change in price causes a large change in quantity demanded, the demand for that product is said to be elastic. If a price change does not result in much of a change in the quantity demanded, that demand is considered inelastic.

The Law of Supply and the Supply Curve

The *law of supply* states as the price rises for a product, the quantity supplied also rises. As the price falls, the quantity supplied falls. The upward-sloping supply curve shows this direct relationship between quantity supplied and price. Four factors determine supply in a market economy: the price of inputs, the number of firms in the industry, taxes, and technology.

Putting Supply and Demand Together

In a free-enterprise economy, prices serve as signals to producers and consumers. The point at which the quantity demanded and the quantity supplied meet is called the *equilibrium price*. A shortage causes prices to rise, signaling producers to produce more and consumers to purchase less. A surplus causes prices to drop, signaling producers to produce less and consumers to purchase more. A price ceiling, which prevents prices from going above a specified amount, often leads to shortages and black market activities. A price floor prevents prices such as a minimum wage from dropping too low.

Microeconomics II: Marketing

Economists classify markets according to conditions that prevail in them. They ask questions such as: How many buyers and suppliers are there? How large are they? Does either have any influence over price? How much competition exists between firms? What kind of product is involved—is everyone trading the exact same product, or are they simply similar? Is it easy or difficult for new firms to enter the market? The answers to these questions help determine market structure, or the nature and degree of competition among firms operating in the same industry.

Competition and Market Structures

Perfect competition is a market structure with large numbers of buyers and sellers, identical economic products, independent action by buyers and sellers, reasonably well-informed participants, and freedom for firms to enter or leave the market. Perfect competition is a largely theoretical situation used as a benchmark to evaluate other market structures. Market situations lacking one or more of these conditions are called imperfect competition. Monopolistic competition has all the characteristics of perfect competition except for identical products. An oligopoly is a market structure dominated by a few very large firms in which the actions by one affect the welfare of others. The monopolist is a single producer with the most control over supply and price. Various forms of monopoly include the natural monopoly, the geographic monopoly, the technological monopoly, and the government monopoly. All private firms, regardless of market structure, maximize profits by producing at the level of output where marginal cost is equal to marginal revenue.

Market Failures

A market failure is a market where any of the requirements for a competitive market—adequate competition, knowledge of prices and opportunities, mobility of resources, or competitive profits—are lacking. Market failures occur when sizable deviations from one or more of the conditions required for perfect competition take place. Three of the five common market failures include inadequate competition, inadequate information, and resource immobility. Externalities, or economic side effects to third parties, are a fourth market failure. A negative externality is a harmful side effect and a positive externality is a beneficial side effect. Externalities are regarded as market failures because they are not reflected in the market prices of the activities that caused the side effects. Another form of market failure shows up in the need for public goods, where a market economy fails to provide public goods such as national defense and public education because it produces only those items that can be withheld if people refuse to pay for them.

The Role of Government

The Sherman Antitrust Act of 1890 was enacted to prohibit trusts, monopolies, and other arrangements that restrain competition. The Clayton Antitrust Act was passed in 1914 to outlaw price discrimination. The Robinson-Patman Act of 1936 was passed to strengthen the price discrimination provisions of the Clayton Antitrust Act. Public disclosure is used as a tool to promote competition. Any corporation that sells its stock publicly is required to supply periodic financial reports to both its investors and to the Securities and Exchange Commission (SEC). Banks are covered by additional disclosure laws and report to various federal agencies. Today, government takes part in economic affairs to promote and encourage competition. As a result, the modern economy is a mixture of different market structures, different forms of business organizations, and some degree of government regulation.

The Changing Role of Marketing

Marketing involves all of the activities needed to move goods and services from the producer to the consumer. In today's economy, marketing's sole purpose is to convince consumers that a certain product or service will add to their utility. Utility—the ability of any good or service to satisfy consumer wants—can be divided into four major types: form utility, place utility, time utility, and ownership utility. Through market research a company gathers, records, and analyzes data about the types of goods and services that people want. The first step in market research is performing a market survey. Before offering a product for national distribution, market researchers will often test-market a product.

The Marketing Mix

A marketing plan combines the "four Ps" of marketing: product, price, place, and promotion. *Product* means determining what services to offer with the product, how to package it, and what kind of product identification to use. In setting a *price,* a company has to consider the costs of producing, advertising, selling, and distributing, as well as the amount of profit it hopes to make. *Place* means determining where a product should be sold (such as through the mail, by telephone, in specialty shops, in department stores, in supermarkets, or on the Internet). *Promotion* is the use of advertising and other methods to inform consumers that a new product is currently available and to convince them to buy it.

Distribution Channels

Deciding what channels of distribution to use is another function of marketing. Businesses that purchase large quantities of goods from producers for resale to other businesses are called *wholesalers*. Businesses that sell consumer goods directly to the public are *retailers*. In the last 10 to 15 years, distribution channels have expanded due to the growth of club warehouse stores and direct marketing, including catalog shopping and e-commerce.

Poverty and the Distribution of Income

The distribution of income is measured by ranking family incomes from lowest to highest and then dividing the ranking into quintiles. The income earned by each quintile is then compared to other quintiles. The Lorenz curve shows that incomes are not evenly distributed, and that they are becoming less equal. Factors accounting for the unequal distribution of income include educational levels, wealth, discrimination, ability, and monopoly power. Poverty is determined by comparing the amount of income earned by families to measures called the *poverty guidelines*. The growing income gap is due to the increased importance of the service industry, the widening workers' skills gap, the decline of union influence, and the changing composition of the American family.

Macroeconomics I: Institutions

Macroeconomics is the branch of economics that deals with the economy as a whole, including employment, gross domestic product, inflation, economic growth, and the distribution of income. Macroeconomics operates on the level of huge aggregates like national production, employment, and the money supply.

Business Cycles and Fluctuations

Business cycles are systematic increases and decreases in real gross domestic product (GDP); unsystematic changes are business fluctuations. The two phases of the cycle are recession and expansion; a peak is when the expansion ends, while a trough is when the recession ends. The Great Depression of the 1930s was the worst economic decline in U.S. history; income distribution inequalities, risky credit practices, weak international economic conditions, and tariff wars all contributed to the Depression. Several short, mild recessions have occurred since World War II. Business cycles are caused by changes in capital and inventory spending by businesses, stimuli supplied by innovations and imitations, monetary factors, and external shocks. Econometric models and the index of leading indicators are used to predict changes in future economic activity.

Unemployment

Unemployed persons are identified monthly by the Census Bureau. The number of unemployed is divided by the civilian labor force to arrive at the unemployment rate. The unemployment rate does not count dropouts (people who have become too frustrated or discouraged to look for work), nor does it distinguish between full- and part-time employment.

There are several different forms of unemployment:

- *Frictional* unemployment is caused by workers changing jobs or waiting to go to new ones.
- *Structural* unemployment is caused by a fundamental change in the economy that reduces the demand for some workers.

- *Cyclical* unemployment is caused by swings in the business cycle.

- *Seasonal* unemployment is caused by changes in the weather or other conditions that prevail at certain times of the year.

- *Technological* unemployment is caused by technological developments or automation that make some workers' skills obsolete.

Inflation

Inflation is the rate of change in the price level as measured by the consumer price index (CPI). Terms used to describe the severity of inflation are *creeping inflation,* a relatively low rate of inflation, usually 1 to 3 percent annually; *galloping inflation,* a relatively intense inflation, usually ranging from 100 to 300 percent annually; and *hyperinflation,* the last stage of a monetary collapse, an abnormal inflation in excess of 500 percent per year. Generous credit conditions and excessive growth of the money supply allow demand-pull, deficit spending, cost-push, and wage-price spiral inflation to take place. Inflation erodes the value of the dollar, makes life difficult for people on fixed incomes, changes the spending habits of consumers and businesses, and alters the distribution of income in favor of debtors.

Macroeconomics II: Policies

A growing economy means an expanding economy, one that continues to provide more people with what they need. The nation's economic growth is the key to a better future for everyone. To stimulate the nation's overall economic growth, macroeoconomic policies are used.

Measuring the Nation's Output

Gross domestic product (GDP) is the most complete measure of total output. GDP excludes intermediate goods and secondhand sales, nonmarket activities, and unreported activities in the underground economy. Gross national product (GNP) is the measure of the total income received by American citizens, regardless of where their productive resources are located. Other measures of income are net nation product, national income, personal income, and disposable personal income, which appears as the take-home pay on paychecks. The four sectors of the macro economy are the consumer (C), investment (I), government (G), and foreign sectors (F). The output-expenditure model, GDP = C + I + G + F, is used to show how GDP is consumed by the four sectors of the economy.

GDP and Changes in the Price Level

A price index tracks price changes over time and can be used to remove the distortions of inflation from other statistics. The price index is computed by dividing the latest prices of the market basket items (a representative collection of goods and services used to compile a price index) by the base-year prices and then multiplying by 100. Three popular indices are the consumer price index, the producer price index, and the implicit GDP price deflator. Current GDP is converted to real GDP, or constant dollar GDP, by dividing the unadjusted number by the price index and then multiplying by 100.

GDP and Population

The rate at which population grows influences GDP and economic growth in several ways. First, for an economy to grow, its factors of production must also grow or become more productive. One of the factors of production, labor, is closely tied to the size of the population. Second, changes in population can distort some macroeconomic measures such as GDP and GNP, which is why they are often expressed on a per-capital, or per-person, basis. If a nation's population grows faster than its output, per-capital output falls and the country could end up with more mouths than it can feed. Or, if a nation's population grows too slowly, there may not be enough workers to sustain economic growth. Population growth also affects the quality of life, especially in fast-growing cities such as Atlanta, Georgia.

The study of population involves more than a simple total of people. The annual population growth in the United States was more than 3 percent until the Civil War, but it has declined steadily to the point where it is now about 0.9 percent annually. The factors that contribute to changing populations are the fertility rate (the number of births that 1,000 women are expected to undergo in their lifetime), life expectancy (the average remaining life span in years for persons who reach a given age), and net immigration (the net population change after accounting for those who leave as well as enter a country). Projections by age and sex show the continuing influence of the baby boom, which will ultimately increase the dependency ratio. The racial and ethnic mix will change with population gains by Asian Americans, Hispanic Americans, and African Americans, so that the white component of the population will be a bare majority by the middle of the next century.

Economic Growth

Because of changes in population, long-term economic growth is usually measured in terms of real GDP per capita. Economic growth is important because it raises the standard of living, increases the tax base, increases employment, and helps the economies of other nations. Economic growth requires an ample supply of productive resources, especially entrepreneurs, to organize production and make the economy grow. When labor productivity is increasing, it helps in raising economic growth and improving living standards.

The Functions and Characteristics of Money

Money has three functions. It can be used as a medium of exchange, a unit of accounting, and a store of value. Anything serving as money must be durable, portable, divisible, stable in value, scarce, and accepted as a medium of exchange in payment for debts. Money that has an alternative use as a commodity—cattle, gems, and tobacco, for example—is considered commodity money. Money that is backed by—or can be exchanged for—gold or silver is known as representative money. Today all United States money is fiat money, or legal tender.

History of American Money and Banking

Throughout American history, people have used commodity money, European coins, privately printed banknotes, and many other forms of notes. To control the amount of money in circulation, Congress established the Federal Reserve System in 1913. It serves as the nation's central bank. In 1914 the system began issuing paper money called Federal Reserve notes, which soon became the major form of currency. The Constitution of the United States gave Congress the power to mint coins. It was not until the Civil War that the government set up a safe, uniform currency. In 1934 the nation switched from a gold standard to a fiat money standard. Electronic funds transfer has revolutionized the banking industry, with customers using automated teller machines (ATMs) and even the Internet to do their banking.

Types of Money in the United States

Money today consists of more than just currency. It also includes deposits in checking accounts as well as debit cards and near moneys (assets such as savings accounts that can be turned into money relatively easily and without the risk of loss of value). Economists measure the amount of money in the economy by adding up M1—currency, all checkable deposits, and traveler's checks. Then they calculate M2—all the items in M1 plus savings deposits, time deposits, small-denomination certificates of deposit, and other account balances.

International and Global Economies

International trade allows nations to specialize, increase the productivity of their resources, and obtain more goods and services. Nations, like individuals and regions of a nation, can gain by specializing in products they can produce efficiently and by trading for goods they cannot produce as efficiently. In order to accomplish economic development, the nations of the world have to overcome the problems that hinder their economic growth, and they must use their resources effectively. Although developing countries are working to increase their production and raise the standard of living of their people, they still face many challenges that may prevent them from reaching their potential, but advances in technology may help.

Characteristics of Developing Nations

Developing nations are those with less industrial development and a relatively low standard of living. Five characteristics of developing nations include a low GDP, an economy based on subsistence agriculture, poor health conditions (including a high infant mortality rate), a low literacy rate, and rapid population growth. Many developing nations have governments that do not support private property rights.

The Process of Economic Development

The three stages of economic development are the agricultural stage, the manufacturing stage, and the service sector stage. A basic problem for developing nations is how to finance the equipment and training necessary to improve their standard of living. Developing nations receive financing through foreign investment and foreign aid. Foreign aid can be given in the form of economic assistance, technical assistance, and/or military assistance. International agencies, including the World Bank and the International Monetary Fund, channel funds to developing nations. Developed countries provide foreign aid for humanitarian, economic, political, and military reasons.

Obstacles to Growth in Developing Nations

Four obstacles hamper economic growth in developing nations: traditional attitudes and beliefs, continued rapid population growth, a misuse of resources (including capital flight—the legal or illegal export of currency or money capital from a nation by that nations' leaders), and trade restrictions. The economic failure of Indonesia highlights some of the problems associated with rapid economic growth—lack of a national identity, massive government corruption and bureaucracies, reliance on a single product, and government interference in trade.

Industrialization and the Future

There are four problems of rapid industrialization: unwise investments, not enough time to adapt to new patterns of living and working, use of inappropriate technology, and inadequate time to move through the stages of development. Factors that spur economic growth include trade with the outside world, an appropriate incentive structure, a supportive political structure, managing natural resources, and reduced population growth. Developing countries can get out of the vicious cycle of poverty if their political system rewards entrepreneurs and promotes private property rights.

The Growth of E-Commerce

Numbers, also called digits, are so vital to our lives today that people have labeled our era "the digital age." Microchips in a network of interconnected computers are changing how people communicate, produce, consume, educate, and entertain themselves. Some economists believe we have entered the age of cybernomics—economics driven by a huge digital machine, the Internet. Websites connecting businesses, private organizations, government offices, and educational institutions make locating information and global communication extraordinarily easy. The Internet provides businesses in particular with the opportunity to directly reach suppliers and consumers. E-commerce is expanding rapidly, affecting both business-to-business relationships and consumers. In this new world of cybernomics, the buyer is ruler. If one seller cannot deliver a superior product at a competitive price in real time, another seller will. Marketers can now track purchases electronically and organize cybercommunities of people whose needs they serve.

A New Economy?

The Information Age may be as significant as the Industrial Revolution was in affecting human society. The knowledge economy includes communications technology, intellectual property, and stored data. Some economists believe that new concepts are needed to explain how the knowledge economy differs from earlier economic concepts and principles. Most economists agree that innovation stimulates economic growth cycles.

Issues in Cybernomics

Cybernomics has raised important issues. Decisions being made by policy makers today will help determine our economic future. Among the important issues today are ensuring safe Internet trade, securing intellectual property rights, protecting consumer privacy, and helping developing nations catch up with the rapidly changing global economy. Communications technology provides access to knowledge and distance education, but we must make wise choices that help create a better economic future.

Behavioral Sciences

The following topics are covered in the Behavioral Sciences portion of the test:

- Sociology
- Anthropology
- Psychology

Sociology

Sociology is the scientific study of social structure (human social behavior). It assumes a group rather than an individual perspective. Sociologists look for patterns in social relationships. A rather young science, sociology started with the writings of European scholars such as Auguste Comte, Harriet Martineau, Herbert Spencer, Karl Marx, Emile Durkheim, and Max Weber. Americans Jane Addams and W. E. B. Du Bois hoped to focus America's attention on social issues; after World War II, America took the lead in developing the field.

Sociology includes three major theoretical perspectives: *Functionalism* views society as an integrated whole; *conflict theory* looks at class, race, and gender struggles; and *symbolic interactionism* examines how group members use shared symbols as they interact.

The Importance of Socialization

Socialization is the cultural process of learning to participate in group life. Without it, we would not develop many of the characteristics we associate with begin human. Studies have shown that animal and human infants who are deprived of intensive and prolonged social contact with others are stunted in their emotional and social growth.

All three theoretical perspectives—functionalism, conflict theory, and symbolic interactionism—agree that socialization is needed if cultural and societal values are to be learned. Symbolic interaction offers the most fully developed perspective for studying socialization. In this approach, the self-concept is developed by using other people as mirrors for learning about ourselves.

During childhood and adolescence, the major agents of socialization are the family, school, peer group, and mass media. The family's role is critical in forming basic values. Schools introduce children to life beyond family. In peer groups, young people learn to relate as equals. The mass media provide role models for full integration into society.

Symbolic interactionism views socialization as a lifelong process. Desocialization is the process of having to give up old norms. Resocialization begins as people adopt new norms and values. Anticipatory socialization and reference groups are concerned with voluntary change as when moving from one life stage to another.

Social Organizations

Groups are classified by how they develop and function:

- *Primary groups* meet emotional and support needs.
- *Secondary groups* are task focused.
- *Reference groups* help us evaluate ourselves and form identities.
- *In-groups* and *out-groups* divide people into "we" and "they."
- *Social networks* extend our contacts and let us form links to many other people.

Five types of social interaction are basic to group life: cooperation, conflict, social exchange, coercion, and conformity. A formal organization is created to achieve some goal. Most are bureaucratic. The existence of primary groups and primary relationships within formal organizations can either help or hinder the achievement of goals.

Social Institutions

A social institution is a cluster of social structures that collectively meet one or more of the basic needs of a society. Institutions include family, education, politics, economy, religion, and sport. While each institution is organized differently, changes in quite different ways, and is responsible for different functions or needs of society, they are also interdependent.

Family

In all societies, the family is the most important of all social institutions. It produces new generations, socializes the young, provides care and affection, regulates sexual behavior, transmits social statutes, and provides economic support.

The family is the very core of human social life. It is not surprising that each of the three major sociological perspectives focuses on the family. Functionalism emphasizes the benefits of the family for society. The conflict perspective looks at the reasons males dominate in the family structure. Symbolic interactionism studies the way the family socializes children and promotes the development of self-concept.

Modern marriages are based primarily on love, but there are many reasons for marrying—and as many reasons for divorce. Although the American family provides social and emotional support, violence in this setting is not uncommon. Child abuse and spousal abuse are serious problems in too many American families.

Many new patterns of marriage and family living have emerged in the United States. They include blended families, single-parent families, child-free families, cohabitation, same-sex domestic partners, and families with boomerang children (young adults who either leave home and return or stay at home and live with parents). In spite of these new arrangements, the traditional nuclear family is not going to be replaced on any broad scale.

Education

Schools are becoming more bureaucratic. Advocates of open classrooms and cooperative learning contend that bureaucratically run schools fail to take into account the emotional and creative needs of individual children.

Functionalists see the emergence of the educational institution as a response to society's needs. The manifest functions of education include transmission of culture, creation of a common identity, selection and screening of talent, and promotion of personal growth and development. Schools also serve latent functions; some are positive, while others are not. Educators do not usually think of schools as day-care facilities for dual-employed couples or single parents. Nor do parents vote for additional school taxes so that their children can find dates or marriage partners. Also, schools are not consciously designed to prevent delinquency by holding juveniles indoors during the daytime. Nor are schools intended as training grounds for athletes. Nonetheless, all of these activities are latent functions of the school system, and positive contributions to society. Some consequences are dysfunctional; thought-tracking, for example, can perpetuate an unequal social-class structure from generation to generation.

In theory, America is a meritocracy in which social status is achieved. Proponents of the conflict perspective identify flaws in this model by pointing to inequality in our schools. Methods and programs aimed at promoting educational equality have been developed.

Symbolic integrationists emphasize the socialization that occurs in schools. Children learn values, norms, beliefs, and attitudes through what is called the hidden curriculum. Much of this socialization helps young people make the transition from home to a larger society.

Political and Economic Institutions

Authority is the sanctioned use of power. Political systems can be based on three types of authority: *Charismatic authority* arises from the personality of an individual; *traditional authority* is a form of authority in which the legitimacy of a leader is rooted in custom; and *rational-legal authority* is a form of authority in which the power of government officials is based on the offices they hold.

There are three different types of political systems: A *representative democracy* is a system of government that uses elected officials to fulfill majority wishes, *totalitarianism* is a political system in which a ruler with absolute power attempts to control all aspects of a society, and *authoritarianism* is a political system controlled by elected or nonelected rulers who usually permit some degree of individual freedom.

The two major models of political power are elitism and pluralism. *Elitism* is a system in which a community or society is controlled from the top by a few individuals or organizations. Advocates of the conflict perspective believe American society is controlled by an elite group. *Pluralism* is a system in which political decisions are made as a result of bargaining and compromise among special-interest groups. Pluralists, whose view is associated with functionalism, depict power as widely distributed among interest groups. Voting does not seem to be an effective means for nonelites to influence political decisions in the United States.

Capitalist economies are based on private property and the pursuit of profit, and government, in theory, plays a minor role in regulating industry. In socialist economies, the means of production are owned collectively, and government has an active role in planning and controlling the economy.

Corporations, especially those with multinational connections, have grown very powerful. Corporate managers affect domestic political decision making and influence the political and economic institutions of countries around the world.

Workers today face a changing job structure. More corporations are downsizing and replacing full-time employees with consultants or temporary workers. Evidence indicates that this trend is having some negative consequences—employees' trust in management appears to be declining.

Religion

Sociologists studying religion face some unique problems. They do not judge the validity of various religions but rather look at those aspects of religion that can be measured and observed in society.

Religion has several functions. It legitimates the structure of society, promotes social unity, and provides a sense of meaning and belonging. German social philosopher and economist Karl Marx argued that religion is used to justify and maintain the group in power. Another sociologist, Max Weber, believed that religion could promote social change. He connected the Protestant ethic and the rise of capitalism.

The major forms of religious organization are churches, denominations, sects, and cults. Religiosity—the ways people express their religious interests and convictions—can be analyzed in terms of five dimensions: belief, ritual, intellect, experience, and consequences.

Through the process of secularization, the sacred and the profane tend to become intermixed. Religious faiths can be analyzed by major social characteristics such as class and political tendencies.

Sport

As a social institution, sport fulfills some important societal needs. One of these is helping individuals identify with other members of society. Sport subcultures have developed around both team and individual sports. For this reason, sport is a reflection of society.

Functionalists see sport positively, as a means for socializing young people, promoting social integration, providing a release for tension, and developing sound character. Conflict theorists believe that organized sports can be harmful to character development. Symbolic integrationists focus on the self-concepts and relationships developed through sport activities.

Sport contributes to upward mobility among collegiate athletes, but the opportunities are few. Minorities still face discrimination in sport in that, historically, minorities are not assigned to positions that involve leadership and decision-making responsibilities. Additionally, there is pay discrimination for minorities, and they are rarely represented in the power structure (head coaches, general managers, owners, executives, commissioners). Women in sport suffer from gender-based stereotypes. Intercollegiate female athletes do not receive treatment equal to the treatment received by males, although this situation is slowly improving.

Cultural Diversity and Similarities

Cultures change according to three major processes. One cause is *discovery,* which is the process of finding something that already exists. Culture is also changed through *invention,* which is the creation of something new. A third cause of cultural change is *diffusion,* which is the borrowing of aspects of culture from other cultures. Cultures contain groups within themselves called subcultures (a group that is part of the dominant culture but that differs from it in some important respects) and countercultures (a subculture that is deliberately and consciously opposed to certain central beliefs or attitudes of the dominant culture). Ethnocentrism is judging others in terms of one's own cultural standards. Cultural universals are general cultural traits that exist in all cultures. Researchers have found more than 70 traits that appear to one degree or another in all cultures. These traits fall into these larger categories: economy, institutions, arts, language, environment, recreation, and beliefs.

Minority, Race, and Ethnicity

Sociologists have specific definitions particular to their field of study for minority, race, and ethnicity. Ethnic minorities have historically been subjected to prejudice and discrimination.

Patterns of racial and ethnic relations take two forms: assimilation and conflict. Patterns of assimilation include Anglo-conformity, melting pot, cultural pluralism, and accommodation. Conflict patterns include genocide, population transfer, and subjugation.

Prejudice involves attitudes, while discrimination is about behavior. Prejudice usually leads to discrimination. Conversely, in some instances, discrimination creates prejudiced attitudes through stereotyping. Each of the three major perspectives—functionalism, conflict theory, and symbolic interactionism—looks at different aspects of prejudice.

Discrimination in the United States has caused some ethnic and racial groups to lag behind the white majority in jobs, income, and education. Progress is being made, but gains remain fragile. African American, Latino, Asian America, Native American, and white ethnics are the largest minority groups in this country.

Inequalities of Gender and Age

All societies expect people to behave in certain ways based on their sex. Through socialization, members of a society acquire an awareness of themselves as masculine or feminine. The functionalist perspective focuses on the origins of gender differences. Conflict theory looks at the reasons gender differences continue to exist. Symbolic interactionism attempts to explain the ways in which gender is acquired. Although great progress has been made, women today are still subject to prejudice and discrimination. This imbalance of power is seen most clearly in the areas of economics, law, and politics.

The relatively low social standing of older people is based on ageism—a set of beliefs, attitudes, norms, and values used to justify age-based prejudice and discrimination. Each of the theoretical perspectives has a unique slant on ageism. According to the functionalists, elderly people in a given society are treated according to the role the aged play in that society. Competition over scarce resources lies at the heart of ageism for the conflict perspective. Elderly people compete with other age groups for economic resources, power, and prestige. According to symbolic interactionists, children learn negative images of older people just as they learn other aspects of culture.

Elderly people are a minority group. The poverty rate for America's elderly population stands at around 10 percent. Members of racial and ethnic minorities are in the poorest rank. The political process offers the major source of power for elderly Americans. Older people exert political influence through their high voting rate and their support of special-interest groups.

Anthropology

Anthropology investigates culture, the customary beliefs and material traits of groups. It is the social science most closely related to sociology.

Human Culture

Culture is the full range of learned human behavior patterns. Culture is powerful human tool for survival, but it is also fragile in that it is constantly changing. There are three layers or levels of culture that are part of learned behavior patterns and perceptions. First is the body of cultural traditions that distinguishes a specific society. The second layer is a subculture—a smaller culture within the larger society that shares a common identity, food tradition, dialect or language, and other cultural traits. The third layer of culture consists of cultural universals—learned behavior patterns that are shared by all of humanity. Examples of such "human cultural" traits include communicating with a verbal language consisting of a limited set of sounds and grammatical rules for constructing sentences; using age and gender to classify people (for example, teenager, senior citizen, man, woman); classifying people based on marriage and descent relationships and having kinship terms to refer to them (for example, wife, mother, uncle, cousin); raising children in some sort of family setting; having a sexual division of labor; having a concept of privacy; having rules to regulate sexual behavior; distinguishing between good and bad behavior; having some sort of body ornamentation; making jokes and playing games; having art; and having some sort of leadership roles for the implementation of community decisions.

Language and Culture

Human language is unique because it is a symbolic communication system that is learned instead of biologically inherited. Because it is a learned system, it is infinitely flexible. Meanings can be changed and new symbols created. This allows us to respond linguistically to major environmental, historical, and social changes. Language is a set of rules for generating speech; a dialect is a variant of a language. Dialects can be regional, if associated with a geographically isolated speech community; or they can be social—based on class, ethnicity, gender, age, and particular social statutes.

Patterns of Subsistence

Anthropologists categorize cultures of the world by looking at the differences in subsistence patterns—that is, the sources and methods a society uses to obtain its food and other necessities. There is a surprisingly high positive correlation between the type of economy and such things as population sizes and densities, social and political systems, scale of warfare, and complexity of science, mathematics, and technology. Using this approach, the cultures of the world can be divided into four basic subsistence types:

- Foraging (hunting and gathering wild plants and animals)
- Pastoralism (herding large domesticated animals)
- Horticulture (small-scale, low intensity farming)
- Intensive agriculture (large-scale intensive farming)

Economic Systems

There are vast differences between the economies of isolated, small, self-sufficient societies and large-scale societies that are integrated into the modern system of global commerce. Their systems of production, distribution, and exchange as well as concepts of property ownership are often radically different. Systems of production refer to how food and other necessities are produced. Systems of distribution and exchange refer to the practices that are involved in getting the goods and services produced by a society to its people. Almost all large-scale societies of the world have complex market economies that are efficient systems of production, distribution, and exchange. These economies are characterized by the use of money as a means of exchange, the ability to accumulate vast amounts of capital, and highly complex economic interactions that are ultimately international in the scale of their inter-relatedness.

Social Organization

Humans are highly social animals. Normally we live in groups all of our lives. The need for human social contact and the rewards that it can bring lead most people to become members of numerous social groups. People may be family members, employees of companies, and citizens of towns, states, and nations. In addition, we are often members of clubs, vocational associations, political parties, and religious groups. Our individual identities and behavior are greatly defined by the groups to which we belong and by our positions within them.

People around the word create social groups based on two broad criteria: kinship identity and non-kinship factors. Kinship refers to the culturally defined relationships among individuals who are commonly thought of as having family ties. All societies use kinship as a basis for forming social groups and for classifying people. However, there is much variability in kinship rules and patterns around the world. Kinship connections are based on two categories of bonds: those created by marriage and those that result from descent. Non-kinship factors include age-based groups, gender-based groups, and groups based on common interests.

Sex and Marriage

Marriage is the socially recognized union of two or more people. Throughout the world, it is an effective method of regulating heterosexual intercourse by defining who is socially acceptable as a sexual partner and who is not. Marriage also functions as a glue in the organization of society. It establishes social relationships that are the foundation for families and households. In many societies, it also is an important tool for creating economically and politically valuable links between families.

Process of Socialization

Human infants are born without any culture. They must be transformed by their parents, teachers, and others into cultural and socially adept animals. The general process of acquiring culture is referred to as socialization. During socialization, we learn the language of the culture we are born into as well as the roles we are to play in life. Socialization is important in the process of personality formation. While much of human personality is the result of our genes, the socialization process can mold it in particular directions by encouraging specific beliefs and attitudes as well as selectively providing experiences.

Ethnicity and Race

Ethnicity refers to selected cultural and sometimes physical characteristics used to classify people into ethnic groups or categories considered to be significantly different from others. A race is a biological subspecies, or variety of a species, consisting of a more or less distinct population with anatomical traits that distinguish it clearly from other races. In the final analysis, it is clear that people, not nature, create our identities. Ethnicity and supposed "racial" groups are largely cultural and historical constructs. They are primarily social rather than biological phenomena. This does not mean that they do not exist. To the contrary, "races" are very real in the world today. In order to understand them, however, we must look into culture and social interaction rather than biological evolution.

Political Organization

If politics is defined broadly as competition for power over people and things, then it is clear that all societies have some sort of political system. There can be a vast difference, however, in what political organizations look like and how they function in different kinds of societies. All societies recognize political leadership roles of some sort. These are roles in which individuals generally have authority related to broad areas of concern for the society. They usually are allowed to make decisions concerning the group as a whole.

Social Control

All societies impose social control on their citizens to some degree. They monitor and regulate behavior formally and informally. This is one of the most important prerogatives of political leaders. In addition to exerting their political will, they strongly influence or manage the mechanisms of social control. To understand a culture's system of social control, one must understand the social norms upon which it is based. There are commonly held conceptions of appropriate and expected behavior in a society. Norms can and do change over time. Often a society's norms change but the laws relating to them have a long delay in catching up. This was the case with antimiscegenation laws in the U.S. southern states. Sometimes the laws change before the norms do for large sections of a society. This was the case with the civil rights acts of the U.S. Congress during the 1960s.

The most effective form of social control is not laws, police, and jails. Rather, it is the internalization of the moral codes by the members of society. As children grow up they normally learn what is proper and improper, right and wrong, good and bad. If a society is able to indoctrinate all of its members to accept its moral code, it will not need to use police or other external means of social control. No society, however, is able to rely solely upon internalization of its normative code, though some are more successful at it than others. All societies have laws to deal with the inevitable disputes that arise. However, laws and their focus vary significantly from culture to culture.

Anthropology of Religion

A religion is a system of beliefs usually involving the worship of supernatural forces or beings. Religious beliefs provide shape and meaning to one's perception of the universe. In other words, they provide a sense of order in what might otherwise be seen as a chaotic existence. Religions also provide understanding and meaning for inexplicable events such as the death of a loved one in an earthquake or some other unpredictable force of nature. For most religious people, their beliefs about the supernatural are at the very core of their world views.

The performance of rituals is an integral part of all religions. Rituals are stylized and usually repetitive acts that take place at a set time and location. Most religious rituals are performed in special places and under special conditions, such as in a dedicated temple or at a sacred spot. This is an intentional separation between the secular and the sacred.

Religions fulfill psychological and social needs. They help us confront and explain death. They help relieve our fears and anxieties about the unknown. Religions help ease the stress during life crises. Religions reinforce group norms, so they help bring about social homogeneity.

Cultural Change

All cultures change through time. However, most cultures are basically conservative in that they tend to resist change. When cultures change, not everything changes entirely. Most often, only the function, form, or principle is new, but not all three.

Psychology

Psychology is the scientific study of behavior and mental processes. Such study can involve both animal and human behaviors. When applied to human beings, psychology covers everything that people think, feel, and do. Overall, psychologists seek to do four things: describe, explain, predict, and influence behavior.

The Life Span

Each of us is born into a world in which we must adapt. From childhood to adolescence to adulthood to old age, we change physically, emotionally, cognitively, socially, and morally. Developmental psychologists study the changes through which human behaviors pass as we grow older.

Infancy and Childhood

Infants are born equipped to experience the world. As infants grow physically, they also develop perceptions and language. Some psychologists believe that most behaviors are the result of genetics—nature. Others believe that most behaviors are the result of experience and learning—nurture. The newborn is capable of certain inherited, automatic, coordinated movement patterns, classed reflexes, which are triggered by the right stimulus. Infants experience rapid development through maturation and learning. Depth perception increases in older infants.

As the thought processes of children develop, they begin to think, communicate and relate with others, and solve problems. Children's knowledge of the world changes through the processes of assimilation and accommodation. Swiss psychologist and philosopher Jean Piaget described the changes that occur in children's understanding in four stages of cognitive development:

1. The *sensorimotor* stage, in which the infant uses schemas (a conceptual framework used to make sense of the world) that primarily involve his or her body and sensations

2. The *preoperational* stage, in which the child begins to use mental images or symbols to understand things

3. The *concrete operations* stage, in which the child is able to use logical schemas, but his or her understanding is limited to concrete objects or problems

4. The *formal operations* stage, in which the child is able to solve abstract problems

Infants begin to develop emotionally by attaching to specific people, usually their mothers. Children face various social decisions as they grow and progress through the stages of life. There are four basic parenting styles: authoritarian, democratic or authoritative, permissive or laissez-faire, and uninvolved. Austrian physician Sigmund Freud's theory of psychosexual development suggests that all children are born with powerful sexual and aggressive urges, and in learning to control these impulses, children acquire a sense of right and wrong. Psychologist Erik Erikson's theory of psychosocial development suggests that the need for social approval is important. The cognitive-developmental theories of development suggest that social development is the result of the child trying to make sense out of his experiences.

Adolescence

Adolescence is the transition period between childhood and adulthood. All adolescents experience dramatic changes in their physical size, shape, and capacities, as well as biological development related to reproduction. In his theory of adolescence, psychologist and theorist G. Stanley Hall portrayed the adolescent as existing in a state of great storm and stress. Other psychologists and social scientists, such as Margaret Mead, regard adolescence as a relatively smooth continuous development out of childhood and into adulthood. The onset of puberty marks the end of childhood; both boys and girls experience a growth spurt just before puberty. The rate and pattern of sexual maturation varies so widely that it is difficult to apply norms or standards to puberty.

The transition from childhood to adulthood involves changes in patterns of reasoning and moral thinking, as well as the development of one's identity. During adolescence, most people reach the stage of formal operations thinking in which thinking becomes abstract and less concrete. According to Erik Erikson, building an identity is a task that is unique to adolescence; most adolescents must go through an identity crisis, a time of inner conflict during which they worry intensely about their identities.

Adolescents undergo many changes in their social relationships, adjusting to new relationships with parents and the influence of peers. Parents and peers exercise much influence in shaping adolescent behavior and attitudes. One of the principal developmental tasks for adolescents is becoming independent of their families. Belonging to a peer group fulfills the need for closeness with others and gives the adolescent a means of establishing an identity.

Females and males have physical and psychological gender differences. Our beliefs about what we think it means to be male or female influence our behavior. During adolescence, individuals develop attitudes about gender and expectations about the gender role they will fill. Most psychologists agree that nature and nurture interact to influence gender differences. The roles of men and women in society are changing. For example, there are more women in the workforce now than there have been in the past. Despite that fact, women in general do not advance as quickly as men, and women occupy lower levels of leadership positions.

Adulthood and Old Age

Adulthood is a time of transition—it involves shifting priorities and outlooks on life from adolescence and throughout the remainder of life. For most adults, the process of physical decline is slow and gradual. The adult years are a time when lifestyle may set the stage for problems that will show up then or in later life. Good physical and mental health seem to be the key factors affecting sexual activity in adulthood. The ability to comprehend new material and to think flexibly improves in early adulthood, and overall intelligence increases with age. An individual's basic character remains relatively stable throughout life.

As we age, our priorities and expectations change to match realities, and we experience losses as well as gains. The misbelief that progressive physical and mental decline is inevitable with age has resulted in a climate of prejudice against the old. The health of older people, for the most part, is related to their health when younger. In late adulthood, life transitions are often negative and reduce responsibilities and increase isolation. The frequency and regularity of sexual activities during earlier years is the best overall predictor of such activities in later years. Crystallized intelligence, or the ability to use accumulated knowledge and learning in appropriate situations, increases with age; fluid intelligence, or the ability to solve abstract relational problems and to generate new hypotheses, decreases with age.

Much of people's fear of aging is rooted in stereotypes of what it means to grow older. The positive side of aging is one of the best-kept secrets in our society—older people can continue to learn and develop skills. While some abilities such as nonverbal tasks and problem solving may decline, other abilities remain normal and even improve with age. Older people can enjoy a guilt-free, healthy sex life. Many older people have more time to enjoy hobbies and companionship, and to travel.

Death is inevitable. Most people face death by going through stages or an adjustment process. In her ground-breaking book *On Death and Dying,* Elisabeth Kübler-Ross identified five stages of psychological adjustment to death: denial, anger, bargaining, depression, and acceptance. A hospice is a special place where terminally ill people go to receive supportive care; it is designed to make the patient's surroundings pleasant and comfortable.

Learning and Cognitive Processes

Learning is a relatively permanent change in a behavioral tendency that results from experience. Not all behaviors are acquired in the same way. Psychologists have studied three basic types of learning, classical conditioning, operant conditioning, and social learning:

- People acquire certain behaviors through *classical conditioning,* a learning procedure in which associations are made between a neutral stimulus and a conditioned response. Russian physiologist Ivan Pavlov discovered the principles of classical conditioning. The four elements involved in classical conditioning are UCS (unconditioned stimulus), UCR (unconditioned response), CS (conditioned stimulus), CR (conditioned response). Generalization and discrimination are complementary processes in which the participant responds to similar stimuli in the same manner or responds differently to dissimilar stimuli. A CR will sometimes reappear spontaneously after extinction in a process called spontaneous recovery. Classical conditioning may be used to affect human behavior, such as taste aversions and fears.

- *Operant conditioning* occurs when the consequences that follow a behavior increase or decrease the likelihood of that behavior occurring again. Operant conditioning, as explained by U.S. psychologist B. F. Skinner, means that human behavior is influenced by one's history of rewards and punishments. Reinforcers (positive and negative, and primary and secondary) are stimuli that increase the likelihood that certain behaviors will be repeated. Behavior is reinforced according to continuous or partial reinforcement schedules that are based on numbers of responses or times of responses. Reinforcing responses that are increasingly similar to the desired behavior is a process called *shaping.* Punishments are stimuli that decrease the likelihood that certain behaviors will be repeated.

- *Social learning,* consisting of cognitive learning and modeling, involves how people make decisions and act upon the information available to them. Latent learning is an alteration of a behavioral tendency that is not demonstrated by an immediately observable change in behavior at the time of learning. Although the learning typically occurs in the absence of a reinforcer, it may not be demonstrated until a reinforcer appears. If people have numerous experiences in which their actions have no effect, they may learn a general strategy of learned helplessness. Modeling is a type of learning that occurs as the result of observation and imitation. Behavior modification uses learning principles to change people's actions or feelings.

Personality Tests and Theories

Personality tests are used to assess personality characteristics and to identify problems. Personality tests can be objective or projective. Objective tests are usually constructed in a limited- or forced-choice format, in which a person must select one of several answers. One of the most widely used objective personality tests is the Minnesota Multiphasic Personality Inventory (MMPI). Projective tests are unstructured tests in which a person is asked to respond freely, giving his or her own interpretation of various ambiguous stimuli. The two major projective personality tests are the Rorschach inkblot test and the Thematic Apperception Test (TAT).

Personality theories provide a way of organizing the many characteristics that people have. Personality theorists try to organize traits by similarities and differences, explore how people cope with life situations, and how people grow and change.

- Sigmund Freud's *psychoanalytic theory* proposes that personality is made up of three components: the id, ego, and superego. Freud believed that every personality has an unconscious component and that childhood experiences, even if not consciously recalled, continue to influence a person's behavior. The id, ego, and superego explain how the mind works and how instinctual energies are regulated.

- Behaviorists are interested in how aspects of personality are *learned*. Behaviorists believe that as individuals differ in the learning experiences, they acquire different behaviors and different personalities. In his social learning theory of development, which emphasizes interaction, Albert Bandura believed that personality is acquired not only by reinforcement but also by observational learning.

- *Humanistic and cognitive theories* of personality stress the positive aspects of human nature. Humanistic psychology is founded on the belief that all human beings strive for self-actualization. Carl Rogers, best known for his role in the development of counseling, believed that many people suffer from a conflict between what they value in themselves and what they believe other people value in them. He believed that people are basically good and can solve their own problems once they realize that they can.

- *Trait theorists* believe that character traits account for consistency of behavior in different situations. Trait theorists believe we understand people by specifying their traits, and we use traits to predict people's future behavior. Gordon W. Allport, an influential psychologist, defined common traits as those that apply to everyone and individual traits as those that apply more to a specific person.

Stress

Stress results from our perceptions of demands placed upon us and our evaluations of situations we encounter. Stress is a normal part of life that goes hand in hand with working toward any goal or facing any challenge. Making difficult decisions between two or more options results in conflicting motives and is a major source of stress. Major life changes are another main source of stress.

Although all people experience stress at some point in their lives, how they react to it varies from individual to individual. The reactions may be beneficial or harmful. The body reacts to stress with the fight-or-flight response. This prepares the individual to either act in potentially dangerous situations or escape them. The general adaptation syndrome identifies three stages in the body's stress reaction: alarm, resistance, and exhaustion. How people react to stress depends on their personality type, their perception of control over stressors, and the social support they receive.

People deal with stress by employing defensive and active coping strategies. A personal interpretation and evaluation of an event helps determine its stress impact. Common defense mechanisms used to cope with stress are denial and intellectualization. Active coping strategies involve changing the environment or modifying a situation to remove stressors or reduce the level of stress.

For many people, college and work involve adjustment and stress. Attending college stimulates change in many students. Students find several ways of coping with the stress of going to college. Job satisfaction is simply the attitude a worker has toward his or her job. Overall, women face a considerable gap between their income and that received by men for the same job.

Psychological Disorders

Psychologists draw the line between normal and abnormal behavior by looking at deviance, adjustment, and psychological health. One approach to defining abnormality is to say that whatever most people do is normal and any deviation from the majority is abnormal. Abnormality can be viewed as an inability to adjust to getting along in the world—physically, emotionally, and socially. No single accepted definition of abnormal behavior exists. Psychiatrists use the DSM-IV (the fifth version of the American Psychiatric Associations' Diagnostic and Statistical Manual of Mental Disorders) to help them classify psychological disorders:

- *Anxiety disorders* are marked by excessive fear, caution, and avoidance. Generalized anxiety is often accompanied by physical symptoms. Other anxiety disorders include phobic, obsessive-compulsive, post-traumatic stress, and panic disorders.

- Dealing with anxiety can lead to *somatoform and dissociative disorders*. Somatoform disorders are psychological problems in which symptoms are focused on the body. Dissociative disorders involve a breakdown in a person's normal conscious experience.

- *Schizophrenia* involves disordered thoughts and is a collection of symptoms relating to impairments in cognition, emotion, perception, and motor movement. Psychologists have classified several types of schizophrenia. *Mood disorders* involve disturbances in the experience and expressions of depression. Types of mood disorders are major depressive disorder, bipolar disorder, and seasonal affective disorder.

- *Personality disorders* and *drug addiction* prohibit normal relationships and normal functioning. People with personality disorder seem unable to establish meaningful relationships with other people or to adapt to the social environment. Abuse of drugs often involves psychosocial dependence, addiction, tolerance, and sometimes withdrawal.

Psychotherapy

Psychotherapy is a general term for the several approaches used by mental health professionals to treat psychological disorders. Mental health professionals who have been trained to deal with the psychological problems of others include counseling and clinical psychologists, psychiatrists, and social workers. An important function of psychotherapy is to help people realize that they are responsible for their own problems and that they are the only ones who can really solve those problems. The primary goal of psychotherapy is to strengthen the patient's control over his or her life. People seeking psychotherapy need to change their thoughts, feelings, and behaviors. Over the years, they have developed not only certain feelings about themselves, but also behaviors that reinforce those feelings. These behaviors and feelings make it difficult or impossible for them to reach their goals. One of the most important factors in effective treatment is the patient's belief or hope that he can change.

Psychoanalysis and Humanistic Therapy

Psychoanalysis, the study of the conscious and unconscious mind, is based on the theories of its founder, Sigmund Freud. Humanistic therapy helps people reach their full potential. A main goal of a psychoanalyst is to help make patients aware of unconscious impulses, desires, or fears that may be causing their anxieties. Humanistic psychology has given rise to several approaches to psychotherapy known as client-centered therapy. Client-centered therapists believe the psychological problems arise when the true sense of self becomes lost and the individual comes to view himself or herself according to the standards of others.

Cognitive and Behavior Therapies

Cognitive and behavior therapists help clients develop new ways of thinking and behaving. Cognitive therapists focus on changing the way people think. Behavior therapists concentrate on determining what is specifically troubling with a patient's life and taking steps to change it.

Biological Approaches to Treatment

Biological approaches to treatment rely on methods such as medications, electric shock, and surgery to help clients. Biological approaches to treatment assume there is an underlying physiological reason for the disturbed behavior, faulty thinking, or inappropriate emotions an individual displays. Drug therapy involves four main types of medications: antipsychotic drugs, antidepressant drugs, lithium carbonate, and antianxiety drugs. Antipsychotic drugs reduce agitation, delusions, and hallucinations by blocking the activity of dopamine in the brain. Antidepressants treat major depression by increasing the amount of one or both of the neurotransmitters noradrenaline and serotonin. Lithium carbonate is a chemical used to counteract mood swings associated with bipolar disorder. Antianxiety drugs relieve anxiety and panic disorders by depressing the activity of the central nervous system. Electroconvulsive therapy (ECT) is a rare, drastic treatment that is used with great caution. It involves sending an electrical current through the brain to try to reduce symptoms of mental disturbance. Psychosurgery involves destroying part of the brain to free the patient of symptoms.

Social Psychology

We depend on others to survive. Social psychologists have provided insights into why people choose to interact with some people and not with others. We are attracted to certain people because of factors such as proximity, reward values, physical appearance, approval, similarity, and complementarity. Psychologists have discovered that people need company most when they are afraid or anxious or when they are unsure of themselves and want to compare their feelings with other people's. The closer two individuals are geographically to one another, the more likely they are to become attracted to each other. Friendships provide three rewards—stimulation, utility, and ego support.

Social Perception

We explain the behavior of others by making judgments about them. Our judgments are influenced by our perceptions of others. Forming impressions about others helps us place these people in categories. We form first impressions of people based on schemas. When people develop schemas for entire groups of people, they are developing stereotypes. People often try to interpret and explain other people's behavior by identifying what caused the behavior. Communication in a relationship consists of both verbal and nonverbal messages (the process through which messages are conveyed using space, body language, and facial expression).

Personal Relationships

People experience different types of love and relationships throughout their lives. Children apply what they have learned from their relationships with parents to relationships with others. There are two common types of love: passionate love and companionate love. Robert Sternberg, a more recent psychologist, contends that love is made of intimacy, passion, and commitment. People tend to marry someone who is from their own social group and who has similar attributes. The success of a marriage seems to depend on whether the couple's needs are compatible, whether the husband's and wife's images of themselves coincide with their images of each other, and whether they agree on what the husband's and wife's roles in the marriage are. Parents and their children may have difficulty adjusting to divorce, but it is usually far more difficult for children because the conflict is not theirs but their parents'. Like their parents, though, most children do eventually come to terms with divorce. Divorce remains an issue with which increasing numbers of children have to cope.

Group Behavior

A group—a collection of people who interact, share common goals, and influence how members think and act—is unified by the attitudes and standards members share and by their commitment to those beliefs. To be classified as a group, a collection of people must demonstrate interdependence, communication, and common goals. Groups serve two general purposes: task functions (activities directed toward getting a job done) and social functions (responses directed toward satisfying the emotional needs of members). To be part of a group, an individual must be responsive to the norms of the group, subscribe to its ideology, and be prepared to make sacrifices in order to be part of it. Research has shown that social facilitation seems to occur when participants perform simple tasks, whereas social inhibition seems to occur when participants perform more complex tasks. Group polarization and groupthink are two processes of group decision making.

You may engage in behavior because of direct or indirect group pressure or in response to orders given by authorities. Psychologists believe that people conform to gain approval. Compliance occurs when an individual changes behavior to avoid discomfort or rejection and to gain approval. Under such circumstances, social pressure often results in only temporary compliance, and attitudes do not really change. Psychologists believe that people learn to obey authority figures and to follow orders and rules.

Conflicts between groups are a fact of everyday life. Individuals often give up responsibility for their actions by perceiving and responding to situations as a group. Aggression is a combination of biological, cognitive, personality, and environmental factors. Psychologists have found that the larger the crowd or group of bystanders, the more likely any given individual is to feel that he or she is not responsible for whatever is going on. Social loafing occurs when people allow their contributions to the group to slack off because they realize that individual contributions are not as apparent and easily measured in a group setting. When deindividuation occurs, people lose their sense of self and follow group behaviors.

Attitudes

Our attitudes are the result of conditioning, observational learning, and cognitive evaluation. Our attitudes help us define ourselves and our place in society, evaluate people and events, and guide our behavior. The culture in which you grew up, the people who raised you, and those with whom you associate all shape your attitude. People living in the same conditions and who frequently communicate with one another tend to have attitudes in common because they are exposed to the same information. Our attitudes serve as guidelines for interpreting and categorizing people, objects, and events.

Attitudes are formed through compliance, identification, and internalization. Attitudes may be changed as a result of cognitive dissonance. People often adapt their actions to the wishes of others to avoid discomfort or rejection and to gain support. Identification occurs when a person wants to define himself or herself in terms of a person or group and therefore adopts the person's or group's attitudes and ways of behaving. Internalization is the most lasting of the three sources of attitude formation or change. People's attitudes change because they are always trying to get things to fit together logically. A person's actions can affect his or her attitudes.

Persuasion is a direct attempt to influence attitudes. We evaluate when, where, and how a message is presented, as well as the message itself, when determining the credibility of the message. The process of communication involves four elements: the message itself, the source of the message, the channel through which it is delivered, and the audience that receives it. The audience may process a message by systematically thinking about it or by using heuristics (a rule of thumb or a shortcut that may lead to but does not guarantee a solution). The most effective messages combine moderate emotional appeal with factual information and argument.

PART II

FULL-LENGTH PRACTICE TESTS

Answer Sheets for Practice Test 1

Section 1

1 Ⓐ Ⓑ Ⓒ Ⓓ
2 Ⓐ Ⓑ Ⓒ Ⓓ
3 Ⓐ Ⓑ Ⓒ Ⓓ
4 Ⓐ Ⓑ Ⓒ Ⓓ
5 Ⓐ Ⓑ Ⓒ Ⓓ

6 Ⓐ Ⓑ Ⓒ Ⓓ
7 Ⓐ Ⓑ Ⓒ Ⓓ
8 Ⓐ Ⓑ Ⓒ Ⓓ
9 Ⓐ Ⓑ Ⓒ Ⓓ
10 Ⓐ Ⓑ Ⓒ Ⓓ

11 Ⓐ Ⓑ Ⓒ Ⓓ
12 Ⓐ Ⓑ Ⓒ Ⓓ
13 Ⓐ Ⓑ Ⓒ Ⓓ
14 Ⓐ Ⓑ Ⓒ Ⓓ
15 Ⓐ Ⓑ Ⓒ Ⓓ

16 Ⓐ Ⓑ Ⓒ Ⓓ
17 Ⓐ Ⓑ Ⓒ Ⓓ
18 Ⓐ Ⓑ Ⓒ Ⓓ
19 Ⓐ Ⓑ Ⓒ Ⓓ
20 Ⓐ Ⓑ Ⓒ Ⓓ

21 Ⓐ Ⓑ Ⓒ Ⓓ
22 Ⓐ Ⓑ Ⓒ Ⓓ
23 Ⓐ Ⓑ Ⓒ Ⓓ
24 Ⓐ Ⓑ Ⓒ Ⓓ
25 Ⓐ Ⓑ Ⓒ Ⓓ

26 Ⓐ Ⓑ Ⓒ Ⓓ
27 Ⓐ Ⓑ Ⓒ Ⓓ
28 Ⓐ Ⓑ Ⓒ Ⓓ
29 Ⓐ Ⓑ Ⓒ Ⓓ

Section 2

30 Ⓐ Ⓑ Ⓒ Ⓓ
31 Ⓐ Ⓑ Ⓒ Ⓓ
32 Ⓐ Ⓑ Ⓒ Ⓓ
33 Ⓐ Ⓑ Ⓒ Ⓓ
34 Ⓐ Ⓑ Ⓒ Ⓓ

35 Ⓐ Ⓑ Ⓒ Ⓓ
36 Ⓐ Ⓑ Ⓒ Ⓓ
37 Ⓐ Ⓑ Ⓒ Ⓓ
38 Ⓐ Ⓑ Ⓒ Ⓓ
39 Ⓐ Ⓑ Ⓒ Ⓓ

40 Ⓐ Ⓑ Ⓒ Ⓓ
41 Ⓐ Ⓑ Ⓒ Ⓓ
42 Ⓐ Ⓑ Ⓒ Ⓓ
43 Ⓐ Ⓑ Ⓒ Ⓓ
44 Ⓐ Ⓑ Ⓒ Ⓓ

45 Ⓐ Ⓑ Ⓒ Ⓓ
46 Ⓐ Ⓑ Ⓒ Ⓓ
47 Ⓐ Ⓑ Ⓒ Ⓓ
48 Ⓐ Ⓑ Ⓒ Ⓓ
49 Ⓐ Ⓑ Ⓒ Ⓓ

50 Ⓐ Ⓑ Ⓒ Ⓓ
51 Ⓐ Ⓑ Ⓒ Ⓓ
52 Ⓐ Ⓑ Ⓒ Ⓓ
53 Ⓐ Ⓑ Ⓒ Ⓓ
54 Ⓐ Ⓑ Ⓒ Ⓓ

55 Ⓐ Ⓑ Ⓒ Ⓓ
56 Ⓐ Ⓑ Ⓒ Ⓓ
57 Ⓐ Ⓑ Ⓒ Ⓓ
58 Ⓐ Ⓑ Ⓒ Ⓓ

Section 3

59 Ⓐ Ⓑ Ⓒ Ⓓ
60 Ⓐ Ⓑ Ⓒ Ⓓ
61 Ⓐ Ⓑ Ⓒ Ⓓ
62 Ⓐ Ⓑ Ⓒ Ⓓ
63 Ⓐ Ⓑ Ⓒ Ⓓ

64 Ⓐ Ⓑ Ⓒ Ⓓ
65 Ⓐ Ⓑ Ⓒ Ⓓ
66 Ⓐ Ⓑ Ⓒ Ⓓ
67 Ⓐ Ⓑ Ⓒ Ⓓ
68 Ⓐ Ⓑ Ⓒ Ⓓ

69 Ⓐ Ⓑ Ⓒ Ⓓ
70 Ⓐ Ⓑ Ⓒ Ⓓ
71 Ⓐ Ⓑ Ⓒ Ⓓ
72 Ⓐ Ⓑ Ⓒ Ⓓ
73 Ⓐ Ⓑ Ⓒ Ⓓ

74 Ⓐ Ⓑ Ⓒ Ⓓ
75 Ⓐ Ⓑ Ⓒ Ⓓ
76 Ⓐ Ⓑ Ⓒ Ⓓ
77 Ⓐ Ⓑ Ⓒ Ⓓ
78 Ⓐ Ⓑ Ⓒ Ⓓ

79 Ⓐ Ⓑ Ⓒ Ⓓ

Section 4

80 Ⓐ Ⓑ Ⓒ Ⓓ
81 Ⓐ Ⓑ Ⓒ Ⓓ
82 Ⓐ Ⓑ Ⓒ Ⓓ
83 Ⓐ Ⓑ Ⓒ Ⓓ
84 Ⓐ Ⓑ Ⓒ Ⓓ

85 Ⓐ Ⓑ Ⓒ Ⓓ
86 Ⓐ Ⓑ Ⓒ Ⓓ
87 Ⓐ Ⓑ Ⓒ Ⓓ
88 Ⓐ Ⓑ Ⓒ Ⓓ
89 Ⓐ Ⓑ Ⓒ Ⓓ

90 Ⓐ Ⓑ Ⓒ Ⓓ
91 Ⓐ Ⓑ Ⓒ Ⓓ
92 Ⓐ Ⓑ Ⓒ Ⓓ
93 Ⓐ Ⓑ Ⓒ Ⓓ
94 Ⓐ Ⓑ Ⓒ Ⓓ

95 Ⓐ Ⓑ Ⓒ Ⓓ
96 Ⓐ Ⓑ Ⓒ Ⓓ
97 Ⓐ Ⓑ Ⓒ Ⓓ
98 Ⓐ Ⓑ Ⓒ Ⓓ

Section 5

99 Ⓐ Ⓑ Ⓒ Ⓓ
100 Ⓐ Ⓑ Ⓒ Ⓓ
101 Ⓐ Ⓑ Ⓒ Ⓓ
102 Ⓐ Ⓑ Ⓒ Ⓓ
103 Ⓐ Ⓑ Ⓒ Ⓓ

104 Ⓐ Ⓑ Ⓒ Ⓓ
105 Ⓐ Ⓑ Ⓒ Ⓓ
106 Ⓐ Ⓑ Ⓒ Ⓓ
107 Ⓐ Ⓑ Ⓒ Ⓓ
109 Ⓐ Ⓑ Ⓒ Ⓓ

110 Ⓐ Ⓑ Ⓒ Ⓓ
111 Ⓐ Ⓑ Ⓒ Ⓓ
112 Ⓐ Ⓑ Ⓒ Ⓓ
113 Ⓐ Ⓑ Ⓒ Ⓓ
114 Ⓐ Ⓑ Ⓒ Ⓓ

115 Ⓐ Ⓑ Ⓒ Ⓓ
116 Ⓐ Ⓑ Ⓒ Ⓓ
117 Ⓐ Ⓑ Ⓒ Ⓓ

Section 6

118 Ⓐ Ⓑ Ⓒ Ⓓ
119 Ⓐ Ⓑ Ⓒ Ⓓ
120 Ⓐ Ⓑ Ⓒ Ⓓ
121 Ⓐ Ⓑ Ⓒ Ⓓ
122 Ⓐ Ⓑ Ⓒ Ⓓ

123 Ⓐ Ⓑ Ⓒ Ⓓ
124 Ⓐ Ⓑ Ⓒ Ⓓ
125 Ⓐ Ⓑ Ⓒ Ⓓ
126 Ⓐ Ⓑ Ⓒ Ⓓ
127 Ⓐ Ⓑ Ⓒ Ⓓ

128 Ⓐ Ⓑ Ⓒ Ⓓ
129 Ⓐ Ⓑ Ⓒ Ⓓ
130 Ⓐ Ⓑ Ⓒ Ⓓ

CUT HERE

Section 1: World History

Directions: For each of the following questions, select the choice that best answers the question or completes the statement.

1. Use the following passage and your knowledge of world history to answer the question.

   From the Ninety-five Theses (1517):

   Ignorant and wicked are the doing of those priests who, in the case of the dying, reserve canonical penances for purgatory.

   Martin Luther's famous document attacked the Catholic Church for which practice?

   A. The Catholic Church had allowed humanism to spread through Europe.
   B. Luther disagreed with the doctrine of predestination.
   C. Many religious leaders sold indulgences.
   D. The Catholic popes were too concerned with worldly affairs.

2. The Silk Road was

   A. a route that covered a distance of about 2,000 miles between China and Egypt.
   B. a path connecting China to Antioch and Constantinople that passed over several bodies of smooth water.
   C. a road in China where people met to trade gold for silk.
   D. a caravan route between China and the Roman Empire used for transporting goods and spreading religion.

3. Which of the following best describes an oligarchy?

   A. A government ruled by a few
   B. A government ruled by the people, or many
   C. A government ruled by a king or queen
   D. A government ruled by women

4. Caesar, Crassus, and Pompey formed a powerful government coalition called the

   A. Republic of the People.
   B. Triumvirate.
   C. Consuls.
   D. Patricians.

5. All of the other cultures EXCEPT which one influenced Islamic art and architecture?

   A. Chinese
   B. Arab
   C. Turkish
   D. Persian

GO ON TO THE NEXT PAGE

6. Refer to the following map to answer the question.

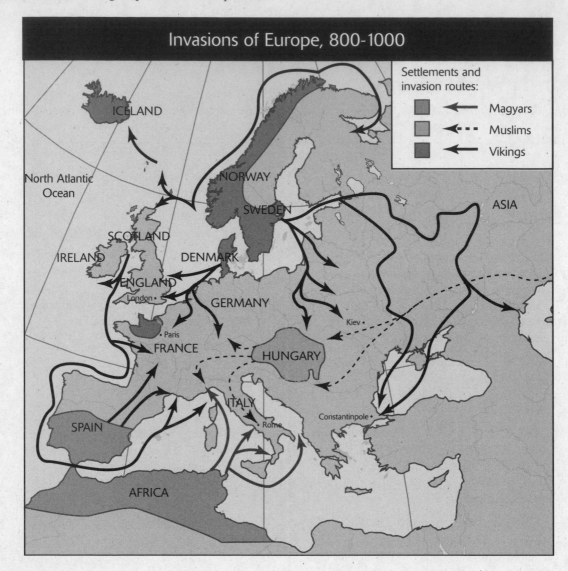

What areas remained free of invasion?

A. France

B. Central Europe

C. Scandinavia

D. England

7. All of the following forces led to Europe's economic growth during the Middle Ages EXCEPT:

   A. Improved agricultural methods
   B. Classical texts that were translated and reintroduced into Europe
   C. Increased trade
   D. Development of a money economy

8. Imagine that you are the first Aztec warrior to see the perched eagle in Lake Texcoco. What you would say about what the eagle means and why it's important to you and your culture?

   A. The gods told us that when we saw an eagle perched on a cactus growing out of a rock, our journey would end; we saw the eagle and we built our city.
   B. The gods told us that eagles were sacred and we should always protect them so that they would protect us.
   C. The gods told us that the eagle would attack the nearby snakes, allowing us to build upon the land.
   D. The gods told us that the eagle would be delivering money.

9. The Portuguese made effective use of naval technology. Which of the following was NOT helpful to the Portuguese?

   A. The compass
   B. Lateen sails
   C. Heavy cannon
   D. The astrolabe

10. What is the essential message of *Don Quixote* by Cervantes?

    A. One needs to risk everything one has for one's true love.
    B. One needs to worship freely and protect one's political privileges.
    C. One needs to try to keep peace with his neighbors, not love war too much, and not overspend.
    D. One needs to balance visionary dreams with the reality of hard work in life.

11. The controversy that led to the English "Glorious Revolution" was

    A. a Tudor-Stuart struggle for the throne.
    B. the restoration of a monarch in England.
    C. increased religious freedom for Catholics.
    D. a power struggle between Parliament and the king.

GO ON TO THE NEXT PAGE

12. Refer to the map to answer the following.

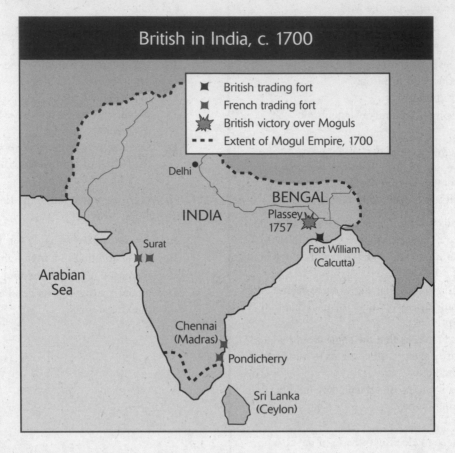

The British East India Company gradually took over more and more land in India. Foreign trading forts in India were

A. always in highly populated locations.
B. always along the coast, usually near a river or bay.
C. started because the British had victory over the Moguls.
D. abundant.

13. How were the Ottoman and the Mogul rulers similar?

A. They controlled the Indian subcontinent.
B. They were principally Shiite Muslims.
C. Although Muslims, they tolerated other religions.
D. They invaded and then controlled the Balkans for about a century.

14. The Great Peloponnesian War from 432 B.C.E. to 405 B.C.E. immediately resulted in

A. the Age of Pericles.
B. the Hellenistic Era.
C. the weakening of the Athenian city-state.
D. a rise of literature and history.

15. In general, women in ancient India

A. could not get an education or inherit property.
B. passed down the Vedas to the younger generation.
C. traded with Chinese merchants.
D. became a force in politics.

16. Use the passage below and your knowledge of world history to answer the following.

"[I]t seems to be quite remarkable ... that in a kingdom of almost limitless expanse and innumerable population ... [that has] a well-equipped army and navy ... neither the King or his people ever think of waging a war or aggression."

—Journals of Matteo Ricci

The author suggests that people in the Ming dynasty

A. lived in a militaristic society.
B. adopted a "closed country" policy.
C. were impoverished and starving.
D. were prosperous but focused inward.

17. All of the following are factors that helped spread Enlightenment ideas throughout Europe EXCEPT:

A. Discussion in salons
B. Use of the scientific method
C. Growth of publishing and reading
D. Writings of philosophers and other Enlightenment thinkers

18. Refer to the following map to answer the question.

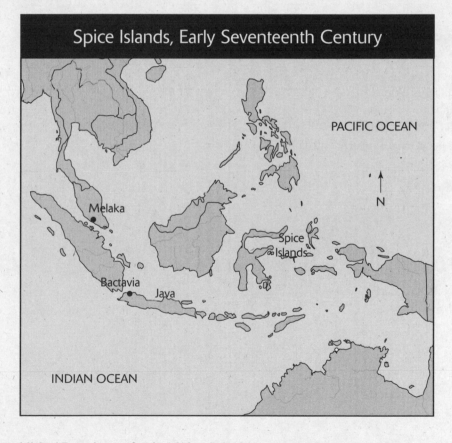

Spice Islands, Early Seventeenth Century

PACIFIC OCEAN

N

Melaka

Spice Islands

Bactavia

Java

INDIAN OCEAN

The Dutch established Batavia as a fort in 1619 to help them edge the Portuguese traders out of the area now called Indonesia. Today, which city is located where Batavia was established?

A. New Delhi
B. Jakarta
C. Phnom Penh
D. Beijing

GO ON TO THE NEXT PAGE

19. Refer to the following timeline to answer the question.

Selected Milestones in Political Thought

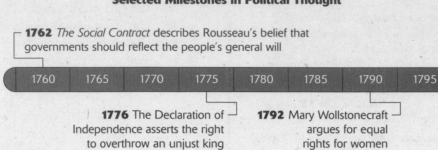

1762 *The Social Contract* describes Rousseau's belief that governments should reflect the people's general will

| 1760 | 1765 | 1770 | 1775 | 1780 | 1785 | 1790 | 1795 |

1776 The Declaration of Independence asserts the right to overthrow an unjust king

1792 Mary Wollstonecraft argues for equal rights for women

Which one of the following statements is supported by the information on the timeline?

A. Most Europeans supported their monarch completely.

B. Many people questioned the nature of their governments.

C. There were few political problems in the 1750s.

D. Only men thought and wrote about politics.

20. What economic event precipitated the American Revolution?

A. Three estates were established in France, determining taxation.

B. British taxation on colonists.

C. The fall of the Bastille.

D. Government finances nearly collapsed in France.

21. Refer to the following map to answer the question.

Revolutions in Europe, 1848-1849

Center of revolution

RUSSIA

PRUSSIA

Berlin

Warsaw

BELGIUM

Frankfurt

Dresden

Krakow

Paris

Prague

GERMANY

Munich

Vienna

Budapest

FRANCE

Lyon

AUSTRIAN EMPIRE

Milan

Venice

Livorno

Florence

OTTOMAN
EMPIRE

Rome

PAPAL
STATES

Naples

KINGDOM
OF THE TWO
SICILIES

GREECE

Palermo

How far south did the revolutions of 1848 and 1849 extend?

A. Palermo in Sicily

B. Naples

C. Kingdom of the two Sicilies

D. Berlin in Prussia

GO ON TO THE NEXT PAGE

22. Use the information below and your knowledge of world history to answer the following question.

British economic conditions during the early 1800s:

Canal miles tripled between 1760 and 1830.

Britain had built more the 6,000 miles of railroad tracks by 1850.

Britain produced nearly 3 million tons of iron ore by 1852.

London's population grew by 236 percent between 1800 and 1850.

Which of the following statements is based on the information above?

A. The Industrial Revolution led to greater urbanization.

B. London neighborhoods in the 1800s were sharply divided between rich and poor.

C. A boom in railroad and canal construction made transportation more difficult.

D. Parliament disagreed with the king over taxes and spending.

23. How did the Impressionists radically change the art of painting in the 1870s?

A. They began to use art to represent reality as accurately as possible.

B. They followed the lead of Pablo Picasso and began painting geometric designs to represent reality.

C. They worked side-by-side with the photographers of the time to make art imitate life.

D. They rejected the studios where artists had traditionally worked and went out into the countryside to paint nature directly.

24. The role Russia played in World War I can best be described as

A. a strong supporter of Germany and Austria.

B. a strong supporter of France and Great Britain.

C. a weak role due to the Russian Revolution.

D. militarily strong because of its vast army.

25. Refer to the following map to answer the question.

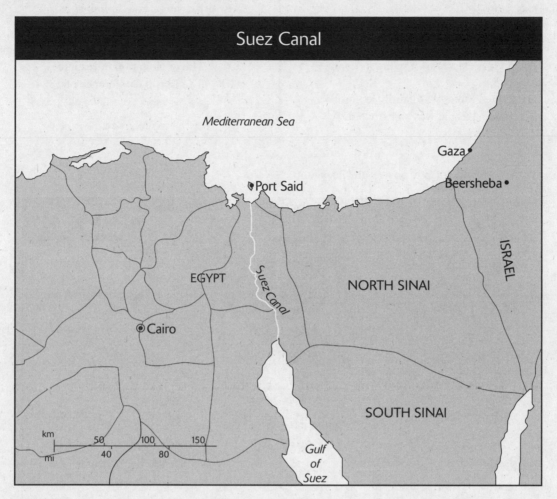

Why is control of the Suez Canal so important?

A.   The Suez Canal helps Cairo.

B.   The Suez Canal is about 100 miles long.

C.   The Suez Canal connects two seas.

D.   The Suez Canal provides a shorter route from Europe to Asia

GO ON TO THE NEXT PAGE

26. What were the British motives for protecting Latin American states?

   A. The British wanted to trade with Latin America.

   B. The middle class was growing in Latin America.

   C. The United States was gaining control.

   D. The Panama Canal was constructed.

27. Which of the following was a consequence of British colonial rule in India?

   A. The defeat of Mogul dynasty

   B. The popularity of the joint-stock company

   C. The exploitation of resources

   D. The Berlin Conference of 1884

28. Refer to the following map to answer the question.

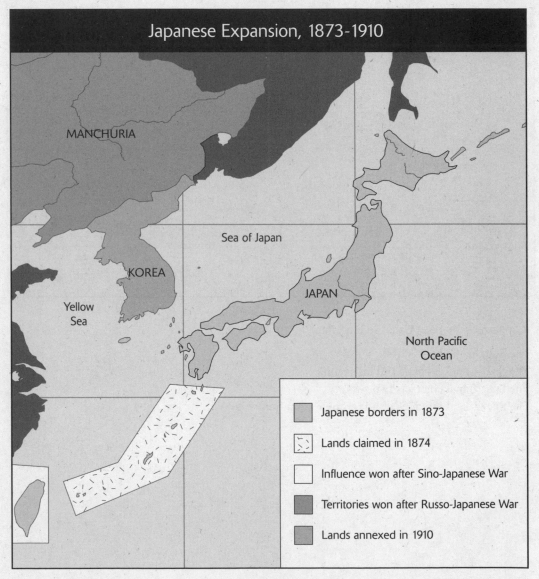

Japanese Expansion, 1873-1910

MANCHURIA

Sea of Japan

KOREA

JAPAN

Yellow Sea

North Pacific Ocean

Legend:
- Japanese borders in 1873
- Lands claimed in 1874
- Influence won after Sino-Japanese War
- Territories won after Russo-Japanese War
- Lands annexed in 1910

Which of the following resulted from Japanese expansion?

   A. Japan was humiliated by its losses.

   B. Japan became an important military force.

   C. Russia and Japan competed for control of China.

   D. China's government was strengthened and reformed.

29. What item was NOT imported from China by the British?

A. Tea
B. Silk
C. Silver
D. Porcelain

Section 2: United States History

Directions: For each of the following questions, select the choice that best answers the question or completes the statement.

30. Which of the following is an *opinion* about the Constitution?

A. By 1790 all states had ratified the Constitution.
B. A major concern in writing the Constitution was how many representatives each state would have.
C. Under the Constitution, the federal government could raise money to operate the government.
D. Because of the Constitution, the United States has a better democracy than other countries.

31. As part of the Columbian Exchange, Spanish explorers brought such things as chocolate and tobacco from the Americas to Europe. What is one thing they brought from Europe to the Americas?

A. Hieroglyphic writing
B. Democratic government
C. Horses
D. Corn

32. President Jefferson wanted to limit the power of the federal government. Which of the following was an action he took to achieve this goal?

A. He increased the size of the army.
B. He proposed renewing the Alien and Sedition Acts.
C. He dissolved the Republican Party to eliminate political conflict.
D. He cut the federal budget.

33. One advantage the Southern states held during the Civil War was that

A. they received military and financial support from the British and the French.
B. many battles occurred on lands with which Southerners were more familiar.
C. the largest weapons factories were located in the South.
D. most people in the country agreed with the position of the Southern states.

34. Which of the following is true about the early colonies of Jamestown and Plymouth?

A. Both colonies were started by people interested in establishing a new nation.
B. Food shortages caused loss of life in both colonies.
C. The primary source of income for both colonies was tobacco.
D. Both colonies were started by religious separatists.

GO ON TO THE NEXT PAGE

35. Read the passages below and answer the question that follows.

Susan B. Anthony, who was raised as a Quaker, was a powerful organizer in the women's rights movement. A dedicated reformer, she joined the temperance movement and worked for the American Antislavery Society.

Sojourner Truth, a former slave, spoke out against slavery and in defense o women's rights. Truth often attended women's rights conventions to remind women that their African American sisters had a place in the movement.

Susan B. Anthony and Sojourner Truth both worked for which of the following reforms?

A. Abolitionism and education
B. Education and temperance
C. Temperance and women's rights
D. Women's rights and abolitionism

36. Women faced all of the following kinds of discrimination in the 1960s EXCEPT:

A. Unequal pay for performing the same tasks as men
B. Being prohibited from attending certain universities
C. Being denied the right to vote
D. The inability to obtain loans and credit

37. All of the following are examples of strong community life in New England colonies EXCEPT:

A. Plantations
B. Schools
C. Town meetings
D. Churches

38. Each of the following is true of the bills passed during the first Hundred Days of FDR's presidency EXCEPT:

A. They were intended to provide immediate relief to American citizens.
B. They were known as the New Deal.
C. They were designed as temporary measures to restart the economy.
D. They were the subject of divisive and protracted debate in Congress.

39. One of the effects of World War I on the American economy was

A. a sharp rise in unemployment.
B. stronger government control over industry.
C. a sharp decrease in taxes.
D. the abolition of labor unions, which were seen as unpatriotic.

40. When Roosevelt signed the Lend-Lease Act in 1941, he said that the United States must become the "arsenal of democracy" in order to

A. end the Depression.
B. help the Axis powers.
C. remain neutral.
D. help Great Britain.

41. Read the following excerpts, taken from the Monroe Doctrine, and then answer the question.

The American continents, by the free and independent condition which they have assured and maintain, are hence forth not to be considered as subjects for future colonization by any European powers.

We should consider any attempt on their part to extend their system to any portion of this hemisphere as dangerous to our peace and safety.

The Monroe Doctrine sent a clear message to European powers from the United States. What was the Doctrine designed to do?

A. Preserve the United States' trade routes with Europe
B. Prohibit European nations from colonizing any lands in the Western Hemisphere
C. Prevent Central American countries from declaring war against the United States
D. Protect the United States from invasion by Central American nations

42. The purpose of the War Powers Act was to ensure that the president would

A. have greater authority over the military.
B. consult Congress before committing troops to extended conflicts.
C. have the authority to sign treaties without Senate approval.
D. have a freer hand in fighting the spread of communism.

43. In 1920 women won an important victory when the Nineteenth Amendment was ratified. What did the amendment accomplish?

   A. It required colleges to accept women.

   B. It guaranteed child care for workers' children.

   C. It granted women the right to vote.

   D. It guaranteed equal wages for equal work.

44. Which of the following concepts is NOT associated with both Social Darwinism and the Gospel of Wealth?

   A. Survival of the fittest

   B. Laissez-faire

   C. Unregulated competition

   D. Philanthropy

45. All of the following were effects of rulings by the Warren Court EXCEPT:

   A. Involved federal courts in the reapportionment of state election districts

   B. Extended rights for people accused of crimes

   C. Protected religious minorities through greater separation of church and state

   D. Increased state authority at the expense of federal authority

46. Which of the following was one of the primary causes of World War I?

   A. A complex set of alliances among European nations

   B. The exile of Mexican General Victoriano Huerta

   C. The dissatisfaction of Russian peasants

   D. The breakup of the Austro-Hungarian Empire

47. One difference between the strategies of Dr. Martin Luther King, Jr., and some later civil rights groups was that King was committed to

   A. ending discrimination in housing and unemployment.

   B. using only nonviolent forms of protest.

   C. demanding equal rights for African Americans.

   D. gaining improvements in living conditions for African Americans.

48. Labor unions were formed for all of these reasons EXCEPT:

   A. To improve workers' wages

   B. To protect factory owners from being sued

   C. To make factories safer

   D. To prevent children from working long hours

49. Several events in the 1850s caused anger in both the North and South, making war more likely. Which of the following was NOT a cause of increasing tension?

   A. The Fugitive Slave Act

   B. The publication of *Uncle Tom's Cabin*

   C. John Brown's Harpers Ferry raid

   D. Crittenden's Compromise

50. The Platt Amendment specified all of the following conditions EXCEPT:

   A. Cuba could not allow another foreign power to gain territory within its borders.

   B. Cuba must allow the United States to buy or lease naval stations in the country.

   C. Cuba would be guaranteed its independence by 1915.

   D. The United States had the right to intervene to protect Cuban independence and to keep order.

51. The colonists complained about having to pay British taxes while not being allowed to vote for members of the British Parliament. Which of the following quotations best expresses their complaint?

   A. "Give me liberty or give me death."

   B. "Taxation without representation is tyranny."

   C. "These are the times that try men's souls."

   D. "Don't fire until you see the whites of their eyes."

52. Which of the following trends of the 1920s did NOT contribute to a renewed nativist movement?

   A. Economic recession

   B. Influx of immigrants

   C. Fear of radicals and communists

   D. Prohibition

GO ON TO THE NEXT PAGE

53. Which of the following did NOT make it easier for settlers to live and farm on the Great Plains?

   A. Government assistance such as the Homestead Act

   B. New technology such as the mechanical reaper and the combine

   C. New farming techniques such as dry farming

   D. The absence of land speculators

54. The Eisenhower administration worked to achieve all of the following EXCEPT:

   A. Ending wage and price controls

   B. Winning passage for the Federal Highway Act

   C. Repealing right-to-work laws

   D. Extending the Social Security system

55. One historical lesson from the McCarthy era is the realization that

   A. loyalty oaths prevent spying.

   B. communism is influential in prosperous times.

   C. communist agents had infiltrated all levels of the U.S. government.

   D. public fear of traitors can lead to intolerance and discrimination.

56. The Sherman Antitrust Act of 1890 declared illegal "any combination ... in restraint of trade or commerce." What *combination* was it originally intended to prevent?

   A. Labor unions

   B. Business mergers

   C. Transcontinental railroads

   D. Farmers' Alliances

57. A major reason for the collapse of the American economy after 1929 was

   A. high interest rates.

   B. decreased farm production.

   C. low tariffs at home and abroad.

   D. overproduction of consumer goods.

58. Which of the following statements about the period of Reconstruction after the Civil War is NOT true?

   A. To maintain their strength in Congress, Radical Republicans wanted to be certain African Americans voted.

   B. Some Northern teachers wanted to help newly emancipated African Americans get education and jobs.

   C. President Johnson was eager to punish the South and insisted on strict control of the region through the Military Reconstruction Act.

   D. Southern state legislatures often passed black codes to limit the rights of African Americans in the South.

Section 3: Government/Political Science/Civics

Directions: For each of the following questions, select the choice that best answers the question or completes the statement.

59. Refer to the following map to answer the question.

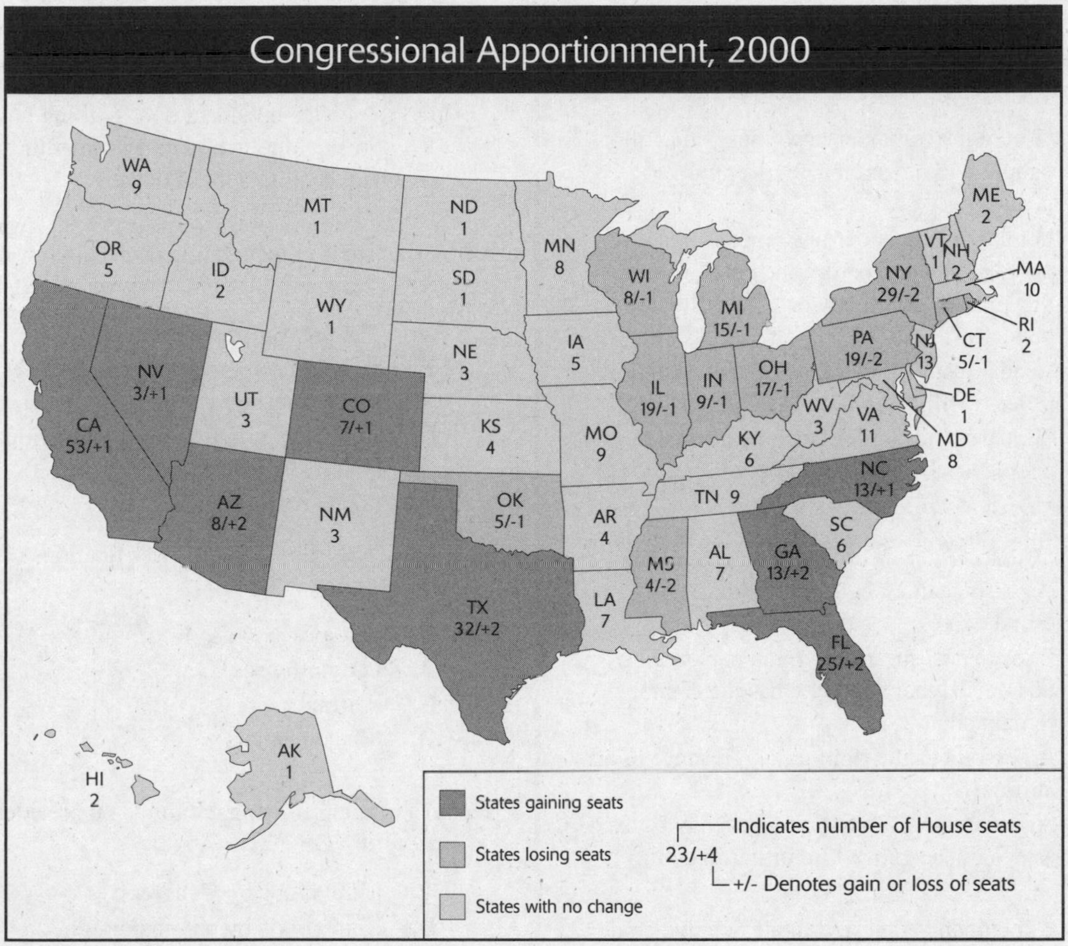

Congressional Apportionment, 2000

WA 9
MT 1
ND 1
MN 8
ME 2
OR 5
ID 2
WY 1
SD 1
WI 8/-1
MI 15/-1
VT 1
NH 2
MA 10
NY 29/-2
PA 19/-2
RI 2
NV 3/+1
UT 3
CO 7/+1
NE 3
IA 5
IL 19/-1
IN 9/-1
OH 17/-1
NJ 13
CT 5/-1
DE 1
CA 53/+1
KS 4
MO 9
WV 3
VA 11
MD 8
AZ 8/+2
NM 3
OK 5/-1
AR 4
TN 9
NC 13/+1
KY 6
SC 6
TX 32/+2
MS 4/-2
AL 7
GA 13/+2
LA 7
FL 25/+2
AK 1
HI 2

States gaining seats
States losing seats
States with no change

Indicates number of House seats
23/+4
+/- Denotes gain or loss of seats

Source: U.S. Census Bureau, 2001

This apportionment map is based on the 2000 census. It will be adjusted after the census of 2010. What is the general trend in reapportionment because of population shifts?

A. The Southeast and Southwest gained seats while the Midwest lost seats.
B. The Northwest gained more seats than the Southwest.
C. The Northeast gained more seats while the far Northeast remained the same.
D. People are moving to different parts of the country.

GO ON TO THE NEXT PAGE

60. The president and Congress share powers. All of the following are powers EXCEPT:

A. Paying expenses
B. Making treaties
C. Declaring war
D. Appointing federal officials

61. How may the principle of "equal justice under law," applied in federal court cases, benefit minorities, poor people, or young people?

A. "Equal justice under law" means that all people will be given a court-appointed lawyer.
B. "Equal justice under law" means that all people are equal before the court, even if they have little money or little political power.
C. "Equal justice under law" means that due process will be applied to all people.
D. "Equal justice under law" means that all people are innocent until proven guilty.

62. All of the following are *Miranda* rules EXCEPT:

A. A person cannot be tried for the same crime twice.
B. Prior to any questioning, the person must be advised that he or she has the right to remain silent.
C. A person has the right to the presence of an attorney.
D. Any statement a person makes may be used as evidence against him or her in court.

63. Which document suggested the legislative branch have a House of Representatives and a Senate?

A. The Virginia Plan
B. The Connecticut Compromise
C. The New Jersey Plan
D. The Three-Fifths Compromise

64. John Adams once said, "I am Vice President. In this I am nothing, but I may be everything." What did he mean?

A. The vice president does not have much official power, but should he become president, he will have a great deal of power.
B. The vice president is a meaningless role unless the president dies.
C. The vice president feels like he has no power, but he is actually very power-hungry.
D. The vice president does nothing unless the president tells him to do something; then he yields quite a lot of power.

65. All of the following are reasons or concerns that cause people to join interest groups EXCEPT:

A. The pressure of mass media
B. To help promote an individual's economic self-interests
C. Because a group shares an individual's beliefs, values, or attitudes
D. Social reasons

66. All of the following are classifications of crimes EXCEPT:

A. Felonies
B. Petty offenses
C. Warrants
D. Misdemeanors

67. All of the following are limits on presidential power EXCEPT:

A. Limitations by Congress
B. Limitations by public opinion
C. Limitations by federal courts
D. Limitations by the vice president

68. Federal programs are designed to provide insurance against such social problems as old age, illness, and unemployment. Those programs are called:

A. Social insurance programs
B. Public assistance programs
C. Urban renewal programs
D. Securities programs

69. The Internet assists citizen activists in all of the following ways EXCEPT:

A. Getting involved in grassroots movements
B. Controlling coverage of certain issues
C. Making it easier to gather information
D. Communicating with candidates

70. How does the winner-take-all system of the Electoral College operate?

A. The electors pledge to vote for a particular presidential candidate.
B. The candidate who loses the states' popular vote still wins the electoral votes if the candidate is from that state.
C. The candidate who wins the most votes wins the election.
D. The candidate who wins the most popular votes in a state wins all of that states' electoral votes.

71. What is the most accurate description of an autocratic government?

A. Power is divided among the national government and state or provincial governments.
B. A small group of people have the power to govern, often because of wealth, military power, or social position.
C. Leaders rule with the consent of the citizens.
D. One person holds the power to rule and may use military or police power to maintain authority.

72. Students with disabilities may have their needs met through which department?

A. Department of Justice
B. Department of State
C. Department of Treasury
D. Department of Education

73. A political cartoon shows a large, bloated figure, which represents baby boomers, falling down a hill. The figure is being supported by Uncle Sam and is singing, "Will you still need me, will you still feed me, when I'm sixty-four?"

According to the political cartoonist, who will financially support retired baby boomers?

A. They will not receive any financial support
B. Social Security
C. Other baby boomers
D. The United States government

74. Why do presidential candidates who represent moderate views usually win elections?

A. Most voters have moderate views.
B. The voters on the two extremes of issues are generally satisfied with a moderate view of an issue.
C. More moderates tend to vote than extremists.
D. Their vice-presidential candidates are usually stronger.

75. In a laissez-faire economic system, the role of government is

A. to own the basic means of production and make most economic decisions.
B. to keep competition free and fair and protect the public interest.
C. to avoid interfering except to ensure free competition in the marketplace.
D. to share equally in industrial production.

76. Why do so few bills actually become laws?

A. They are poorly written.
B. The process provides opportunities to kill a bill.
C. The line-item veto is used too often.
D. There are seldom enough representatives present.

GO ON TO THE NEXT PAGE

77. In a political cartoon, two students are looking at a parking meter on a desk. The students are saying, "The state decided to leave per-pupil spending up to the individual."

What is the subject of this cartoon?

- **A.** State funding of education and schools
- **B.** High prices of public parking in downtown areas
- **C.** The attitudes of today's youth
- **D.** College tuition

78. Federal grants influence the states in all of the following ways EXCEPT:

- **A.** Federal grants set certain minimum standards in the states.
- **B.** Federal grants establish different types of local government.
- **C.** Federal grants supply funds for programs that states otherwise might not be able to afford.
- **D.** Federal grants stimulate programs and goals that the federal government believes are necessary.

79. A well-established government with fair elections, competing political parties, and some form of market economy is known as a

- **A.** parliamentary government.
- **B.** consolidated democracy.
- **C.** supranational organization.
- **D.** state-sponsored terrorism.

Section 4: Geography

Directions: For each of the following questions, select the choice that best answers the question or completes the statement.

80. Which of the following is a challenge that rapid population growth presents to the global community?

- **A.** Shortages of metropolitan areas
- **B.** Shortages of housing
- **C.** Low population density
- **D.** Disloyal military forces

81. In Russia, nuclear power plants built during the Soviet era

- **A.** have been shut down.
- **B.** provide much of Russia's electricity.
- **C.** are now safer than ever before.
- **D.** have been replaced by coal-fired generators.

82. Refer to the following graph to answer the question.

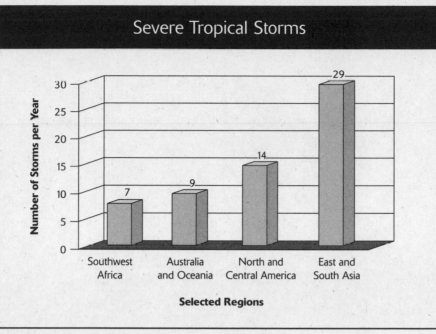

Source: Encyclopedia Britannica.

Which of the following statements can be inferred from the graph?

A. Severe tropical storms are rare in Oceania.
B. East and South Asia have about four times as many severe tropical storms as Southwest Africa.
C. North and Central America never go through a month without a storm.
D. South America does not have tropical storms.

GO ON TO THE NEXT PAGE

83. Refer to the following circle graph to answer the question.

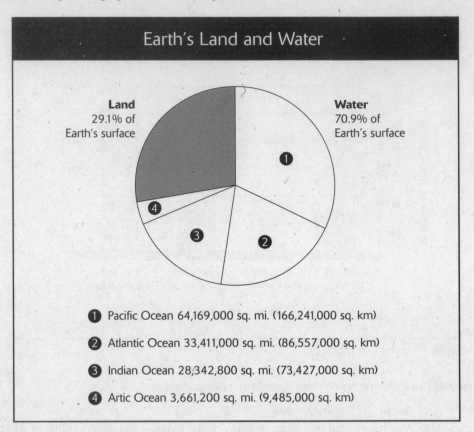

Earth's Land and Water

Land
29.1% of
Earth's surface

Water
70.9% of
Earth's surface

❶ Pacific Ocean 64,169,000 sq. mi. (166,241,000 sq. km)

❷ Atlantic Ocean 33,411,000 sq. mi. (86,557,000 sq. km)

❸ Indian Ocean 28,342,800 sq. mi. (73,427,000 sq. km)

❹ Artic Ocean 3,661,200 sq. mi. (9,485,000 sq. km)

Which ocean covers about as much of the earth's surface as land does?

A. Indian
B. Pacific
C. Arctic
D. Atlantic

84. Refer to the map to answer the following.

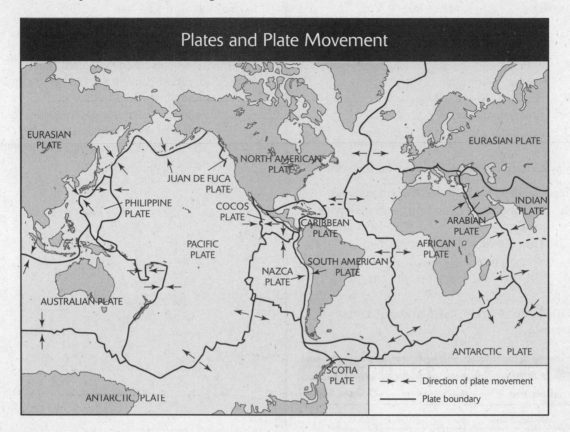

Plates and Plate Movement

All of the following are physical features that are the result of plate movement EXCEPT:

A. Mountains
B. Volcanoes
C. Trenches
D. Oceans

85. Which of the following statements about languages in Latin America is true?

    A. Few Latin Americans speak Native American languages.

    B. Portuguese is the official language of only one Latin American country.

    C. French is the official language in most Latin American countries.

    D. Few Latin Americans are bilingual.

86. Why do the mid-latitudes have a temperate climate?

    A. Ocean winds moderate the temperatures.

    B. The mid-range latitude presents mid-range temperatures.

    C. The cold currents cool off the high temperatures.

    D. The sun shines longer on these regions.

87. Refer to the following table to complete the statement.

Notable Volcanic Eruptions			
Year	**Volcano**	**Location**	**Deaths (est.)**
1631	Mt. Vesuvius	Italy	4,000
1783	Laki	Iceland	9,350
1883	Krakatua	Indonesia	36,000
1902	Mt. Pelee	Martinique	28,000
1980	Mt. St. Helens	United States	57
1991	Mt. Pinatubo	Philippines	800

The table probably contains data from the past 300+ years because

    A. more volcanoes erupted then.

    B. more information is available.

    C. no volcanoes erupted before 1631.

    D. eruptions are getting closer together.

88. The mountains have all of the following effects on the climate of East Asia EXCEPT:

    A. Crops may fail if there is too much or too little rain.

    B. Mountains block the humid summer monsoon, causing a cooler, drier climate north of the Qin Ling range.

    C. Rain shadow causes desert conditions in Mongolia and inland northern China.

    D. The highlands are cool or cold, depending on their elevation.

89. Refer to the following map to answer the question.

Selected Countries in Eastern Europe

GERMANY

POLAND

BELARUS

CZECH REPUBLIC

SLOVAKIA

AUSTRIA

HUNGARY

ROMANIA

SLOVENIA

CROATIA

BOSNIA

SERBIA

BULGARIA

How might the location of the Czech Republic, Slovakia, and Hungary affect their role in world trade?

A. They are smaller.

B. They are landlocked.

C. They are communist.

D. They have many resources.

GO ON TO THE NEXT PAGE

90. In part of the region of North Africa, Southwest Asia, and Central Asia, people earn their living by growing citrus fruits, olives, and grapes, as well as from the tourist trade. This region probably has a

A. highlands climate.
B. steppe climate.
C. Mediterranean climate.
D. desert climate.

91. Imagine that you are hired to create a sketch map of Egypt to show the importance of the Nile River to Egypt's people. What combination of information would be the most useful to show?

A. Coastal areas, mountains, and oil and phosphate resources
B. Population density, commercial farming, and deserts
C. Population density, subsistence farming, and city locations
D. Deserts, plateaus, and mountains

92. Refer to the following table to answer the question.

Facts About Tanzania		
	1996	*2003*
Population	29,058,470	35,400,000
Percent urban	21	22
Percent rural	79	78
Population density of entire country	80 per sq. mi. (31 per sq. km)	97 per sq. mi. (38 per sq. km)
Population of current capital, Dar es Salaam	1,400,000	2,347,000

Sources: World Almanac, 1997, 2001; 2003 World Population Data Sheet

Which of the following statements regarding Tanzania's population is implied by the chart?

A. Dar es Salaam's population increased by about 100,000 people.
B. Tanzania's population density was lower in 1996 than it was in 2003.
C. The percentage of Tanzanians living in urban areas increased from 21 percent to 40 percent.
D. Between 1996 and 2003, many of Tanzania's residents moved from cities to rural areas.

93. Refer to the following graph to answer the question.

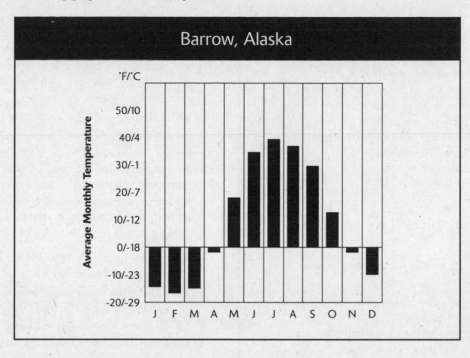

As a regional geographer for an oil company, you need to determine the best time for a survey team to work near Barrow, Alaska. Given the information on the bar graph, during which three-month period should the survey take place?

A. January, February, March
B. September, October, November
C. March, April, May
D. June, July, August

GO ON TO THE NEXT PAGE

94. Use the following passage to answer the question.

"And so I have finally come to understand that while I am hopelessly American, accustomed to (and dependent on) the relentless pressures and fierce energies of the New World ... there are moments when I want to escape to a different place with a beauty and a beat of its own. And when that happens, when I want to disappear from who I am, and where I live, the place I think of is Paris."

—David Halberstam, "Paris," *National Geographic Traveler,* October 1999

What kind of place does the author want to escape to sometimes?

A. He wants a place where there is a lot of pressure and energy.

B. He wants a beautiful place halfway around the world.

C. He wants a unique, beautiful place that is different from where he lives.

D. He wants a place where he can disappear into the crowds.

95. How do prevailing winds affect the acid rain that falls in Europe?

A. Prevailing winds disperse acid rain across national borders.

B. Prevailing winds help clear away the acid rain, which results in less pollution.

C. Acid rain is heavier than air, so prevailing winds do not affect acid rain at all.

D. Europe's industrial belt lies in an area with no prevailing wind.

96. How might global warming affect Europe?

A. Global warming might cause rising sea levels and severe drought.

B. Global warming might make temperatures intolerably hot.

C. Global warming might cause an increase in the acid rain.

D. Global warming might cause rivers and lakes to go dry.

97. Researchers using GIS and GPS technology to correlate water quality indexes, zoning maps, census figures, and maps of area rivers and aquifers are most likely trying to determine which of the following?

A. The relationship between the location of industrial plants and water quality

B. The water pressure for new fire hydrants for a developing community

C. The location of scenic hiking trails

D. The lung disease rates for various areas in the region

98. Refer to the following chart to answer the question.

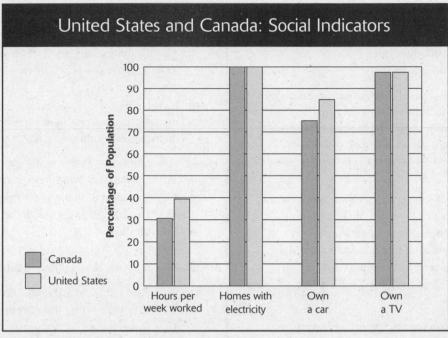

United States and Canada: Social Indicators

Source: Brittanica Book of the Year, 2000.

What can you infer about the social indicators in the United States and Canada?

A. Neither country is worried about electricity.

B. Cars are more important than televisions.

C. Both countries have highly developed economies.

D. Citizens do not work very hard.

Section 5: Economics

Directions: For each of the following questions, select the choice that best answers the question or completes the statement.

99. Your friend says, "I need some new clothes." Under what conditions would this be expressing a need?

A. If the clothes were needed to auction off at a charity auction.

B. If the clothes were wanted as additional clothes.

C. If the clothes were needed for a weekend party.

D. If the clothes were an absolute necessity to keep warm.

100. All of the following are stages required to establish the federal budget EXCEPT:

A. Executive formulation, in which the president prepares the budget and submits it to Congress

B. Initial formulation, in which Congress reviews the main points of the budget

C. Final approval, in which the president signs or vetoes the budget

D. Congressional action, during which Congress reviews, modifies, and approves the budget

GO ON TO THE NEXT PAGE

101. All of the following are examples of oligopolies in the United States EXCEPT:

A. Franchises
B. Domestic airlines
C. The fast-food industry
D. The soft drink industry

102. Alan Greenspan says "The American economy, clearly more than most, is in the grip of what the eminent Harvard professor, Joseph Schumpeter, many years ago called 'creative destruction'...." What do you think Greenspan means by "creative destruction"?

A. The continuous process by which new technologies push out old technologies.
B. Technological innovations are revolutionizing medicine and agriculture.
C. There is very little imprecision.
D. The standard of living for the average worker has gone up.

103. All of the following are important buying principles EXCEPT:

A. Comparison shopping
B. Gathering information
C. Using advertising wisely
D. Respecting the rights of producers and sellers

104. What is the major source of income for the national government?

A. Importing/exporting
B. Income taxes
C. Gifts
D. Grants

105. All of the following are types of unemployment EXCEPT:

A. Frictional unemployment
B. Full unemployment
C. Structural unemployment
D. Seasonal unemployment

106. A free-enterprise system has all of the following characteristics EXCEPT:

A. Economic freedom
B. Public property
C. Voluntary exchange
D. Competition

107. How will the economic growth and development of developing countries affect the future?

A. International trade will increase.
B. There will be overpopulation.
C. Communication will improve.
D. There will be high interest rates.

108. Imagine that you have just started a business manufacturing toothbrushes. What would a quota on imported toothbrushes do to your business?

A. Quotas will push up the price of the product.
B. Quotas will bring more foreign competition.
C. Quotas will make you work harder.
D. Quotas will bring down the price of the product.

109. How are roles defined in a traditional economy?

A. Roles are set by popular vote.
B. Roles are set by the government.
C. Roles are set by consumers.
D. Roles are set by long-standing customs.

110. If we were to enter a period of recession, all of the following would likely happen EXCEPT:

A. Inflation would fall.
B. Unemployment would rise.
C. Poverty would rise.
D. Inflation would rise.

111. Owning private property gives people all of the following incentives EXCEPT:

A. The incentive to work harder
B. The incentive to buy/sell
C. The incentive to save
D. The incentive to invest

112. All of the following are major renewable resources EXCEPT:

A. Hydroelectric power
B. Wind power
C. Oil
D. Solar power

113. All of the following are explanations for why unions have lost members, as well as influence, in recent years EXCEPT:

   A. Additions to the labor force have little loyalty to organized labor.

   B. Unions are victims of their own success.

   C. Nobody likes unions and what they stand for.

   D. Many employers have kept unions out.

114. Refer to the following chart to answer the question.

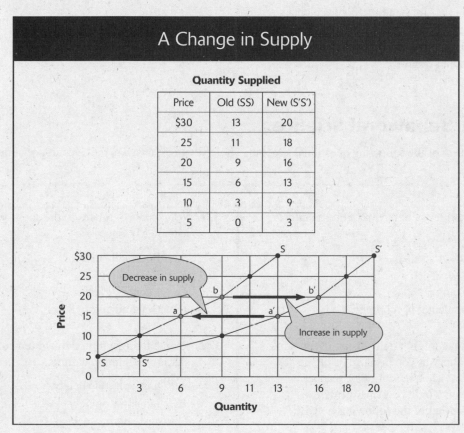

A change in supply means that a different quantity is supplied at every price. What does a shift of the supply curve to the right show?

   A. An increase in supply at each price

   B. A decrease in supply for the new price but an increase in price for the old price

   C. An increase in quantity at the old price

   D. An increase in supply at the old price but a decrease in price for the new price

GO ON TO THE NEXT PAGE

115. What economic goal is being met by the following action: Juan moves to Seattle to work for a Web page designer?

A. Economic security
B. Economic equity
C. Economic competition
D. Economic freedom

116. Banks are using all of the following actions to earn more profits EXCEPT:

A. Charging a fee for returning canceled checks
B. Raising fees for handling bounced checks
C. Taking a portion of the customers' interest
D. Charging customers for using live tellers and other banks' ATMs

117. A society must make choices because of scarcity. All of the following are choices EXCEPT:

A. For whom to produce
B. Why to produce
C. What to produce
D. How to produce

Section 6: Behavioral Sciences

Directions: For each of the following questions, select the choice that best answers the question or completes the statement.

118. Learning the rules of behavior of one's culture is called

A. maturation.
B. schema.
C. socialization.
D. developmental psychology.

119. What technique might you be using if you think a teacher is angry at you because he or she gave a difficult test, when in reality the teacher is not angry? You would be using the defense mechanisms of all of the following EXCEPT:

A. Regression
B. Reinforcement
C. Rationalization
D. Projection

120. The study of how people perceive, store, and retrieve information about social interactions is called

A. social cognition.
B. generational identity.
C. attribution theory.
D. utility value.

121. What concept relates to the song lyric, "Walk a Mile in My Shoes"?

A. Resocialization
B. Role taking
C. Looking-glass self
D. Generalization

122. People living within defined territorial borders and sharing a common culture are called a

A. horticultural society.
B. industrial society.
C. agricultural society.
D. society.

123. Treating people differently because of their ethnicity, race, religion, or culture is called

A. discrimination.
B. subjugation.
C. racism.
D. prejudice.

124. A religious movement based on the desire to adhere closely to traditional beliefs, rituals, and doctrines is called

- **A.** spirit of capitalism.
- **B.** legitimation.
- **C.** secularization.
- **D.** fundamentalism.

125. Religions fill psychological and social needs for all of the following EXCEPT:

- **A.** They help us confront and explain death.
- **B.** They help ease stress during life crises.
- **C.** They reinforce social norms.
- **D.** They allow us to classify ourselves in society.

126. The most effective form of social control is

- **A.** police.
- **B.** moral code.
- **C.** laws.
- **D.** jails.

127. Dialects can be categorized by all of the following EXCEPT:

- **A.** Region
- **B.** Class
- **C.** Inheritance
- **D.** Age

128. The set of beliefs, attitudes, norms, and values used to justify age-based prejudice and discrimination is called

- **A.** biological determinism.
- **B.** age stratification.
- **C.** ageism.
- **D.** segregation.

129. All of the following are midlife issues faced by adult women EXCEPT:

- **A.** Menopause
- **B.** Empty-nest syndrome
- **C.** Concerns over physical attractiveness
- **D.** Depression

130. According to Erik Erikson, adolescents go through a(n) _____, a time of inner conflict in which they worry about their identities.

- **A.** identity crisis
- **B.** gender identity
- **C.** conformity
- **D.** individual struggle

Answer Key for Practice Test 1

Section 1: World History

1. C	9. C	17. B	25. D
2. D	10. D	18. B	26. A
3. A	11. D	19. B	27. C
4. B	12. B	20. B	28. B
5. A	13. C	21. A	29. C
6. C	14. C	22. A	
7. B	15. A	23. D	
8. A	16. D	24. C	

Section 2: United States History

30. D	38. D	46. A	54. C
31. C	39. B	47. B	55. C
32. D	40. D	48. B	56. B
33. B	41. B	49. D	57. D
34. B	42. B	50. C	58. C
35. D	43. C	51. B	
36. C	44. D	52. D	
37. A	45. D	53. D	

Section 3: Government/Political Science/Civics

59. A	65. A	71. D	77. A
60. C	66. C	72. D	78. B
61. B	67. D	73. D	79. B
62. A	68. A	74. A	
63. B	69. B	75. C	
64. A	70. D	76. B	

Section 4: Geography

80. B	**85.** B	**90.** C	**95.** A
81. B	**86.** A	**91.** C	**96.** A
82. B	**87.** B	**92.** B	**97.** A
83. B	**88.** A	**93.** D	**98.** C
84. D	**89.** B	**94.** C	

Section 5: Economics

99. D	**104.** A	**109.** D	**114.** A
100. B	**105.** B	**110.** D	**115.** D
101. A	**106.** B	**111.** A	**116.** C
102. A	**107.** A	**112.** C	**117.** B
103. D	**108.** A	**113.** C	

Section 6: Behavioral Sciences

118. C	**122.** D	**126.** B	**130.** A
119. B	**123.** A	**127.** C	
120. A	**124.** D	**128.** C	
121. B	**125.** D	**129.** D	

Answer Explanations for Practice Test 1

Section 1: World History

1. **C.** If the question asks you to read a quote, look for clues that reveal its historical context. Such clues can be found in the title and date of the text as well as in the quote itself. Determining the historical context will help you to determine the quote's *historical significance* or the importance it has gained over time.

2. **D.** The Silk Road extended from China to Southwest Asia. It was a route for transporting luxury items, and it provided the means for spreading the religions of Buddhism, Christianity, and Islam.

3. **A.** Oligarchy is rule by a few. Democracy is rule by the people. Monarchy is rule by a king or queen.

4. **B.** A triumvirate is a government by three people with equal power. Crassus, Pompey, and Julius Caesar emerged as victors of 50 years of Roman civil wars. They combined wealth and power to form a government.

5. **A.** Islamic art is a blend of Arab, Turkish, and Persian traditions. The best expression of Islamic art is found in the magnificent Muslim mosques.

6. **C.** Scandinavia remained free; England, France, and central Europe experienced multiple invasions.

7. **B.** You are looking for the exception in this question, so you want to identify the one force that did *not* lead to growth during the Middle Ages. Improved agricultural methods, increased trade, and development of a money economy all led to growth. Classical texts did not lead to growth.

8. **A.** The Aztecs survived, strengthened by their belief in a sign that would come from their god of war and of the sun. The god had told them that when they saw an eagle perched on a cactus growing out of a rock, their journey would end. When they saw that, they built Tenochtitlan (or "place of the prickly pear cactus"). They believed they had found the land promised to them, they would have peace for their people, and they would want for nothing.

9. **C.** The compass and astrolabe aided in exploration, allowing them to determine what direction they were moving and to navigate; lateen sails made ships more maneuverable and allowed them to carry heavy cannon and more goods.

10. **D.** Through the story of *Don Quixote* and the development of the characters (Don Quixote is the visionary so involved in his lofty ideals that he does not see the hard realities around him; his squire, Sancho Panza, is a realist), we are left with the conviction that both visionary dreams and the hard work of reality are necessary to the human condition.

11. **D.** Remembering the dates of the Glorious Revolution (1688) will help you eliminate answers. In 1688, a son was born to Kin James II, and the possibility of a Catholic monarchy loomed large.

12. **B.** Look at the map carefully and make sure your answer fits with the question. Foreign trading forts in India were always along the coast, usually near a river or bay.

13. **C.** Make sure that the statement is true for *both* empires.

14. **C.** The key word is *immediately*, so the correct answer is a *direct result* of the war. Although many of the events stated in the answer choices happened around this time, you want the answer that happened directly after the Great Peloponnesian War.

15. **A.** Women were not traders or politicians, and they did not pass down traditions to younger generations. So, B, C, and D do not describe women in ancient India.

16. **D.** Look at each answer choice and check it against the quote. Answers B and D may seem very similar. Answer D, however, matches the issues addressed in the quote more closely than B.

17. **B.** The growth of both publishing and the reading public meant more people were reading and becoming aware of the Enlightenment. Enlightenment ideas were also spread through the salon—elegant drawing rooms of the wealthy upper class's great urban houses—where writers, artists, aristocrats, government officials, and wealthy middle-class people would gather.

18. B. Make sure you read the title of the map and look at the map carefully for information before you try to answer the question. Use your knowledge of world geography to help you answer the question.

19. B. With a timeline question, you may need to make an inference. Look for clues in the test question and timeline. In this case, think about what the events on the timeline have in common. These clues can help you make an inference that is supported by the timeline. Obviously, there was not complete support, there *were* problems, and, clearly, women wrote about politics, too. So the only plausible answer is B.

20. B. The British taxation on colonists was the most important event that precipitated the American Revolution.

21. A. Look carefully at the map. The revolutions extended to Palermo in Sicily.

22. A. This question asks for an answer that is supported by the facts provided. Find the answer choice that is *proven true* by the information listed. Answer A is the only statement based on the information.

23. D. Impressionism was a movement that began in France in the 1870s, when a group of artists rejected the studios where artists had traditionally worked and went out into the countryside to paint nature directly. One important Impressionist is Claude Monet. Others include Renoir and Morisot.

24. C. An important word in this question is *best*. Although it is true that Russia entered on the side of France and Great Britain, it could never provide strong support due to internal weaknesses. It may help to remember the domestic history in Russia during World War I, especially that of the Russian Revolution in 1917. Once Lenin established a Bolshevik government, he immediately pulled Russia out of the war. The best answer is C.

25. D. Look carefully at the map and the questions. All of the answer choices are true about the Suez Canal, but you want to find the answer choice that most thoroughly answers the question. Control of the Suez Canal would provide a shorter route form Europe to Asia. Therefore, D is the correct answer.

26. A. All of the other answer choices were things that were happening, but they do not directly relate to the British motives for protecting Latin American states.

27. C. You can automatically eliminate answers not related to India, such as D.

28. B. Any time you get a map, pay careful attention to the title and to the map legend. The legend gives information crucial to understanding the map. The information in the legend may also help you eliminate answer choices that are incorrect. The amount of land gained indicates that answer A is obviously incorrect.

29. C. You are looking for the exception in this question, so you want to find the item that was not imported from China. Tea, silk, and porcelain were all imported from China. Silver was not. So, C is the correct answer.

Section 2: United States History

30. D. The question is asking for an opinion, so you should look for subjective words such as *good, important, think, like* (and synonyms and antonyms of those words). Choice D talks about "better democracy."

31. C. Eliminate answers that don't make sense. The Spanish had a monarchy, not a democracy, so it would be illogical for them to bring democratic government to the Americas. If you attach an approximate date or culture to each answer, that might help. Hieroglyphic writing was prevalent in ancient America and Native American peoples of Mesoamerica were cultivating maize (corn) long before Spanish explorers arrived. Therefore, you can rule out A and D.

32. D. Think about the word *limit*. It means to reduce or restrict. Therefore, you can eliminate answer B—it gave the government more power. You can also eliminate C because dissolving a party would not reduce governmental power.

33. B. *Advantage* and *Southern states* are key words. You probably remember that the North was more populated and "advanced" than the South, so you can eliminate C and D. Also, the South did not have the support of the British and the French, so you can eliminate A.

34. B. The important word in this question is *and*. Look for the answer that applies to both colonies. For example, while it is true that the Pilgrims founded Plymouth Colony for religious reasons, the Jamestown founders were primarily looking for gold and adventure, so you can eliminate answer D. And the primary source of income for Jamestown was tobacco, but there is no evidence that the Pilgrims grew tobacco. Therefore, you can rule out C.

35. D. The important word in this question is *both*. Several reform movements are mentioned, but the question asks about the reforms *both* women supported. Look for clues in the passage—Sojourner Truth was a former slave, so she likely supported abolition. Therefore, you can narrow the choices to A and D. Since Susan B. Anthony was a powerful organizer in the women's right movement, the best answer is D.

36. C. This question is looking for the *exception*. Three of the answer choices describe types of discrimination that women faced in the 1960s. Women gained the rights to vote in 1920, when the Nineteenth Amendment was ratified.

37. A. Think about New England's geography and society. Which of the answers does not describe New England's society? The key words in this question are *community life* and *New England*.

38. D. Remember, this question asks for the *exception*. Read through each answer carefully to see if it is true of FDR's first Hundred Days. You are looking for the answer that is false. The bills were intended to combat the effects of the Great Depression, so since A is true, it is not the correct answer. Since the bills were new, they were known as the New Deal, so B is true, and it cannot be the correct answer. Since the bills were only temporary at the beginning, C is true, and it is not the correct answer. Also, 100 days is less than four months. It does not seem likely that much could have been accomplished if Congress was involved in divisive and protracted debate. Therefore, the correct answer is D.

39. B. This question is asking for a cause-and-effect relationship, so you should look for an answer that can be *directly related* to the needs of a wartime economy. During the war, it was necessary to produce supplies and munitions for the armed forces (which also needed more personnel), so answer A must be incorrect. In fact, there were more jobs and fewer workers to fill them, so unemployment is not a logical choice. The United States had to raise revenue to pay for the war, which led to a rise in taxes during the war, so answer C is incorrect. And, labor unions were not abolished, so, D is incorrect. That leaves B as the correct answer.

40. D. An *arsenal* is a stockpile or storehouse of weapons. Eliminate any answer that does not relate to using weapons to protect democracy. Also think about the timing of the event. This will help you rule out A, since the Depression was largely over by this time. If you think about who the Axis powers were, you can rule out B, since Germany, Italy, and Japan were not democratic countries. Finally, supplying aid to one side is likely to allow the country to remain neutral, so you can rule out C. The answer that is left is D.

41. B. Look in the passage to find clues to support your answer. Try not to get confused by the long sentences or old-fashioned language in this passage. Ask yourself what the main idea is. Underline the key phrases from the excerpt, such as *free and independent* and *not ... for future colonization*. This will help identify the answer.

42. B. After Vietnam and Watergate, Congress wanted legislation to limit the president's power during wartime. Three of the answers actually do the opposite, give the president *more* power. Some of the answers actually state "greater authority" and "freer hand," so the correct answer is B.

43. C. You can eliminate some answers with your own knowledge. For example, you probably know that child care is still an issue for parents today, so it cannot be guaranteed in the Nineteenth Amendment. Therefore, you can eliminate answer B. Also, equal wages is still an issue facing women today, so you can eliminate answer D. In the 1920s, most women were not worried about attending college, so you can eliminate answer A.

44. D. From the wording of the question, you can see that Social Darwinism and the Gospel of Wealth *do* have three of these concepts in common. So, you have to find the answer that is part of only *one* of these philosophies. For each answer, you should ask yourself if the concept in the answer choice is associated with *both*. If the answer is yes, you can eliminate the answer.

45. D. You're looking for an answer that does *not* accurately complete the statement. The Warren Court expanded individual civil liberties and the power of the judicial branch. Eliminate answers that had either of those effects. The correct answer is D.

46. A. Eliminate answers you know are incorrect. For example, the breakup of Austria-Hungary took place after World War I, so you can eliminate that answer. The exile of Huerta occurred in Mexico, which had little effect on European nations, so you can eliminate B. One of the results of World War I was the breakup of several empires. This makes D less likely to be the correct answer. So, the correct answer is A.

47. B. The question is asking for one *difference* in civil rights strategies. Three of the answer choices represent *common goals*. Think about what some of the later civil rights groups advocated. The one issue on this list that some of the later groups did not support was nonviolence. The correct answer is B.

48. B. Remember, you're looking for the answer that does not fit. Unions were formed to try to help workers. Which answer is least likely to help workers? Answers A, C, and D can be eliminated, leaving B as the correct answer.

49. D. When the question stem has a negative, you should try to reword the sentence or phrase to make it positive. For example, which of the following was a cause of tension? Since D refers to a compromise, it does not suggest a cause of anger/tension.

50. C. Because the question has the word *not* in it, look for an answer that seems opposed to the other answers. Which of the answers is opposite of the rest? The Cubans did not readily accept the Platt Amendment and they reluctantly added it to their constitution. So, you can eliminate the answers that place restrictions on Cuba: A, B, and D.

51. B. Use the process of elimination to rule out any answers that you know are wrong. For example, two of the answers suggest that the colonists and the British may already be at war, while only one answer mentions the main issue. Look for the main idea in the question. This question is related to taxes and voting for representation in Parliament. Answer B is the only answer that mentions taxes and representation.

52. D. Know that nativism means favoring native-born people over immigrants. An influx of immigrants contributed to nativism, so you can eliminate choice B. Although some fundamentalists were nativists, fundamentalist beliefs were not anti-immigrant. Therefore you can infer that the correct answer is D.

53. D. Eliminate the answers you know are incorrect. For instance, machinery such as the reaper *did* make it easier for farmers to work more land at a quicker pace. Therefore you can eliminate answer B. The Homestead Act was a form of government assistance, and it did make it easier for settlers to live and farm on the Great Plains. Therefore, you can eliminate answer A. Obviously, new farming techniques would make it easier to farm, so you can eliminate answer C.

54. C. Remember that three of the four choices were part of Eisenhower's programs. If you consider the goals of dynamic conservatism, and think about which answers are most consistent with those goals, you can eliminate A, B, and D.

55. C. Think about the definition of McCarthyism, the use of unsubstantiated accusations to discredit people. So, you're looking for the answer that best relates to this definition.

56. B. Make sure your answer reflects the original goal of the Antitrust Act. Only one answer reflects the reason Congress passed the law. Think about each of the choices—which could realistically restrain trade? Labor unions and the Farmers' Alliances were a combination of workers and did not have the power to restrain trade. Railroads could not restrain trade, either. By eliminating those answers, you are left with choice B.

57. D. You can use the process of elimination. For example, farmers were not prosperous in the 1920s because their huge crops forced down agricultural prices. Therefore, answer B is incorrect. The Hawley-Smoot Tariff, passed in 1930, was the highest tariff ever. This means you can eliminate choice C. Because interest rates were low, business leaders continued to overproduce. This means you can eliminate choice A. The correct answer is D.

58. C. Pay careful attention to the wording of this question. This question asks you to select the answer that is *not* true. That means three of the four statements must be true, and you should find the one that is not. Answers A, B, and D are all true, so the correct answer is C.

Section 3: Government/Political Science/Civics

59. A. Look carefully at the map, and make sure both parts of the answer are correct. The Southeast and Southwest gained seats while the Midwest lost seats, so the correct answer is A.

60. C. Because you are looking for the exception, you have to find the one duty that is *not* shared by Congress and the president. Therefore, C is the correct answer.

61. B. "Equal justice under law" means that every person, regardless of wealth, social status, ethnic group, gender, or age, is entitled to the full protection of the law. All people are equal before the court, even if they have little money or little political power. Even though the other answer choices are aspects of the law, they do not directly answer the question.

62. A. Again, you are looking for the exception, so you must find the answer that is *not* a Miranda rule. While not being retried for the same case is a rule—double jeopardy—it is not a Miranda rule, and B, C, and D are all Miranda rules. Therefore, A is the correct answer.

63. B. The Virginia Plan proposed a government based on three principles: 1) a national legislature with two chambers, 2) a national executive, and 3) a national judiciary, so answer A can be eliminated. The New Jersey Plan called for government based on keeping the major feature of the Articles of Confederation—a unicameral legislature, with one vote for each state, so you can rule out C. The Three-Fifths Compromise settled a disagreement over how to determine how many representatives each state would have in the House, so C is not the correct answer The Connecticut Compromise suggested that the legislative branch have two parts, so B is the correct answer.

64. A. Read all of the answer choices carefully, comparing them to the question. Knowing that the vice president does not have much power unless he becomes president, choice A is the best answer.

65. A. Since you are looking for the exception, you are looking for the answer that does *not* influence people to join an interest group. While mass media might be influential, it does not force one to join an interest group. Therefore, the correct answer is A.

66. C. You are looking for the one answer that is *not* a classification of crime. Since felonies, petty offenses, and misdemeanors are all types of crimes, C is the only possible answer.

67. D. Again you are looking for the exception. Congress, public opinion, and the federal courts all can put some limitations on the president. The vice president, however, does not have any limitations on the presidential power, so D is the correct answer.

68. A. Public assistance programs provide a certain minimum standard of living to those who do not earn enough income. The federal government supports urban renewal in cities to help replace old buildings. Stocks and bonds are forms of securities. Federal social insurance programs are designed to provide insurance against such social problems as old age, illness, and unemployment. Therefore, the correct answer is A.

69. B. Again, you are looking for the exception. You know that the Internet makes everything easier—to gather information, to communicate, and to get involved, and there's very little control. Therefore, B is the correct answer.

70. D. Remember to read the question carefully. You are looking for the "winner-take-all" system. While answer A is correct about the Electoral College, it does not explain the "winner-take-all" system. Choice C is too vague. Choice B is incorrect. Choice D is the correct answer.

71. D. In an autocracy, power and authority to rule are in the hands of a single individual, so A, B, and C are incorrect.

72. D. The Department of Justice oversees the nation's legal affairs, so answer A can be eliminated. The Department of State is responsible for the overall foreign policy of the United States, so you can rule out answer B. The Department of Treasury manages the monetary resources, so C can be eliminated. The Department of Education addresses educational needs, especially programs to help students with special needs, so the correct answer is D.

73. D. In the cartoon the baby boomers are represented by the large, bloated figure falling down the hill. The baby boomer in the cartoon is singing "Will you still need me, will you still feed me, when I'm sixty-four?" as a way of asking, "Will you financially support me?" Uncle Sam, who represents the United States government, is the one holding up the baby boomer. So, the cartoon is implying that the United States government will financially support the baby boomers.

74. A. There are no proven statistics on whether more moderates vote than extremists, so answer C is eliminated. Usually vice-presidential candidates are not the main reason voters vote for a presidential candidate, so you can rule out choice D. While it is possible that the voters on the two extremes are generally satisfied with a moderate view of an issue, it is more likely that most voters have moderate views, so A is the correct answer.

75. C. A laissez-faire economic system is a hands-off approach to government, so C is the best choice.

76. B. While A, C, and D might be true some of the time, the most logical answer is B. The process of a bill becoming a law has several opportunities in which a bill can be killed.

77. A. In the cartoon, the two students are looking at a parking meter on a desk. The parking meter implies that each student will have to pay "per session" to sit and learn and get an education. The students are saying, "The state decided to leave per-pupil spending up to the individual." Differences in the total amount of spending per pupil exist among the states and among localities within states. Differences in spending on education between rich and poor school districts have become vast in some states. Many state courts have claimed such differences are unconstitutional. The cartoonist jokes about the capability of some students to pay for their education. Therefore, the correct answer is A.

78. B. You are looking for the exception, so you want to find that choice that does *not* reflect ways federal grants influence the states. Federal grants do not establish different types of local government, so B is the correct answer.

79. B. In a parliamentary government both the executive and the legislative functions are found in the elected assembly, so you can rule out A. The European Union has evolved from a regional body into a supranational organization, so that eliminates choice C. State-sponsored terrorism is terrorism secretly supported by the government, so you can rule out D. A consolidated democracy is a well-established government with fair elections, competing political parties, and some form of market economy, so B is the correct answer.

Section 4: Geography

80. B. Read the question carefully to determine what is being asked. Look for the key words and phrases that will help you identify the correct answer. The phrase *rapid population growth* is key. Then you must figure out the best choice. The best choice that presents a *challenge* from *rapid population growth* is B.

81. B. Only one answer is completely true. Some reactors have been shut down, and some safety standards were improved. But you must choose the answer that is completely true. That answer is B.

82. B. Read the title and labels on the graph carefully to determine what is being presented. For example, the label on the bottom of the graph tells you that only selected regions are shown. The label on the left indicates the number of storms per year, but not the month in which they occur. Based on the information on the graph, B is the correct answer.

83. B. Study the information shown on the circle graph for the areas of the earth covered by land and by oceans. Then compare the relative sizes of thee different graph segments. By comparing the segments you will be able to determine the correct answer.

84. D. You are looking for the exception, so you want to find the physical feature that is *not* the result of plate movement. The only physical feature that is not the result of plate movement is oceans. So, D is the correct answer.

85. B. Remember to read each answer choice carefully. This question asks you to identify the statement that is true, so you will have to eliminate the answers you know to be false in order to select the correct answer—B.

86. A. You have to read each choice carefully, and best match the answer to the question. The best answer is A.

87. B. Look at the table title to see what kind of information is presented. The statement asks you to infer causes. If you note the table's title, you will have a clue to the answer.

88. A. You are looking for the exception in this question. So, you want to find all of the answers that are effects on the climate. B, C, and D are all effects on the climate. A may be true, but it is not an effect on the climate from the East Asian mountains, so A is the correct answer.

89. B. Notice that the question asks you to base your answer on location. Three of the choices deal with resources, form of government, and size. Choice B, however, focuses on the countries' locations away from seas, which would influence their role in world trade.

90. C. Think about the condition needed to grow the specific crops. Desert climates are too dry, as are steppe climates. Highlands climates are wet but may be too cold. Eliminating wrong choices helps you to choose the correct answer.

91. C. Use the process of elimination to answer this question. First, consider the physical features, land use, resources, and population patterns near the Nile River. Then, eliminate answer choices that contain even one feature or resource that is not likely to be found along the river. Choose your answer from those that remain. The best answer is C.

92. B. Read the question, then skim the table. Next, read each answer choice, deciding whether it is correct or incorrect by referring to the table. Finally, choose the answer that is correct according to the table.

93. D. Study the information shown on the bar graph for an average monthly temperature. Look for three consecutive months in which temperatures would be the most favorable for people and equipment to function outside.

94. C. Sometimes more than one option may seem correct, but read the question carefully, and then look in the reading for information about the kind of place. Compare each answer with that information.

95. A. Some of the answer choices do not answer what the question asks. Study the question closely. Based on the question and the answer choice, A is the best answer.

96. A. Global warming will raise the earth's average temperature. A warmer global climate will melt polar ice caps and mountain glaciers and cause oceans to submerge coastal areas. Weather patterns might change, producing new extremes of rainfall and drought. Looking at the answer choices, knowing what global warming is and what it does, the best answer choice is A.

97. A. Several of the data elements correlated by the researchers relate to water. Eliminate those answers that do not relate to water—C and D. Also, if you know that GPS technology deals with precise positioning data, you can eliminate B. So, the correct answer is A.

98. C. When you are making an inference, you will not find the exact answer on the table. So you need to read each answer choice and compare it to the table and make some assumptions. The best answer is C.

Section 5: Economics

99. D. While you may think that choices A, B, and C seem like needs, they are not; they are wants. D is the only absolute need.

100. B. You are looking for the exception, so you want to find a stage that is *not* involved in the process. A, C, and D are all stages in the process of establishing a federal budget.

101. A. An oligopoly is an industry dominated by *several* suppliers who exercise some control over price. Usually there are a few large firms responsible for 70 to 80 percent of the market, capital costs are high, the goods are very similar, and advertising emphasizes minor differences and attempts to build customer loyalty. With this knowledge, B, C, and D are all oligopolies. Franchises are not, and since you are looking for the exception, the correct answer is A.

102. A. You have to infer on this answer. You have to think about what "creative destruction" might mean and then compare your definition to the answer choices. While B, C, and D are all true situations, the description that best describes "creative destruction" is the notion of new technologies pushing out old technologies, so A is the correct answer.

103. D. You are looking for the one answer choice that is *not* an important buying principle. While respecting the rights of producers and sellers is important, it is not an important buying principle. A, B, and C are all important buying principles, so the correct answer is D.

104. A. While all of these answer choices may bring in income, the major source of income is importing/exporting—choice A.

105. B. You are looking for the exception here, so you want the answer choice that is *not* a type of unemployment. Frictional unemployment is temporary unemployment between jobs because of firings, layoffs, voluntary searches for new jobs, or retraining. Structural unemployment is unemployment caused by changes in the economy, such as technological advances or discoveries of natural resources. Seasonal unemployment is unemployment caused by changes in the seasons or weather. Full unemployment is not a type of unemployment, so B is the correct answer.

106. B. You are looking for the answer choice that is *not* a characteristic of a free-enterprise system. Free-enterprise systems have six important characteristics: limited government involvement, freedom of enterprise, freedom of choice, private property, profit incentive, and competition. The only choice not in this list is answer B.

107. A. Think through the answer choices here, and choose the *best* one. If developing countries are growing and developing, there might be overpopulation, communication might improve for them, there might be high interest rates there, but the most likely answer is that international trade will increase—A.

108. A. Think through the answer choices, and choose the *best* one to answer the question. A quota is a limit on the amount of a good that can be allowed into a country. Because there is a limit on how many toothbrushes can come into the country, the prices of the product will go up. So the correct answer is A.

109. D. If you read the question carefully, there is a clue that can help you determine the answer. The question is asking about a *traditional economy,* or an economy based on traditions. So, roles are defined by long-standing customs, making D the correct answer.

110. D. You are looking for the exception here. If we were to enter a period of recession, the unemployment rate would rise, inflation would fall, and poverty would rise. So, the answer choice that is the exception is D.

111. A. Again, you are looking fore the exception. And you have to find the *best* exception. Owning private property gives people the incentive to buy-sell, to save, and to invest. While all of those incentives *might* cause one to work harder, A is the best choice as the answer that is *not* an incentive.

112. C. Because you are looking for the exception, you should find the resource that is *not* renewable. Of the resources listed, only oil is not renewable. So the correct answer is C.

113. C. Again, you are looking for the exception, so you should find the answer that is *not* a reason for unions losing members and influence. Choice C is not a reason. It may be your opinion, or the opinion of other people you know, but because it is not a fact, we cannot categorize it as a reason, so C is the correct answer.

114. A. Look at the chart carefully. A change in supply means that a different quantity is supplied at every price. So, a shift of the supply curve to the right show an increase in supply at each price—choice A.

115. D. Economic equity is fair and just economic policies, promoted by our government. Economic security is protection against risks beyond our control. If Juan moves to Seattle to work for a Web page designer, he is exhibiting his economic freedom—allowing each citizen to make choices. So D is the correct answer.

116. C. You are looking for the one way that banks do *not* earn more profits. Look at the answers carefully and compare each answer to the question. You can probably use your own banking knowledge to answer this question. Banks are charging fees for returning canceled checks, they are raising fees for handling bounced checks, and they are charging to use live tellers and other banks' ATMs. Banks are not, however, taking people's interest, so the correct answer is C.

117. B. Again, you are looking for the exception. Because we live in a world of relatively scarce resources, we have to make wise economic decisions. The three basic questions we have to ask are What should we produce? How should we produce it? For whom shall we produce it? Therefore, B—Why to produce?—is not a question we ask, so B is the correct answer.

Section 6: Behavioral Sciences

118. C. Maturation is internally programmed growth. Schema is prior knowledge, or mental representations of the world. Developmental psychology is the study of changes that occur as an individual matures. Learning the rule of behavior of one's culture is called socialization, so the correct answer is C.

119. B. You are trying to identify the one defense mechanism that you are *not* using. Regression is a defense mechanism in which an individual retreats to an earlier stage of development or pattern of behavior in order to deal with a threatening or stressful situation. Rationalization is a process whereby an individual seeks to explain an often unpleasant emotion or behavior in a way that will preserve his or her self-esteem. Projection is unconsciously transferring one's own undesirable attitudes, feelings, or thoughts to others. Reinforcement is a stimulus or event that follows a response and increases the likelihood that the response will be repeated. So, B is the correct answer, as you are not displaying reinforcement.

120. A. Generational identity is the theory that people of different ages tend to think differently about certain issues because of different formative experiences. Attribution theory is a collection of principles based on our explanations of the causes of events, other people's behaviors. Utility value is the ability of a person or participant to help another achieve his or her goals. Cognition means knowing/knowledge, so social cognition is the study of how people perceive, store, and retrieve information about social interactions. The correct answer is A.

121. B. Resocialization is the process of adopting new norms, values, attitudes, and behaviors. Looking-glass self is an image of yourself based on what you believe others think of you. The song lyric suggests empathy—walking in another's shoes—so the concept of role taking (assuming the viewpoint of another person and using that viewpoint to shape the self-concept) is what relates to the song lyric. B is the correct answer.

122. D. A, B, and C all suggest more specific types of society. This question is actually a little more general— society is a group of people living within defined territorial borders and sharing a common culture, so the correct answer is D.

123. A. Subjugation is the process by which a minority group is denied equal access to the benefits of a society. Racism is an extreme form of prejudice that assumes superiority of one group over others. Prejudice is widely held negative attitudes toward a group (minority or majority) and its individual members. Discrimination is treating people differently based on ethnicity, race, religion, or culture. A is the correct answer.

124. D. The spirit of capitalism is the obligation to reinvest money in business rather than to spend it. Legitimation is not a term. Secularization is the process through which the sacred loses influence over society. Fundamentalism is the desire to resist secularization and to adhere closely to traditional religious beliefs, rituals, and doctrines, so D is the correct answer.

125. D. You are looking for the exception. So, you need to find the answer choice that does *not* address how religions fill psychological and social needs. While it is possible that religions allow us to classify ourselves in society, religions help us best to confront and explain death, ease stress during life crises, and reinforce social norms. So, the best answer is D.

126. B. While the police, laws, and jails do control society, the *best* form of social control is a society's moral code, so the correct answer is B.

127. C. You are looking for the exception in this question. So, you want to identify the answer that is *not* a categorization of dialect. Dialect is a variant in language. Region, class, and age can all play a part in dialect. Perhaps inheritance plays a part in the way a person speaks, but not the way region, class, and age do. Therefore, C is the answer.

128. C. Biological determinism is the principle that behavioral differences are the result of inherited physical characteristics. Age stratification is the unequal distribution of scarce resources based on age. Segregation is racial imbalance. Ageism is a set of beliefs, attitudes, norms, and values used to justify age-based prejudice and discrimination, so C is the correct answer.

129. D. You are looking for the exception here. While some middle-aged women might be depressed, depression is not as common a midlife issue as menopause, empty-nest syndrome, and concerns over physical attractiveness are. So, the correct answer is D.

130. A. Gender identity is a person's physical and biological makeup. Conformity is becoming a part of one's peer group. Individual struggle sounds a lot like identity crisis, but an identity crisis is the time of inner conflict in which adolescents worry about their identities, so A is the correct answer.

Answer Sheets for Practice Test 2

Section 1

1 Ⓐ Ⓑ Ⓒ Ⓓ
2 Ⓐ Ⓑ Ⓒ Ⓓ
3 Ⓐ Ⓑ Ⓒ Ⓓ
4 Ⓐ Ⓑ Ⓒ Ⓓ
5 Ⓐ Ⓑ Ⓒ Ⓓ
6 Ⓐ Ⓑ Ⓒ Ⓓ
7 Ⓐ Ⓑ Ⓒ Ⓓ
8 Ⓐ Ⓑ Ⓒ Ⓓ
9 Ⓐ Ⓑ Ⓒ Ⓓ
10 Ⓐ Ⓑ Ⓒ Ⓓ
11 Ⓐ Ⓑ Ⓒ Ⓓ
12 Ⓐ Ⓑ Ⓒ Ⓓ
13 Ⓐ Ⓑ Ⓒ Ⓓ
14 Ⓐ Ⓑ Ⓒ Ⓓ
15 Ⓐ Ⓑ Ⓒ Ⓓ
16 Ⓐ Ⓑ Ⓒ Ⓓ
17 Ⓐ Ⓑ Ⓒ Ⓓ
18 Ⓐ Ⓑ Ⓒ Ⓓ
19 Ⓐ Ⓑ Ⓒ Ⓓ
20 Ⓐ Ⓑ Ⓒ Ⓓ
21 Ⓐ Ⓑ Ⓒ Ⓓ
22 Ⓐ Ⓑ Ⓒ Ⓓ
23 Ⓐ Ⓑ Ⓒ Ⓓ
24 Ⓐ Ⓑ Ⓒ Ⓓ
25 Ⓐ Ⓑ Ⓒ Ⓓ
26 Ⓐ Ⓑ Ⓒ Ⓓ
27 Ⓐ Ⓑ Ⓒ Ⓓ
28 Ⓐ Ⓑ Ⓒ Ⓓ
29 Ⓐ Ⓑ Ⓒ Ⓓ

Section 2

30 Ⓐ Ⓑ Ⓒ Ⓓ
31 Ⓐ Ⓑ Ⓒ Ⓓ
32 Ⓐ Ⓑ Ⓒ Ⓓ
33 Ⓐ Ⓑ Ⓒ Ⓓ
34 Ⓐ Ⓑ Ⓒ Ⓓ
35 Ⓐ Ⓑ Ⓒ Ⓓ
36 Ⓐ Ⓑ Ⓒ Ⓓ
37 Ⓐ Ⓑ Ⓒ Ⓓ
38 Ⓐ Ⓑ Ⓒ Ⓓ
39 Ⓐ Ⓑ Ⓒ Ⓓ
40 Ⓐ Ⓑ Ⓒ Ⓓ
41 Ⓐ Ⓑ Ⓒ Ⓓ
42 Ⓐ Ⓑ Ⓒ Ⓓ
43 Ⓐ Ⓑ Ⓒ Ⓓ
44 Ⓐ Ⓑ Ⓒ Ⓓ
45 Ⓐ Ⓑ Ⓒ Ⓓ
46 Ⓐ Ⓑ Ⓒ Ⓓ
47 Ⓐ Ⓑ Ⓒ Ⓓ
48 Ⓐ Ⓑ Ⓒ Ⓓ
49 Ⓐ Ⓑ Ⓒ Ⓓ
50 Ⓐ Ⓑ Ⓒ Ⓓ
51 Ⓐ Ⓑ Ⓒ Ⓓ
52 Ⓐ Ⓑ Ⓒ Ⓓ
53 Ⓐ Ⓑ Ⓒ Ⓓ
54 Ⓐ Ⓑ Ⓒ Ⓓ
55 Ⓐ Ⓑ Ⓒ Ⓓ
56 Ⓐ Ⓑ Ⓒ Ⓓ
57 Ⓐ Ⓑ Ⓒ Ⓓ
58 Ⓐ Ⓑ Ⓒ Ⓓ

Section 3

59 Ⓐ Ⓑ Ⓒ Ⓓ
60 Ⓐ Ⓑ Ⓒ Ⓓ
61 Ⓐ Ⓑ Ⓒ Ⓓ
62 Ⓐ Ⓑ Ⓒ Ⓓ
63 Ⓐ Ⓑ Ⓒ Ⓓ
64 Ⓐ Ⓑ Ⓒ Ⓓ
65 Ⓐ Ⓑ Ⓒ Ⓓ
66 Ⓐ Ⓑ Ⓒ Ⓓ
67 Ⓐ Ⓑ Ⓒ Ⓓ
68 Ⓐ Ⓑ Ⓒ Ⓓ
69 Ⓐ Ⓑ Ⓒ Ⓓ
70 Ⓐ Ⓑ Ⓒ Ⓓ
71 Ⓐ Ⓑ Ⓒ Ⓓ
72 Ⓐ Ⓑ Ⓒ Ⓓ
73 Ⓐ Ⓑ Ⓒ Ⓓ
74 Ⓐ Ⓑ Ⓒ Ⓓ
75 Ⓐ Ⓑ Ⓒ Ⓓ
76 Ⓐ Ⓑ Ⓒ Ⓓ
77 Ⓐ Ⓑ Ⓒ Ⓓ
78 Ⓐ Ⓑ Ⓒ Ⓓ
79 Ⓐ Ⓑ Ⓒ Ⓓ

Section 4

80 Ⓐ Ⓑ Ⓒ Ⓓ
81 Ⓐ Ⓑ Ⓒ Ⓓ
82 Ⓐ Ⓑ Ⓒ Ⓓ
83 Ⓐ Ⓑ Ⓒ Ⓓ
84 Ⓐ Ⓑ Ⓒ Ⓓ
85 Ⓐ Ⓑ Ⓒ Ⓓ
86 Ⓐ Ⓑ Ⓒ Ⓓ
87 Ⓐ Ⓑ Ⓒ Ⓓ
88 Ⓐ Ⓑ Ⓒ Ⓓ
89 Ⓐ Ⓑ Ⓒ Ⓓ
90 Ⓐ Ⓑ Ⓒ Ⓓ
91 Ⓐ Ⓑ Ⓒ Ⓓ
92 Ⓐ Ⓑ Ⓒ Ⓓ
93 Ⓐ Ⓑ Ⓒ Ⓓ
94 Ⓐ Ⓑ Ⓒ Ⓓ
95 Ⓐ Ⓑ Ⓒ Ⓓ
96 Ⓐ Ⓑ Ⓒ Ⓓ
97 Ⓐ Ⓑ Ⓒ Ⓓ
98 Ⓐ Ⓑ Ⓒ Ⓓ

Section 5

99 Ⓐ Ⓑ Ⓒ Ⓓ
100 Ⓐ Ⓑ Ⓒ Ⓓ
101 Ⓐ Ⓑ Ⓒ Ⓓ
102 Ⓐ Ⓑ Ⓒ Ⓓ
103 Ⓐ Ⓑ Ⓒ Ⓓ
104 Ⓐ Ⓑ Ⓒ Ⓓ
105 Ⓐ Ⓑ Ⓒ Ⓓ
106 Ⓐ Ⓑ Ⓒ Ⓓ
107 Ⓐ Ⓑ Ⓒ Ⓓ
109 Ⓐ Ⓑ Ⓒ Ⓓ
110 Ⓐ Ⓑ Ⓒ Ⓓ
111 Ⓐ Ⓑ Ⓒ Ⓓ
112 Ⓐ Ⓑ Ⓒ Ⓓ
113 Ⓐ Ⓑ Ⓒ Ⓓ
114 Ⓐ Ⓑ Ⓒ Ⓓ
115 Ⓐ Ⓑ Ⓒ Ⓓ
116 Ⓐ Ⓑ Ⓒ Ⓓ
117 Ⓐ Ⓑ Ⓒ Ⓓ

Section 6

118 Ⓐ Ⓑ Ⓒ Ⓓ
119 Ⓐ Ⓑ Ⓒ Ⓓ
120 Ⓐ Ⓑ Ⓒ Ⓓ
121 Ⓐ Ⓑ Ⓒ Ⓓ
122 Ⓐ Ⓑ Ⓒ Ⓓ
123 Ⓐ Ⓑ Ⓒ Ⓓ
124 Ⓐ Ⓑ Ⓒ Ⓓ
125 Ⓐ Ⓑ Ⓒ Ⓓ
126 Ⓐ Ⓑ Ⓒ Ⓓ
127 Ⓐ Ⓑ Ⓒ Ⓓ
128 Ⓐ Ⓑ Ⓒ Ⓓ
129 Ⓐ Ⓑ Ⓒ Ⓓ
130 Ⓐ Ⓑ Ⓒ Ⓓ

CUT HERE

Practice Test 2

Section 1: World History

Directions: For each of the following questions, select the choice that best answers the question or completes the statement.

1. The basic change that occurred with the Neolithic Revolution was

   A. an increase in human population.
   B. the cultivation of rice.
   C. the shift to raising animals as a regular source of food.
   D. an increase in the importance of hunting.

2. What is a similarity between the religions of Islam and Christianity?

   A. They are both monotheistic.
   B. They both believe that Allah and Muhammad are prophets.
   C. Both religions forbid the eating of pork.
   D. Believers of both religions were persecuted by the Romans.

3. The emergence of different factions in the Balkan Peninsula at the end of the nineteenth century was a result of

   A. shifting power as the Ottoman Empire waned.
   B. Serbia's dominance of the region.
   C. America's victory in the Spanish-American War.
   D. Nicholas II of Russia's repressive regime.

GO ON TO THE NEXT PAGE

4. Refer to the following map to answer the question.

What geographic factors influenced German military advances?

- **A.** German troops had to cover long distances.
- **B.** Colder climates created problems that the German military could not overcome.
- **C.** The blitzkrieg relied on tanks that were most effective on flatter terrain.
- **D.** All of the above.

5. Why are Latin American countries economically important to the United States?

    A. American banks need countries such as Brazil and Mexico to default on their loans.

    B. Latin American countries are popular destinations for American tourists.

    C. Latin American countries are colonies of European nations.

    D. America imports raw goods such as oil, coffee, and copper from Mexico, El Salvador, Colombia, and Chile.

6. Between 1966 and 1976, the destruction of many temples, the seizure of many books, and the imprisonment of some artists and intellectuals were closely related to which movement?

    A. China's Cultural Revolution

    B. Conservatism

    C. Women's rights movement

    D. Humanism

7. What did the Nazis mean by the Final Solution?

    A. The extermination of the Jewish people was meant to be the Final Solution to the "Jewish problem."

    B. The elimination of racial struggle was the Final Solution for peaceful living.

    C. Arresting and killing the leading citizens of the Slavic peoples was meant to be the Final Solution for the clergy, intellectuals, civil leaders, judges, and lawyers.

    D. The creation of labor camps was the Final Solution to the need to have more laborers.

8. Read the following comment by an Aztec describing the Spanish conquerors and answer the question.

"[They] longed and lusted for gold. Their bodies swelled with greed, and their hunger was ravenous; they hungered like pigs for that gold."

Based on this quote, what might the Aztecs inferred about the Spaniards and their civilization?

    A. The Aztecs thought the Spaniards were starving.

    B. The Aztecs questioned the Spaniards' morals and values.

    C. The Aztecs thought the Spaniards were greedy.

    D. The Aztecs wondered why the Spaniards were on their land.

9. All of the following are characteristics of Italian Renaissance humanism EXCEPT:

    A. It was based on the study of the classics.

    B. It focused on the intellectual life.

    C. It was based on learning more about what it means to be human.

    D. It was noticeable in the artistic accomplishments of the period.

GO ON TO THE NEXT PAGE

10. Refer to the following map to answer the question.

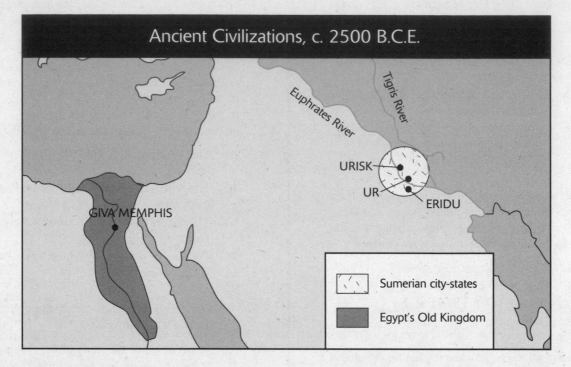

How did geography influence both Egypt and Sumeria?

A. Geography provided natural borders for protecting these civilizations.

B. Floods from nearby rivers irrigated crops.

C. Challenges helped people unite and work together.

D. The flooding rivers caused people to have a dark outlook on the world.

11. What effect did the Black Death have on Europe?

A. The plague resulted in an increase in the number of universities and their scholasticism.

B. The plague led to an acute labor shortage that resulted in higher wages and the emancipation of many serfs.

C. The plague inspired new ideas about faith that led to the formation of the Cistercian, Franciscan, and Dominican orders.

D. The plague sparked the Hundred Years' War between France and England.

12. The rule of Robespierre was a time when the French Revolution

A. was controlled by royalists who supported King Louis XVI.

B. established a long-lasting constitutional monarchy.

C. became a centralized military force under Napoleon.

D. grew more violent as extremists took control.

13. What happened after the Communist Party collapsed in Czechoslovakia?

A. Rival ethnic states could not agree on national borders.

B. East Germany remained loyal to the Soviets.

C. Conservative movements came to power in America and Great Britain.

D. Mikhail Gorbachev invaded Czechoslovakia to regain control.

14. Refer to the following timeline to answer the question.

Selected Events in Middle Eastern Politics

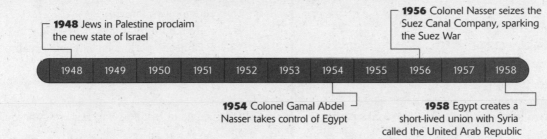

1948 Jews in Palestine proclaim the new state of Israel

1956 Colonel Nasser seizes the Suez Canal Company, sparking the Suez War

1948 1949 1950 1951 1952 1953 1954 1955 1956 1957 1958

1954 Colonel Gamal Abdel Nasser takes control of Egypt

1958 Egypt creates a short-lived union with Syria called the United Arab Republic

Which of the following events resulted from the events on this timeline?

A. Shock over the Holocaust helped Jews realize their goals for a homeland.

B. Nasser imposed a blockade against Israeli shipping.

C. Iraq launched an attack on its enemy, Iran.

D. The Balfour Declaration gave support to Zionist Jews.

15. The most important body within the United Nations and its many subagencies is

A. the General Assembly.

B. UNESCO (United Nations Education, Scientific, and Cultural Organization).

C. WHO (World Health Organization).

D. the Security Council.

16. All of the following are changes during the Neolithic Revolution that led to the emergence of civilization EXCEPT:

A. The acquisition of food on a regular basis

B. The rise of permanent villages

C. The trading of goods and the division of labor

D. The finding of religion

17. The slogan of grassroots public interests groups is "Think globally, act locally." These groups address all of the following issues EXCEPT:

A. Environmental problems

B. Higher education

C. Appropriate technology

D. Nonviolence

18. Read the following poem by Virgil, and answer the question.

"Let others fashion from bronze more lifelike, breathing images—For so they shall—and evoke living faces from marble; Others excel as orators, others track with their instruments The planet circling in heaven and predict when stars will appear. But, Romans, never forget that government is your medium! Be this your art: to practice men in the habit of peace, generosity to the conquered, and firmness against aggressors."

How does this poem summarize the fundamental ideas of Western civilization that originated in Rome?

A. The role of government is to promote peace and to defend.

B. The study of the heavens is very important.

C. The arts will be crucial to the survival of civilization.

D. The role of government is to rule with a strong hand.

19. A crucial part of every Muslim city or town was the covered market, called the

A. mosque.

B. downtown.

C. bazaar.

D. center of town.

GO ON TO THE NEXT PAGE

20. World War I involved a complete mobilization of resources and people that affected the lives of all citizens in the warring countries—a situation called

    A. mobilization.
    B. trench warfare.
    C. war of attrition.
    D. total war.

21. What two important functions did monks perform?

    A. They taught people the importance of prayer, and they stressed education.
    B. They were Christian missionaries, and they spread learning.
    C. They were Christian leaders, and they taught nuns how to withdraw from the world.
    D. They lived an isolated spiritual life, and they fought battles.

22. All of the following are roles of lineage groups in African society EXCEPT:

    A. In lineage groups, women are seen as equal to men.
    B. Lineage groups serve as the basic building blocks of African society.
    C. Elders have much power over others in the group, but the group is a source of mutual support for all its members.
    D. All members of a lineage group claim a common ancestor.

23. Indian advances in science and mathematics have impacted our world today in all of the following ways EXCEPT:

    A. Ancient Indians recognized earth was a sphere that rotated on its axis and revolved around the sun.
    B. Ancient Indians were the first people to use pillars in their architecture.
    C. Ancient Indians were the first people to devise a decimal system.
    D. Ancient Indians introduced the concept of zero.

24. Between the twelfth and fourteenth centuries, both England and France

    A. defeated Frankish rulers and established autonomous kingdoms.
    B. were rebuilt by Emperor Justinian.
    C. established parliaments to help royal authorities rule.
    D. were accomplished shipbuilders and sailors.

25. The League of Iroquois was important because it

    A. protected the Aztec from Hernan Cortes.
    B. was created by Deganawida and Hiawatha.
    C. was an early American form of the democratic assembly.
    D. established the Mayan calendar.

26. Refer to the quote to answer the following.

    "And even today woman is heavily handicapped, though her situation is beginning to change. Almost nowhere is her legal statue the same as man's, and frequently it is much to her disadvantage. Even when her rights are legally recognized in the abstract, long-standing custom prevents their full expression..."

    —*The Second Sex*, Simone de Beauvoir

    Simone de Beauvoir's book, *The Second Sex,* was published in 1949. Her book was influential because it

    A. helped women gain the right to vote.
    B. contributed to the women's movement in the 1950s and 1960s.
    C. greatly increased the number of married women in the labor force.
    D. influenced and shaped the student protest movement.

27. All of the following are products that were sent from the Americas to Europe EXCEPT:

    A. Potatoes
    B. Cocoa
    C. Silk
    D. Tobacco

28. During the Reign of Terror, thousands of people, including aristocrats and the queen of France, were killed by the guillotine. Why did the revolutionaries decide to use the guillotine to execute people?

    A. They could hold executions in places that had openly rebelled against the authority of the National Convention.

    B. The guillotine was relatively inexpensive to maintain.

    C. Executing people with the guillotine drew huge crowds to the town center.

    D. The guillotine was believed to kill quickly and humanely.

29. One lasting contribution of the Roman Empire was

    A. the idea of the Triumvirate.

    B. the Christian Church.

    C. the gladiatorial shows.

    D. its system of law.

Section 2: United States History

Directions: For each of the following questions, select the choice that best answers the question or completes the statement.

30. Why did tensions between western settlers and Native Americans increase during Washington's presidency?

    A. Tensions rose because the settlers did not agree with Washington's foreign policy.

    B. Tensions rose because Little Turtle formed a confederacy of several groups of Native Americans.

    C. Tensions rose because across much of the country, settlers held public meetings condemning Jay's Treaty.

    D. Tensions rose because of the increase in the number of settlers moving West.

31. The Strategic Defense Initiative (SDI) was proposed to strengthen the military by

    A. preventing the expansion of communist countries.

    B. reemphasizing the use of infantry troops in future wars.

    C. developing weapons that would intercept and destroy incoming nuclear missiles.

    D. severely reducing the number of American troops stationed worldwide.

32. How did World War I change attitudes among African Americans toward themselves and their country?

    A. African Americans saw themselves as defenders of democracy and thus entitled to all the rights of citizens.

    B. African Americans were given a chance to perform and their music helped shape the national identity.

    C. Marcus Garvey's Universal Negro Improvement Association advocated African American self-reliance and separation from whites.

    D. The NAACP continued to lobby and protest against the horrors of lynching.

GO ON TO THE NEXT PAGE

33. In his 1789 textbook *The American Geography,* Reverend Jedidiah Morse discussed the defects of the Articles of Confederation. Read the following excerpt and answer the question.

"[The Articles of Confederation] were framed during the rage of war, when a principle of common safety supplied the place of a coercive power in government ... when resolutions were passed in Congress, there was no power to compel obedience. ... Had one state been invaded by its neighbour, the union was not constitutionally bound to assist in repelling the invasion..."

—quoted in *Readings in American History*

Why does Morse think the Articles were effective during the American Revolution but not afterward?

A. They were effective during the Revolution because everyone rallies together during wartime.

B. They were effective during the Revolution because the states had a common goal.

C. They were effective during the Revolution because there were no separate branches of government.

D. They were effective during the Revolution because Congress passed the Northwest Ordinance, which provided the basis for governing much of the western territory.

34. Researchers believe that people arrived in America

A. between 3,000 and 10,000 years ago.

B. between 15,000 and 30,000 years ago.

C. between 30,000 and 60,000 years ago.

D. between 80,000 and 100,000 years ago.

35. Lyndon Johnson said, "...many Americans live on the outskirts of hope..." Why was President Johnson so concerned about poverty?

A. He felt sorry for the nation's impoverished.

B. He thought that his support of the poor would help the nation move past Kennedy's death.

C. He had earned the reputation of a man who gets things done, and he wanted to continue his legacy.

D. He had known hard times and felt a wealthy nation should try to improve living standards for all.

36. Which of the following was NOT a condition set by Mexico for American settlers coming to live in Texas?

A. They received a 10-year exemption from paying taxes.

B. They could never return to live in the United States.

C. They were required to become Mexican citizens.

D. They were required to convert to the Roman Catholic faith.

37. To fight the Depression, Roosevelt believed the first thing to do was

A. provide direct relief for people.

B. set up public works programs.

C. restore confidence in the banks.

D. provide relief for the farmers.

38. Railroads boosted the settlement of the West in all of these ways EXCEPT:

A. Railroad companies traveled across the country frequently.

B. Railroad companies provided credit to prospective settlers.

C. Railroad companies sold land along rail lines at low prices.

D. Railroad companies advertised the benefits of booking passage to the Plains.

39. Why did the French establish forts and settlements along the Mississippi?

    A. To be close to the river for fishing

    B. To ensure control of the river

    C. To be nearby when explorers canoed along the river

    D. To have plenty of land for the enslaved people to work

40. Women played a role in the war effort during World War I. They filled all of the following positions during the war EXCEPT:

    A. Nurses

    B. Clerical help

    C. Newspaper reporters

    D. Other jobs vacated by men who had become soldiers

41. The following graph plots the number of patents issued between 1810 and 1840. Use the graph to answer the question.

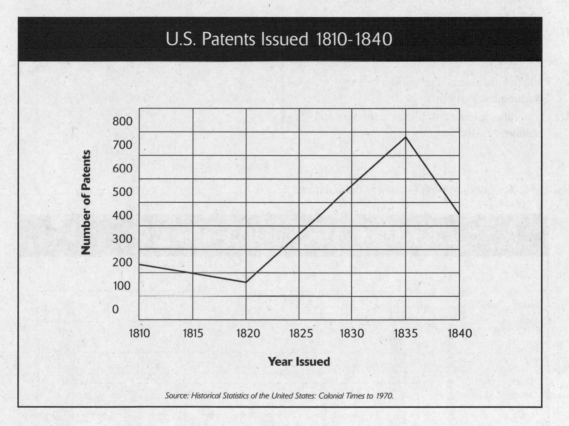

Source: Historical Statistics of the United States: Colonial Times to 1970.

During what time span did the number of patents issued increase the most?

    A. 1835-1840

    B. 1810-1820

    C. 1815-1820

    D. 1820-1835

GO ON TO THE NEXT PAGE

42. Why were the victories on Iwo Jima and Okinawa so vital to the Allies during World War II?

    A. It gave the Allies two more victories, and victories were vital.

    B. It gave Americans landing areas within striking distance of Japan.

    C. It allowed the Allies to punish the Axis leaders.

    D. It allowed the Americans to island-hop.

43. The Contract with America involved

    A. a commitment by Russia to eliminate land-based nuclear weapons.

    B. a campaign promise by President Clinton to create a national health care system for all Americans.

    C. a legislative agenda promoted by the Republican Party in 1994.

    D. programs intended to increase the size and readiness of the military.

44. What was the ruling in *Brown v. Board of Education?*

    A. Public school segregation was ruled unconstitutional because it violated the Fourteenth Amendment.

    B. In the field of public education, the doctrine of separate but equal will prevail.

    C. Public schools would remain mostly segregated, but if a child's parents wanted to take their child to another school, they could.

    D. The Fourteenth Amendment would be rewritten.

45. Use the following bar graph to answer the question.

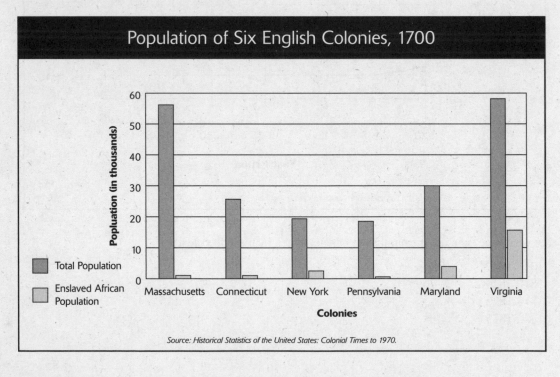

Population of Six English Colonies, 1700

Source: Historical Statistics of the United States: Colonial Times to 1970.

Approximately what percentage of Maryland's total population was enslaved Africans?

    A. 5 percent

    B. 10 percent

    C. 20 percent

    D. 25 percent

46. All of the following are characteristics of the economy of the United States after World War II EXCEPT:

- **A.** Abundant goods
- **B.** Low unemployment
- **C.** Television was the newest form of mass media
- **D.** Housing boom

47. What was President Carter's main foreign policy theme?

- **A.** The singling out of the Soviet Union as a violator of human rights
- **B.** The treaty—the Camp David Accords—between Israel and Egypt
- **C.** The removal of the control of the Panama Canal
- **D.** The need to be honest, truthful, and decent in foreign relations

48. Some people did not support free public education in the early 1800s. The following excerpt was an editorial written to the members of the legislature. It appeared in the *Raleigh Register* of November 9, 1829. Read the excerpt and answer the question that follows.

"Common schools indeed! Money is very scarce, and the times are unusually hard. ... Gentlemen, it appears to me that schools are sufficiently plenty, and that the people have no desire they should be increased. Those now in operation are not all filled, and it is very doubtful if they are productive or of much real benefit. Would it not redound as much to the advantage of young persons, and to the honour of the State, if they should pass their days in the cotton patch, or at the plow, or in the cornfield, instead of being [confined] in a school house, where they are earning nothing?"

All of the following are reasons the author gives for opposing free public education EXCEPT:

- **A.** Scarcity of money
- **B.** Scarcity of school buildings
- **C.** Available space in existing schools
- **D.** Questionable benefit of schooling

49. Why did Congress pass the Enforcement Acts?

- **A.** To allow people to vote
- **B.** To supervise the election of federal marshals
- **C.** To combat violence in the South and outlaw the activities of the Ku Klux Klan
- **D.** To enforce laws

50. In 1766 Benjamin Franklin testified before Parliament about the colonists' reactions to the Stamp Act. Read the following excerpt from his testimony and answer the question that follows.

Q: What is your name, and place of abode?
A: Franklin, of Philadelphia.
Q: Are not the colonies ... very able to pay the stamp [tax]?
A: In my opinion there is not enough in the colonies to pay the stamp duty for one year.
Q: Don't you know that the money arising from the stamps was all to be laid out in America?
A: I know it is appropriated by the act to the American service; but it will be spent in the conquered colonies where the soldiers are, not in the colonies that pay it...
Q: Do you think it right that Americans should be protected by this country and pay no part of the expense?
A: That is not the case. The colonies raised, clothed, and paid, during the last war, near 25,000 men and spent many millions.
Q: Were you not reimbursed by Parliament?
A: We were only reimbursed what, in your opinion, we had advanced beyond our proportion, or beyond what might reasonably be expected form us; and it was a very small part of what we spent. Pennsylvania, in particular, disbursed about 500,000 pounds, and the reimbursements, in the whole, did not exceed 60,000 pounds.

Why does Franklin say that the stamp taxes are unfair?

- **A.** The money did not really get disbursed to the colonies after all.
- **B.** The colonies were not able to pay taxes or any portion of the taxes.
- **C.** The colonies were not obligated to help any more soldiers.
- **D.** The colonies were already paying more than their share.

GO ON TO THE NEXT PAGE

51. What were the Zoot Suit Riots during the time of World War II?

    A. A combination of racism against Mexican Americans and the fear of juvenile crime.

    B. Attacks between Mexican American teenagers and police officers.

    C. The title of a song by the Cherry Poppin' Daddies.

    D. A way to keep Mexican Americans out of the war.

52. All of the following were tactics adopted by the United States to fight the Vietcong EXCEPT:

    A. Search and destroy missions

    B. Bombing

    C. Guerilla tactics

    D. The use of napalm and Agent Orange

53. At the beginning of the Civil War, Robert E. Lee wrote to his sister, Mrs. Anne Marshall, of his decision to resign from the U.S. Army. Read the following excerpt and answer the question.

"My Dear Sister: ... With all my devotion to the Union and the feeling of loyalty and duty of an American citizen, I have not been able to make up my mind to raise my hand against my relatives, my children, my home. I have, therefore, resigned my commission in the Army, and save in defense of my native state. ... I hope I may never be called on to draw my sword. I know you will blame me; but you must think as kindly of me as you can..."

    —from *Personal Reminiscences, Anecdotes, and Letters of General Robert E. Lee*

Why did Robert E. Lee feel it necessary to resign from the Union army and become commander of the Virginia army?

    A. He wanted to show his loyalty to America by fighting with the South.

    B. He did not want to stay in the Union army and have to fight against others from Virginia.

    C. He did not want to draw his sword.

    D. He wanted to impress his sister with his patriotism and willingness to fight.

54. The counterculture, or "hippies" of the 1960s, impacted the nation. All of the following were lasting impacts the counterculture had on the nation EXCEPT:

    A. The idea that vans were an acceptable means of transportation

    B. Changes in fashion

    C. Changes in music and dance

    D. The idea that alternatives to mainstream culture were possible

55. Why did the farmers of the 1890s dislike Eastern bankers?

    A. Farmers thought that their problems were due to a shortage of currency and that Eastern bankers had pressured Congress into reducing the money supply.

    B. The falling prices of the period of deflation meant the farmers sold their crops for less.

    C. Farmers, especially those in the West where new silver mines had been found, wanted the government to begin minting silver coins.

    D. Farmers formed cooperatives to pool their crops in an effort to get higher prices for them.

56. A political cartoon shows a car salesman talking to Uncle Sam. The car salesman says, "So Russia launched a satellite, but has it made cars with fins yet?"

In this cartoon, the speaker is comparing American prosperity with the Soviets' launching of *Sputnik*. What is the cartoonist's intent?

    A. To criticize the American government.

    B. To convey anxiety over the fact that the United States has built fancy consumer goods, but it is behind in space technology.

    C. To express dissatisfaction with the cars with fins and the importance the American public has put on those cars.

    D. To convey pride in the fact that America has such beautiful consumer goods and how far this country has come in the way of modes of transportation.

57. All of the following were innovations that retailers introduced in the late 1800s to sell good to consumers EXCEPT:

 A. Large display ads in newspapers
 B. Monopolies
 C. Chain stores
 D. Mail-order catalogs

58. The Progressive Era brought about reforms in all of these areas EXCEPT:

 A. Economic reforms
 B. Business reforms
 C. Political reforms
 D. Social welfare reforms

Section 3: Government/Political Science/Civics

Directions: For each of the following questions, select the choice that best answers the question or completes the statement.

59. Why is widespread educational opportunity necessary for a nation to develop a democratic system?

 A. The only fair thing is to have education available to the masses.
 B. Without education, people do not have the skills and knowledge to make informed, intelligent choices.
 C. The young people of today will be the future politicians.
 D. Educated people are better voters.

60. Newly developed nations are located in all of the following places EXCEPT:

 A. Africa
 B. Eastern Europe
 C. The Middle East
 D. South America

61. Although many women have enlisted in the armed forces, in 1981, the Supreme Court—in the Reasonableness Standard of the *Reed* decision—decided that Congress could exclude women from the draft. Why would the Court allow Congress to exclude women from the draft?

 A. The Court would claim that some gender differences will always remain as differences.
 B. The Court would claim that it's in the government's best interest to not have young women in combat.
 C. The Court would claim that this gender classification is constitutional because it serves important governmental objectives and is reasonable.
 D. The Court would claim that it is not discrimination.

62. Why does the Constitution provide for free and unlimited debate in Congress?

 A. To ensure that legislators would have the freedom to express their ideas and opinions
 B. To prevent a filibuster
 C. To allow for gerrymandering
 D. To allow legislators to protest the opponents' beliefs

GO ON TO THE NEXT PAGE

63. A political cartoon shows Bill Clinton walking through a "forest" of cacti labeled "Bosnia," "North Korea," "Haiti," and "Rwanda." He is carrying a balloon with the label "Foreign Policy."

How does this cartoon characterize a president's role in foreign policy?

A. The president is the main leader of his nation's foreign policy.

B. The most important thing for a president to do is settle disputes with other nations.

C. A president must carefully plan and conduct his nation's foreign policy, as it may burst if the president does not plan his path and navigate well.

D. There are clearly problems with other nations that can potentially affect other nations, including the United States.

64. In 1948, by executive order, President Harry S. Truman desegregated the armed forces, which affected U.S. troops, which later fought in the Korean War. Truman enhanced his presidential powers by taking decisive action without Congress's consent. Under which presidential duty does this action fall?

A. Chief executive

B. Head of state

C. Chief legislator

D. Chief diplomat

65. What are independent voters?

A. Voters who consistently vote early

B. Independent voters is synonymous with weak party voters

C. Voters who voted for Ross Perot in 1992

D. Voters who think of themselves as neither Republicans nor Democrats

66. Why does the Tenth Amendment use the term *reserved* to describe the powers that belong to the people and the states?

A. Those are the powers that are indirectly stated for the people and the states.

B. Those are the powers that are given to the people and the states simply because they are the people and the states.

C. Those are the powers that are set aside for the people and the states.

D. Those are the powers that are directly stated to be for the people and the states.

67. Refer to the following graph to answer the question.

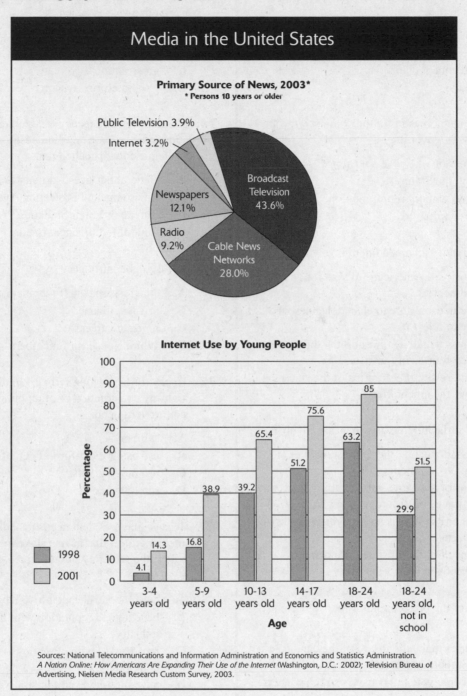

Media in the United States

Primary Source of News, 2003*
* Persons 10 years or older

Public Television 3.9%
Internet 3.2%
Newspapers 12.1%
Radio 9.2%
Cable News Networks 28.0%
Broadcast Television 43.6%

Internet Use by Young People

Legend: 1998, 2001

Age	1998	2001
3-4 years old	4.1	14.3
5-9 years old	16.8	38.9
10-13 years old	39.2	65.4
14-17 years old	51.2	75.6
18-24 years old	63.2	85
18-24 years old, not in school	29.9	51.5

Sources: National Telecommunications and Information Administration and Economics and Statistics Administration.
A Nation Online: How Americans Are Expanding Their Use of the Internet (Washington, D.C.: 2002); Television Bureau of Advertising, Nielsen Media Research Custom Survey, 2003.

Although Internet use has steadily increased over the last decade, television remains the primary source of news for most Americans. Between 1998 and 2001, which age group saw the largest increase in Internet use?

A. 10-13 years old

B. 14-17 years old

C. 18-24 years old

D. 18-24 years old, not in school

GO ON TO THE NEXT PAGE

68. The Constitution of the United States guarantees basic rights in the

   A.   Bill of Rights.
   B.   slander laws.
   C.   establishment clause.
   D.   libel laws.

69. The fundamental reason for the colonists' revolt was because of government

   A.   suppression of Locke's writings.
   B.   passing the Stamp Act.
   C.   taxation without representation.
   D.   oppression.

70. One way to ratify an amendment is for

   A.   a majority of Americans to vote for an amendment.
   B.   people in each state to elect delegates who pledge to reject it.
   C.   Congress to call a convention at the request of three-fourths of the states.
   D.   legislatures in three-fourths of the states to approve the amendment.

71. Concurrent jurisdiction exists in a case involving

   A.   ambassadors and other representatives of foreign governments.
   B.   citizens of the same state claiming lands under grants of different states.
   C.   a state or its citizens and a foreign country or its citizens.
   D.   citizens of different states in a dispute concerning at least $75,000.

72. Supporters of the presidential primary system agree that

   A.   primaries make the image of the candidate more important than the issues.
   B.   few people vote in primaries so the winners look more popular than they are.
   C.   it is a great improvement over the previous method of selecting delegates.
   D.   the primaries extend over too long a time during an election year.

73. The sum of all goods and services produced in the nation in a year is called the

   A.   budget deficit.
   B.   national debt.
   C.   gross national product.
   D.   free-enterprise system.

74. The independent agency that gathers information about other countries, evaluates it, and passes it on to the president is called the

   A.   General Services Administration.
   B.   Environmental Protection Agency.
   C.   Bureau of Labor Statistics.
   D.   Central Intelligence Agency.

75. A bill can be introduced by

   A.   congressional staff members.
   B.   private citizens.
   C.   representatives.
   D.   White House staff members.

76. To pay for large, long-term expenditures such as highway construction or other building projects, state governments

   A.   sell bonds.
   B.   use categorical-formula grants.
   C.   use block grants.
   D.   run lotteries.

77. Because the president needs to satisfy powerful interest groups that have a stake in a department's policy, the secretary of commerce, for example, is expected to

   A.   be someone acceptable to labor unions.
   B.   have a good reputation with business and industry.
   C.   be a banker with close ties to the financial community.
   D.   have high-level administrative skills.

78. A campaign manager is responsible for

    A. overall planning and strategy within the organization.

    B. contacting voters and holding local rallies.

    C. ringing doorbells and canvassing voters over the telephone.

    D. making sure voters turn out to vote on Election Day.

79. The goal of the American court system to treat all persons alike is called the principle of

    A. due process of law.

    B. the adversary system of justice.

    C. equal justice under the law.

    D. the presumption of innocence.

Section 4: Geography

Directions: For each of the following questions, select the choice that best answers the question or completes the statement.

80. All of the following are distinct geographic zones or geographic elements in Africa EXCEPT:

    A. The northern fringe, on the coast, which is mountainous

    B. Central Africa, which is colder than average

    C. The Sahara

    D. The Great Rift Valley, Congo River basin, which has tropical rain forests

81. Human geographers analyze human aspects of culture—population, language, ethnicity, religion, and government. Human geographers who are studying the effects of population growth might gather information for their research in all of the following ways EXCEPT:

    A. Geographic information systems

    B. Interviews

    C. Statistics

    D. Satellite images

82. Read the following selection and then answer the question.

"Rabbits are one of the more destructive wild animals that have been introduced into Australia. They damage the environment and reduce agricultural production. They compete with native wildlife for food and shelter, which reduces the populations of many native plants and animals. Because rabbits eat seedlings, there are fewer young plants to replace those that die naturally. Rabbits also compete with livestock for the same plants, eating them to below ground level. This loss of plant cover results in soil erosion."

—from *World Geography*

Based on the information in the paragraph, how do rabbits reduce agricultural production?

    A. They live in wheat-growing regions and eat the wheat seedlings.

    B. They compete with native wildlife for food.

    C. Dead plants are not replaced by enough new plants to prevent soil erosion.

    D. They eat the plants that provide food for livestock and cause soil erosion by eliminating plant cover.

GO ON TO THE NEXT PAGE

Practice Test 2

83. Refer to the following graph to answer the question.

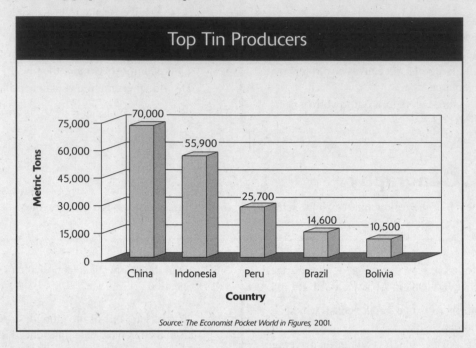

Top Tin Producers

Source: The Economist Pocket World in Figures, 2001.

About how much tin does Indonesia produce each year?

A. 55,900 metric tons

B. 55,000,900 metric tons

C. 55.9 million metric tons

D. 55.9 billion metric tons

84. Lignite, or brown coal, is easily and inexpensively mined. Why should European cities be discouraged from using lignite as a main fuel source?

A. Mining of the lignite creates unsightly open pits that are dangerous to children.

B. Acid rain in European cities would be reduced by burning lignite.

C. European cities, especially in the east, use natural gas more than lignite.

D. Sulfur dioxide emissions from lignite cause high levels of air pollution.

85. Geographers use all of the following research methods EXCEPT:

A. Culture

B. Art

C. Economics

D. History and government

86. Refer to the following table to answer the question.

Arable Land in Selected Countries				
	Russia	*Canada*	*United States*	*France*
Arable land	8%	5%	19%	33%
Permanent crops	0%	0%	0%	2%
Permanent pastures	4%	3%	25%	20%
Forests and woodlands	46%	54%	30%	27%
Other	42%	38%	26%	18%

Source: CIA World Factbook 2000

What factor may help explain why Russia and Canada have a lower percentage of arable land than the United States?

A. Russia and Canada have been settled longer.
B. Russia and Canada extend farther into cold northern regions.
C. Russia and Canada have larger land masses.
D. Russia and Canada are less industrialized.

87. Read the following passage and then answer the question.

"Raindrops keep falling on the head of anyone who takes a summer trip to Mawsynram, a hill town in northeast India. And falling. And falling. Two Indian meteorologists claim, and many U.S. specialists agree, that Mawsynram has ousted Hawaii's Waialeale as [the] earth's wettest spot, measured by average annual rainfall. Mawsynram gets an average 467.44 inches of rain a year, compared with 459.99 for Waialeale."

—"Geographica," *National Geographic,* May 1993

According to the reading, which of the following statements is a fact?

A. All Indian and U.S. meteorologists agree that the average annual rainfall in Mawsynram, India, is greater than that in Waialeale, Hawaii.
B. Mawsynram and Waialeale have always been wetter than other places on earth.
C. The average annual rainfall in Waialeale, Hawaii, is less than that of Mawsynram, India.
D. In the view of many Indians, the town of Mawsynram is earth's wettest spot.

88. Part of Uzbekistan has a desert climate. What kind of vegetation can grow in a desert climate?

A. No vegetation at all
B. Drought-resistant shrubs and cacti
C. Drought-resistant shrubs, cacti, and occasional small-scale farm crops in areas with underground water
D. Short grasses for grazing

89. Ships at sea use GPS technology

A. as a communication device.
B. as a navigational aid.
C. for inventory control.
D. to maintain personnel files.

90. Which of the following is a challenge that rapid population growth presents to the global community?

A. Shortages of metropolitan areas
B. Shortages of housing
C. Low population density
D. Disloyal military forces

GO ON TO THE NEXT PAGE

Practice Test 2

161

91. Refer to the following bar graph to answer the question.

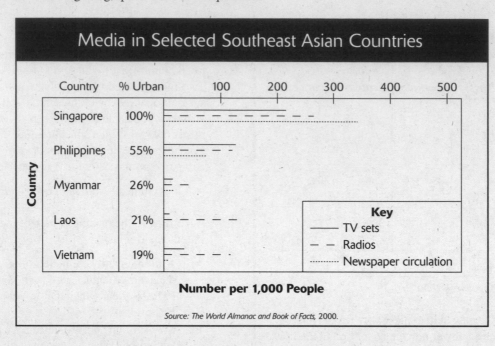

What conclusions can you draw from the graph?

A. Newspapers are censored in Laos.

B. People in rural areas have less access to literacy programs.

C. Urban populations have more access to news sources.

D. Televisions are less expensive in Singapore than in other countries in Southeast Asia.

92. Which of the following is a reason why Southeast Asia is a region of highly diverse cultures?

A. High population density in many areas causes a variety of traditions.

B. Similar physical geography encourages peoples to create their own traditions.

C. Trade and colonization from many regions spread new ideas.

D. Lack of contact with the outside world enables many local cultures to develop.

93. All of the following are types of migration that occur in the Latin American region EXCEPT:

A. Internal migration within a country or region

B. Inflow of immigrants into the region

C. Outflow of emigrants to other countries

D. High population density in some cities and on some islands

94. Study the following table, then answer the question.

Economic Activities in East Asia				
	Taiwan	**China**	**Japan**	**South Korea**
Economic Activity	%	%	%	%
Agriculture	2.9	18.4	1.7	4.9
Industry	34.0	48.7	36.0	43.5
Services	63.1	32.9	62.3	51.6
Labor Force				
Agriculture	8.0	50.0	5.0	12.0
Mining and manufacturing	37.0	23.0	32.0	27.0
Services and other	55.0	27.0	63.0	61.0

Source: The Economist Pocket World in Figures, 2001

Based on the table, which two countries have economic activities that are the most similar in all areas?

A. South Korea and Taiwan
B. Taiwan and Japan
C. Taiwan and China
D. China and Japan

95. In Russia, which of these challenges affects the transportation of both petroleum products and other goods?

A. Poorly repaired roads
B. Harsh weather and vast distances
C. Frozen waterways
D. Separatists movements

GO ON TO THE NEXT PAGE

96. Refer to the following graph to answer the question.

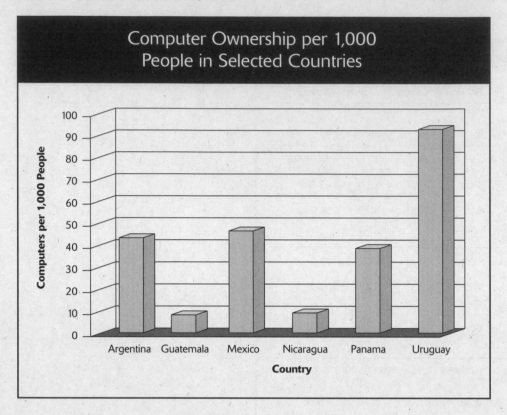

On average, 34 of every 1,000 Latin Americans owned computers in 1998. Which countries had higher rates of computer ownership than the regional average?

A. Nicaragua and Panama
B. Argentina, Mexico, Panama, and Uruguay
C. Argentina, Mexico, and Uruguay
D. Guatemala, Nicaragua, and Panama

97. Read the following excerpt about Chinese writer Gao Xingjian, who won the Nobel Prize for literature in 2000. Then complete the statement.

"Born in 1940 in Jiangxi province in eastern China, Mr. Gao earned a degree in French in Beijing and embarked on a life of letters [writing literature]. During the Cultural Revolution [1966-1976], he was sent to a re-education camp, where he spent six years at hard labor in the fields. He also burned a suitcase full of his early manuscripts. ...[In] 1979 ... he was first able to publish his work and to travel abroad..."

—*New York Times On the Web* (online), October 12, 2000

Xingjian's relationship with the Chinese government can best be described as

A. subservient.
B. manipulative.
C. passive.
D. turbulent.

98. Refer to the following table to answer the question.

Australian City	Average Yearly Precipitation (inches)	Average Temperature Range	
		January (°F)	July (°F)
Alice Springs	10-20	75°-85°	45°-55°
Brisbane	over 30	75°-85°	55°-65°
Darwin	over 30	75°-85°	over 75°
Melbourne	20-30	65°-75°	45°-55°
Perth	over 30	75°-85°	45°-55°
Sydney	over 30	65°-75°	45°-55°

If tourists were traveling to Australia in January and wanted to avoid both excessive heat and heavy rainfall, to which city should they travel?

A. Melbourne
B. Brisbane
C. Darwin
D. Sydney

Section 5: Economics

Directions: For each of the following questions, select the choice that best answers the question or completes the statement.

99. Which of the following has the most value?

A. Diamonds
B. Water
C. Home computer
D. Tickets to a rock concert

100. A city administrator with a $100,000 annual budget is trying to decide between fixing potholes or directing traffic at several busy intersections after school. Studies have shown that 15 cars hit potholes every week, causing average damages of $200 to the cars. Collisions at the intersections are less frequent, averaging one per month at an average cost of $6,000, although none has ever caused injuries or deaths. What are the annual costs due to damage from collisions?

A. $2,400
B. $30,000
C. $72,000
D. $10,400

GO ON TO THE NEXT PAGE

101. A city administrator with a $100,000 annual budget is trying to decide between fixing potholes or directing traffic at several busy intersections after school. Studies have shown that 15 cars hit potholes every week, causing average damages of $200 to the cars. Collisions at the intersections are less frequent, averaging one per month at an average cost of $6,000, although none has ever caused injuries or deaths. Given the size of the annual budget, what should the recommendation be as to which project should be undertaken?

A. Fixing the potholes
B. Directing the traffic
C. Doing both
D. Doing neither

102. What type of economy is demonstrated in the following situation? After hearing complaints about postal service, Jack starts a delivery service.

A. Producer-consumer
B. Command
C. Traditional
D. Market

103. The law of supply states that

A. the quantity supplied varies inversely with its price.
B. the quantity supplied varies irregularly with its price.
C. the quantity demanded varies inversely with its price.
D. the quantity supplied varies directly with its price.

104. Opponents of the minimum wage believe that if the minimum wage were abolished,

A. wages for unskilled workers would rise and employment would fall.
B. wages for unskilled workers would fall and employment would rise.
C. wages for unskilled workers would rise and employment would rise.
D. wages for unskilled workers would fall and employment would fall.

105. In the 1990s the federal debt surpassed $5 trillion. The federal debt impacts the economy in all of the following ways EXCEPT:

A. The federal debt reduces the purchasing power of the economy.
B. The federal debt affects the distribution of income.
C. The federal debt affects the debt of individual citizens.
D. The federal debt causes a rise in interest rates.

106. The dollar value of all final goods, services, and structures produced in one year with labor and property supplied by United States residents is called the

A. Gross Labor Production.
B. Gross National Product.
C. Average National Product.
D. Average Labor Production.

107. Alpha can produce either 10 apples or 3 oranges. Beta can produce either 12 apples or 3 oranges. Therefore,

A. Alpha has an absolute advantage in the production of apples.
B. Alpha has an absolute advantage in the production of oranges.
C. Beta has an absolute advantage in the production of apples.
D. Beta has a comparative advantage in the production of oranges.

108. Which of the following statements about the use of technology in production is TRUE?

A. The technological advance in which machines oversee people who are actually doing the work is known as automation.
B. Robotics refers to sophisticated computer-controlled machinery that operates the assembly line.
C. With mechanization, skilled handiwork became even more important to a company's production process.
D. Because the assembly line results in more efficient use of machines and labor, the costs of production are greatly increased.

109. Important facts for a firm to know when it is considering where to sell its products include all the following EXCEPT:

    A. It is best for a company to get its start by using direct-mail advertising and wait for calls from potential consumers.

    B. A business may choose to sell its goods over the Internet if it thinks that the items may be of special interest to a select group of consumers.

    C. If a company thinks the product will appeal to a limited market, it may choose to sell its goods only in a specialty shop.

    D. Sometimes there is an existing marketplace established for the product.

110. Which of the following statements about job categories is TRUE?

    A. Professionals are workers whose jobs require some training, often using modern technology.

    B. Skilled workers are workers who have college degrees, and often, additional education or training.

    C. Semiskilled workers are workers who have learned a trade or a craft, either through a vocational school or as an apprentice to an experienced worker.

    D. Unskilled workers have jobs that require no specialized training but do require good general employment skills.

111. All of the following are drawbacks for customers using electronic funds transfer EXCEPT:

    A. The increased risks of tampering

    B. The increased lack of privacy

    C. The reduced time, trouble, and costs

    D. The possibility of altering account information

112. If your city made a trade-off to spend $1 million on a recycling facility instead of a fitness and health center, the opportunity cost of a cleaner environment would be

    A. fewer fit and healthy people.

    B. fewer colleges and universities.

    C. less garbage to dispose of.

    D. fewer employed people.

113. The basic issues that every nation's economic system addresses are

    A. the type of goods and services that should be produced, the quantity of each type of good and service produced, and who should share in their use.

    B. the type of goods and services that should be produced, what labor should be used to produce them, and who should distribute the goods and services.

    C. the types of goods and services that should be produced, the trade-offs required by producing each type of good and service, and who should produce them.

    D. the types of goods and services that should be produced, how the goods and services should be produced, and who should share in what is produced.

114. Which of the following pairs of items would NOT be substitutes for each other if the price of one increased dramatically?

    A. Fitness center membership, exercise bicycle

    B. Broccoli, pizza

    C. Home perms, salon hair styling

    D. Concert tickets, movie rentals

115. After making the decision to start a business, entrepreneurs must do all of the following EXCEPT:

    A. Be willing to take a risk.

    B. Gather the factors of production.

    C. Learn as much as possible about the businesses they plan to start.

    D. Do all the work in their businesses themselves.

GO ON TO THE NEXT PAGE

116. Agriculture is an example of perfect competition because

    A. the costs of renting farmland are relatively high, making entry into the market difficult.

    B. demand for some agricultural products, such as wheat, is inelastic.

    C. demand for some agricultural products, such as wheat, is elastic.

    D. individual farmers exert control over the market prices of their goods.

117. Improved telecommunications have affected global integration in all the following ways EXCEPT:

    A. Increasing the cost of computing

    B. Teaching people in developing nations about the rest of the world

    C. Spreading fads and fashion

    D. Encouraging more of the world's people to learn English

Section 6: Behavioral Sciences

Directions: For each of the following questions, select the choice that best answers the question or completes the statement.

118. All of the following are causes of cultural change EXCEPT:

    A. Discovery

    B. Counterculture

    C. Invention

    D. Diffusion

119. What is the hidden curriculum?

    A. The teaching of the curriculum that an individual teacher thinks is important

    B. The teaching of the rules and regulations of activities

    C. The teaching of time

    D. The teaching of the informal and unofficial aspects of culture to prepare children for life

120. Read the following scenario, then answer the question.

Two people are in a 20-mile race. The winner will receive a prize of $100,000. Two of the competitors—Lynn and Tony—are very good runners, and both are in good physical condition. At the beginning of the race Tony is told to put a set of 10-pound ankle weights on each leg, but Lynn is not. In fact, Lynn does not even know about the weights. When Lynn reaches the 13-mile marker, Tony is 2 miles behind. He is not only exhausted but is also experiencing a shortened running stride and is off-rhythm because of the weights. The judges decide to remove the ankle weights from Tony.

What should be done to provide an equal opportunity for Tony?

    A. A policy would need to be enacted to guarantee that Tony could get a fair chance.

    B. Let the situation work itself out.

    C. Allow Tony to win, regardless of the actual end result, as compensation for having the disadvantage for over half of the race.

    D. Let Tony and Lynn finish the race and then have a rematch.

121. A student is told by teachers that he will not amount to anything. He then begins to fail subjects he has normally passed. What term would sociologists use to describe this occurrence?

A. Sexism

B. Cultural bias

C. Meritocracy

D. Self-fulfilling prophecy

122. Pretend that you are attending a professional tennis match with an economist, a political scientist, a psychologist, and a sociologist. Which of those people would ask, "Why do some athletes fall apart after a bad call?"

A. Economist

B. Political scientist

C. Psychologist

D. Sociologist

123. Pretend that you are attending a professional tennis match with an economist, a political scientist, a psychologist, and a sociologist. Which of those people would ask, "How did Americans lose their dominance in this sport?"

A. Economist

B. Political scientist

C. Psychologist

D. Sociologist

124. Which of the following statements is true concerning marriage partner selection?

A. Love and sexual compatibility is the basis for marriage partner selection in all societies.

B. When romantic love is an important criterion, physical beauty is frequently a key factor.

C. The rules governing marriage partner selection vary little from society to society.

D. All of the above.

125. The principle bonds that hold kinship groups together are

A. marriage and descent.

B. marriage and fictive relationships.

C. marriage and law.

D. descent.

126. How might a child who displays avoidant attachment react when placed alone in a strange room?

A. The child will welcome the mother back when she returns, free of anger.

B. The child may avoid or ignore the mother when she leaves and returns.

C. The child will reject or act angrily toward the mother when she returns.

D. It cannot be determined, as the child will behave inconsistently.

127. What is the main reason adolescents form cliques?

A. Cliques allow an adolescent to grow socially and to form close friendships.

B. Cliques encourage conformity.

C. Cliques provide the basic means for forming beliefs and values.

D. Cliques are cool.

128. How would a behaviorist explain a person's persistence in becoming an accomplished tennis player?

A. It is genetic.

B. The drive to succeed in tennis has been reinforced in a variety of tangible and intangible ways.

C. Because the player watched accomplished players consistently, he became an accomplished tennis player himself.

D. A mix of cognitive factors such as expectations and intentions and environmental factors such as the influence of people the tennis player respects all lend to the player's success.

GO ON TO THE NEXT PAGE

129. If you want people to think you're smart, should you try to do your best on the first, second, third, or last test in a class?

   A. First
   B. Second
   C. Third
   D. Last

130. How does the cognitive theory explain aggression?

   A. The cognitive theory assumes aggression is learned through reinforcements.
   B. The cognitive theory assumes aggression is hereditary; it is something you inherit from your parent or parents.
   C. The cognitive theory assumes aggression evolves over time in response to peer groups.
   D. The cognitive theory assumes aggression is learned in childhood by observing and imitating the behavior of models.

Answer Key for Practice Test 2

Section 1: World History

1. C	9. C	17. B	25. C
2. A	10. B	18. A	26. B
3. A	11. B	19. C	27. C
4. D	12. D	20. D	28. D
5. D	13. A	21. B	29. D
6. A	14. B	22. A	
7. A	15. D	23. B	
8. B	16. C	24. C	

Section 2: United States History

30. D	38. A	46. C	54. A
31. C	39. B	47. D	55. A
32. A	40. C	48. B	56. B
33. B	41. D	49. C	57. B
34. B	42. B	50. D	58. B
35. D	43. C	51. A	
36. B	44. A	52. C	
37. C	45. B	53. B	

Section 3: Government/Political Science/Civics

59. B	65. D	71. D	77. B
60. A	66. C	72. C	78. A
61. C	67. A	73. C	79. C
62. A	68. A	74. D	
63. C	69. C	75. C	
64. A	70. D	76. A	

Section 4: Geography

80. B	**85.** C	**90.** B	**95.** B
81. A	**86.** B	**91.** C	**96.** C
82. A	**87.** C	**92.** C	**97.** D
83. A	**88.** C	**93.** D	**98.** A
84. D	**89.** B	**94.** B	

Section 5: Economics

99. A	**104.** B	**109.** A	**114.** B
100. C	**105.** C	**110.** D	**115.** D
101. A	**106.** B	**111.** C	**116.** B
102. C	**107.** C	**112.** A	**117.** A
103. D	**108.** B	**113.** D	

Section 6: Behavioral Sciences

118. B	**122.** C	**126.** B	**130.** D
119. D	**123.** D	**127.** A	
120. A	**124.** B	**128.** B	
121. D	**125.** A	**129.** A	

Answer Explanations for Practice Test 2

Section 1: World History

1. **C.** Read all of the answer choices. Do not simply choose the first answer that seems to have something to do with the topic. In this question, you want the choice that comes closest to defining the Neolithic Revolution. Some of the answer choices represent results of the Neolithic Revolution, rather than its main development. The basic change that occurred was the shift to raising animals as a regular source of food, so C is the correct answer.

2. **A.** When a question asks for a similarity, check that your answer is true for both parts of the comparison. In this case, you need something that is true for both faiths. Wrong answer choices often describe only *one half* of the comparison. The only answer that is true for both religions is that they are both monotheistic, or believe in one God, so A is correct.

3. **A.** This question asks you for a cause. Because causes always happen before effects, think about which answer choices happened before the disintegration of the Balkan Peninsula. The shift in power as the Ottoman Empire waned is the only one of the options given that would facilitate the emergence of different factions in the Balkan Peninsula, so the correct answer is A.

4. **D.** To answer this question about how geography affected history, look at the map carefully. Notice which areas the German military did not occupy. Use these clues to make an inference about how geography affected the German army. All of these answer choices include influential factors, so D is the correct answer.

5. **D.** Read test questions carefully because every word is important. This question asks why Latin America is *economically* important. Therefore, you can eliminate any answer choices that do not offer explanations about their economic importance. Choices A, B, and C do not benefit the United States, so the correct answer is D.

6. **A.** Even if you know the correct answer immediately, read all of the answer choices and eliminate those you know are wrong. Doing so will help you confirm that the answer choice you think is correct is indeed correct. In 1966, Mao launched the Great Proletarian Cultural Revolution, which was established to create a working class culture. Revolutionary groups set out to eliminate the old ideas, old culture, old customs, and old habits. They destroyed temples, books written by foreigners, and foreign music. Therefore, A is the correct answer.

7. **A.** This question offers four answers that all apply to the work of the Nazis, so you will need to think through your answer. Hitler believed that the Jews were parasites who were trying to destroy the Aryans. The Final Solution to the Jewish problem was genocide—physical extermination—of the Jewish people. Therefore, the correct answer is A.

8. **B.** This question is asking you to infer. When you infer, you are using your own knowledge and combining it with what is written in the text. In this quotation, the Aztecs describe the Spaniards as greedy, "hungering like pigs for gold." Because you are inferring, you can eliminate choices A and C, as those choices offer information that is directly in the quotation, and inferences aren't "right there" in the text. Clearly, comparing the Spaniards to hungry pigs is not a compliment, so the best answer is B.

9. **C.** You are looking for the exception in this question, so you will want to compare each answer choice to the question, trying to find the one that is *not* representative of the Italian Renaissance humanism movement. Humanism was an intellectual movement based on the study of the classics. Characteristics of the Renaissance are most noticeable in the intellectual and artistic accomplishments of the period. Humanism is *not* the study of being human, so C is the correct answer.

10. **B.** This question asks for an example of how geography influenced history. Eliminate any answer choices that do not mention anything about geography. Then study the map thoroughly and choose from the answer choices that remain. The best answer is that floods from nearby rivers irrigated crops. So the correct answer is B.

11. **B.** Using common sense can help you arrive at the correct answer. For example, think about what you know about the Black Death first and then read the answer choices. Some peasants bargained with their lords to pay rent instead of owing service, thus freeing them from serfdom, so B is the best answer.

12. **D.** If you do not know the answer to a question, eliminate any answer choices that you know are incorrect. Robespierre dominated the Committee of Public Safety, which set in motion an effort that came to be known as the Reign of Terror. Revolutionary courts were set up to prosecute internal enemies of the revolutionary republic. During the Reign of Terror, close to 40,000 people were killed, including Marie Antoinette. Therefore, the best answer choice is D.

13. **A.** If you do not know the correct answer to this question, read the answer choices carefully. Eliminate any statement that is historically incorrect. This will help you focus on the remaining answer choices and increase your chances of choosing the correct answer. When the Communist Party collapsed, Czechoslovakia became two separate nations, so A is the correct answer.

14. **B.** Timelines show chronology, or the order in which events happened. You can use your knowledge of chronology to eliminate incorrect answer choices. Thing about what events happened *before* this timeline begins. Those answer choices must be wrong. Answer B includes the same subject as the timeline entries.

15. **D.** Eliminating answers is a good way to begin on many questions. You may be able to see that UNESCO and WHO each address a specific area and that these areas seem equally important. Since it would be difficult to pick between them, you can conclude that these two answers can be eliminated. The General Assembly might be considered, but it is general, so it probably includes all members. So, the best choice is D.

16. **D.** You are looking for the exception in this question, so you need to find the one element that did *not* lead to civilization. While religion was important during the rise of civilization, it did not lead to civilization the way choices A, B, and C did. So, D is the correct answer.

17. **B.** Again, you are looking for the exception in this question, so you need to find the one issue that is *not* addressed by grassroots public interest groups. Grassroots public interest groups deal with issues such as environmental problems, women's and men's liberation, human potential, appropriate technology, and nonviolence. They do not address educational issues, so the best answer is B.

18. **A.** To answer this question you will need to analyze the poem a little, focusing on figurative language. Then look at the choices again. Choices B and C are too literally addressed in the poem for it to be a summarization of the fundamental ideas of Western civilization. Choice D addresses government, which is clearly the focus of the poem, but ruling with a strong hand is not the best summary of the role of government. The best summary is that the role of government is to promote peace and to defend. So, A is the correct answer.

19. **C.** To answer this question, you will need to know about Muslim culture. A mosque is a Muslim house of worship, and while they were very important to the culture, they are not the covered market. Very often the covered markets were located in the center of town or "downtown" (in our terms), but the covered markets were called bazaars. So, the correct answer is C.

20. **D.** It might help you to reread the question, looking at the key phrase *of all citizens*. Mobilization, which is already stated in the question, is the process of assembling troops and preparing them for war. Trench warfare is fighting from ditches. War of attrition is a war based on wearing the other side down by constant attacks and heavy losses. Total war is a war that involves the complete mobilization of resources and people, affecting the lives of all citizens in the warring countries, even those remote from the battlefields. Therefore, D is the correct answer.

21. **B.** You need to know what monks are and what their roles were in order to answer this question. Monks were men who separated themselves from ordinary human society in order to pursue a life of total dedication to God. Their community was seen as the ideal Christian society. The monks' dedication to God became the highest ideal of Christian life. Their homes, called monasteries, became centers of religious learning. Although the first monks were men, women, called nuns, also began to withdraw from the world to dedicate themselves to God. With this knowledge, of the choices given, B is the best answer.

22. **A.** You can use your knowledge of today's history to help you answer this question. Lineage groups serve as the basic building blocks of African society. All members claim to be descended from a real or legendary common ancestor. There are leading members of each lineage group, but the group provided mutual support for all its members. Women were usually subordinate to men in Africa (as is still the case today), so the correct answer is A.

23. **B.** You are looking for the exception in this question, so you want to find the one contribution that was *not* an advance in science and mathematics that impacts our world today. Eliminating some answers will help you. Answer choices A, C, and D were all advances in science and mathematics. Answer choice B was a contribution from the ancient Indians, but it is not in the field of science and mathematics, so the correct answer is B.

24. **C.** Questions that ask about a specific fact can be difficult if you do not know the answer. Increase your chances of choosing the correct answer by looking at each answer choice and eliminating choices you know are wrong. Then ask yourself which remaining choice makes the most sense and select that as your answer. The English Parliament emerged during the reign of Edward I and the French Parliament during the reign of Philip IV.

25. **C.** Read all the choices carefully before you pick your answer. You are looking for the *best* answer to the question. While Deganawida and Hiawatha did create the Great Peace, which created an alliance of five groups called the League of Iroquois, there is a better answer. The Grand Council (the council of representatives) was an experiment in democracy, and some scholars believe that in 1754, Benjamin Franklin used the Iroquois League as a model for a Plan of Union for the British colonies. So, the best answer choice is C.

26. **B.** A date can be an important clue. When a question contains a date, think about major events that occurred during or around that time. Then eliminate answer choices that do not reflect that history. All of these answer choices address women's issues, but if you look closely at choice B, you will see that is it discussing the same subject as the quote.

27. **C.** You are looking for an exception here—an item that was *not* sent from the Americas to Europe. Your knowledge about what was available in the Americas that was "new and different" to Europe will help you answer this question. Silver, dyes, gold, cotton, vanilla, hides, potatoes, cocoa, corn, and tobacco were all sent from the Americas to Europe. Silk was not. So, C is the correct answer.

28. **D.** You need to read the question and the answers very carefully here. While many of the answer choices present information that was true about the guillotine and executions, you need to focus on why the guillotine was used for executions. It was believed to kill quickly and humanely, so the best answer choice is D.

29. **D.** Do not pick an answer just because it sounds good. Sometimes a choice is deliberately meant to sound correct but is not. Read all the answer choices very carefully before you select the best one and avoid making any hasty decisions. For example, while the Christian Church began during the Roman Empire, it was not directly created by the Empire. And while the Triumvirate and the gladiatorial shows might have been nice, they were not lasting contributions. The best answer choice is D.

Section 2: United States History

30. **D.** Remember to read the question and the answer choices carefully. The question is asking about tensions between the western settlers and the Native Americans. While choices A, B, and C all happened during Washington's term as president, the only answer choice that suggests tension *between* the Native Americans and the western settlers is choice D.

31. **C.** Eliminate answers that do not make sense. Reducing the number of American troops probably would not strengthen the military, so you can eliminate choice D. Obviously we want to prevent the expansion of communist countries, but that is not currently a really big issue. Another name of the Strategic Defense Initiative is Star Wars. That leads you to the fact that the initiative is probably technologically advanced, so C would be the answer most focused on technology. Therefore, C is the correct answer.

32. **A.** Read the question and the answer choices carefully. The question is asking how World War I changed the attitudes of African Americans. Choices B, C, and D all relate to African American history around the time of World War I, but only answer A addresses the change in attitudes based on their involvement in the war itself. So, the correct answer is A.

33. **B.** Read the answer choices carefully. Then reread the excerpt and the question. You can eliminate choices C and D because they do not make sense given the question. Answers A and B are very similar, but B is a better choice because it better explains the reason that the Articles of Confederation were effective at that time.

34. B. No one can say for certain when the first people arrived in America. In Folsom, New Mexico, George McJunkin discovered a bone that belonged to a type of bison that had been extinct for 10,000 years. More recent research, however, suggests that humans arrived much earlier. Presently, scientific speculation points to a period between 15, 000 and 30,000 years ago.

35. D. You have to know a little bit about Lyndon Johnson to answer this question, but you can also infer part of the answer. Johnson had known hard times, and he had also seen extreme poverty firsthand in his brief career as a teacher in a low-income area. He understood suffering and he believed deeply in social action. He felt that a wealthy, powerful government could and should try to improve the lives of its citizens. This makes the best answer D.

36. B. Be careful to look for the exception. So you need to find the answer choice that was *not* a condition. Since a tax exemption *was* a benefit for Texas newcomers, you can eliminate answer A. Choice C simply does not make sense. You're left with choices B and D, and of those two, B is the better choice.

37. C. On his very first night in office, Roosevelt told the Secretary of the Treasury that he wanted an emergency banking bill ready for Congress within five days. In his "fireside chats," FDR assured people that it was safer to keep their money in a re-opened bank than under the mattress. The banking crisis was over quickly. Therefore, the answer is C.

38. A. You are looking for the exception in this question, so you want to find one way that railroads did *not* boost the settlement of the West. At first glance, all of these answers look good. But read more carefully and think about the ways railroads could have boosted the settlement. Just traveling across the country (choice A) did not boost the settlement quite the way the other three choices did. So A is the correct answer.

39. B. Remember that European countries wanted to gain as much land as "theirs" as possible in America. With that in mind, it would make sense to ensure control of the Mississippi River, so the correct answer is B.

40. C. Keep in mind that you are looking for the exception in this question. So you are looking for the one position that women did *not* fill during the war. The process of elimination might help you. Remember that World War I took place from 1914-1920 and women did not have a lot of choices in the types of jobs they held. Women filled noncombat positions such as nurses, clerical help, and other jobs vacated by men who had become soldiers, so C is the best answer.

41. D. Make sure you read the question carefully. Look at the key words *the most*. The correct answer is D.

42. B. Many times, several answer choices seem correct, so you have to look for the *best* answer. C and D both happened during World War II, but neither choice addresses why the victories on Iwo Jima and Okinawa were so vital to the Allies. And while any victory was vital (choice A), the *best* answer is that those victories allowed Americans to have landing areas within striking distance of Japan. The best answer is B.

43. C. This question requires that you remember details about a specific program. Use the process of elimination if you are unsure. Does the Contract with America sound like a foreign policy agreement between two countries? It may help to put a face with the Contract with America. Even if you cannot remember Newt Gingrich's name, you might remember that the Contract with America was not a Clinton initiative. The Contract with America was created by congressional Republicans, led by Newt Gingrich. The program proposed 10 major changes, including lower taxes, welfare reform, tougher anti-crime laws, term limits for members of Congress, and a balanced budget amendment. The correct answer is C.

44. A. In 1954 the Supreme Court decided to combine several different cases and issue a general ruling on segregation in schools. One of the cases involved a young African American girl named Linda Brown, who was denied admission to her neighborhood school in Topeka, Kansas, because of her race. She was told to attend an all-black school across town. With the help of the NAACP, her parents sued the Topeka school board, and on May 17, 1954, the Supreme Court ruled unanimously in the case that segregation in public schools was unconstitutional and violated the equal protection clause of the Fourteenth Amendment. Chief Justice Earl Warren summed up the Court's decision when he wrote: "In the field of public education, the doctrine of separate but equal has no place. Separate educational facilities are inherently unequal."

45. B. Look at the graph carefully and study the information. The correct answer is 10 percent, so B is the correct answer.

46. C. Read this question carefully. You are looking for the exception in this question. So, you will have to find the one answer choice that was *not* a characteristic of the United States economy after World War II. *Economy* is a key word in this question. All of the answer choices were characteristics in the U.S. after WWII, but one answer choice does not deal with the economy, and that answer choice is C.

47. D. Remember that a main theme is the general, overall feeling of something. You're looking for Carter's main foreign policy theme. Answer choices A, B, and C were all part of Carter's foreign policy, but the answer choice that addresses main theme is D: the need to be honest, truthful, and decent in foreign relations.

48. B. You are looking for the exception here, so you need to identify one reason the author does *not* give for opposing free public education. If you reread the excerpt, you will find that his reasons include scarcity of money, existence of plenty of schools, available space in existing schools, questionable benefit of schooling, and lack of earning for children while they are in school. There *are* plenty of buildings, so choice B is the correct answer.

49. C. Sometimes more than one answer choice seems correct, so you need to read carefully. In 1870 and 1871, Congress passed three Enforcement Acts to combat the violence in the South. The first act made it a federal crime to interfere with a citizen's right to vote. The second act put federal elections under the supervision of federal marshals. The third act, also known as the Ku Klux Klan Act, outlawed the activities of the Klan. So, the correct answer is C.

50. D. Once you have read the answer choices, reread the excerpt again. The question is asking you to infer, or read between the lines. Part or all of the answer choices are mentioned in the text, so you have to decide which one is *best*. The text says the money does go to the colonies, but only to the *conquered* colonies, so you can eliminate choice A. You can rule out B because the text does not say that the colonies cannot pay any portion of the taxes—only that in Franklin's *opinion* they cannot pay the stamp duty for one year. Eliminate choice C because the text does not mention anything about being obligated to soldiers in the future—it mentions how much they helped soldiers during the *last* war. In the excerpt, Franklin implies that the colonies are already paying more than their share, so D is the correct answer.

51. A. A zoot suit had very baggy, pleated pants and an overstuffed, knee-length jacket with wide lapels. Zoot-suit wearers usually wore their hair long, gathered into a ducktail. The zoot suit angered many Americans. In order to save fabric for the war, most men wore a suit with no vest, no cuffs, a short jacket, and narrow lapels. By comparison, the zoot suit seemed excessive and thus, unpatriotic. In California, Mexican American teenagers adopted the zoot suit. In June 1943, after hearing rumors that zoot suiters had attacked several sailors, 2,500 soldiers and sailor stormed into Mexican American neighborhoods in Los Angeles. They attacked Mexican American teenagers, cut their hair, and tore off their zoot suits. The police did not intervene, and the violence continued for several days. Despite the Zoot Suit Riots, Mexican Americans were not deterred from joining the war effort. Therefore, the correct answer is A.

52. C. You are looking for the exception in this question, so you want to identify a war tactic that was *not* used by the United States. The United States used search and destroy missions, bombing, napalm, and Agent Orange. The Vietcong used guerilla tactics. So, C is the correct answer.

53. B. Be sure to read the excerpt and the question carefully. Several of the answer choices may seem correct, so using the process of elimination will help you. You can eliminate choice A because although Robert E. Lee wanted to show his loyalty to his country, it wasn't through fighting with the South that he'd be doing that. Rule out choice D because Lee very clearly realized he would not be impressing his sister. Choice C appears correct, because Lee said he didn't want to be called on to draw his sword. But choice B contains a little more specificity by addressing the reason Lee didn't want to stay in the Union army—because he didn't want to have to fight against his fellow Virginians. So, the correct answer is B.

54. A. Again, you are looking for the exception in this question, so you want to find something that did *not* have a lasting impact on the nation. All of the answer choices may, at first glance, appear to be impacts on the nation, so you will have to find the *least likely* choice. The counterculture had a lasting impact on the nation in art, music and dance, fashion, and the idea that alternatives to mainstream culture were possible. While some "hippies" drove buses and vans, it did not have a major impact on transportation ideals in this country, so A is the correct answer.

55. A. Read the question carefully. All of these choices are true about farmers of the 1890s, but only one answer choice describes how the farmers disliked Eastern bankers. So, the correct answer is A.

56. B. Read the answer choices carefully, and think about the effects of *Sputnik* on the United States. *Sputnik* "scared" the United States, as we realized we were behind other nations in technology and the space race. Therefore, B is the correct answer.

57. B. You are looking for the exception, so you want to identify the one answer that was *not* an innovation that retailers introduced in the late 1800s. Monopolies were not a new innovation to sell goods to consumers, so the correct answer is B.

58. B. Because you are looking for the exception, you need to find the one area in which there were *no* reforms during the Progressive Era. It may seem that all of the answers are areas of reform. But because business is a subset of economic reform, B is the best answer.

Section 3: Government/Political Science/Civics

59. B. Make sure you read the question carefully and choose the answer that *best* answers the question. Oftentimes more than one answer choice will seem correct. Choices A, C, and D are all assumptions we can make about education in the United States. Choice B, however, more accurately answers why widespread educational opportunities are necessary for a nation to develop a democratic system, so the correct answer is B.

60. A. You are looking for the exception in this question, so you need to find where there are *not* the most newly developed nations. Newly developed nations are states that have had significant or rapid industrial growth in recent years. These countries, mostly in Eastern Europe, the Middle East, Asia, and South America, have begun to influence the world economy. Therefore, A is the correct answer.

61. C. Several of the answer choices may seem correct or partially correct. Remember you're looking for the *best* answer. Aspects of A, B, and D are correct, but they are either too vague or not explanatory enough. The Reasonableness Standard of the *Reed* decision states that the Supreme Court said any law that classifies people on the basis of gender "must be reasonable, not arbitrary, and must rest on some ground of difference." That difference must serve "important governmental objectives." The reason Congress can exclude women from the draft is because it is "reasonable" and it serves important governmental objectives. Therefore, the correct answer is C.

62. A. Make sure you read each answer choice carefully and compare it to the question. Then you should begin the process of elimination. You can eliminate choice B because a filibuster is a method of defeating a bill in the Senate by stalling the legislative process and preventing a vote. Choice C can be ruled out because gerrymandering is to draw a district's boundaries to gain an advantage in decisions. It is possible that choice D looks like the right answer. But the better choice for this question is A.

63. C. Although it may seem that more than one answer is correct, you need to identify the *best* answer. All of the answer choices address the president and/or foreign policy, but the answer choice that best relates the president's role in foreign policy to the political cartoon is C, because it most closely and in the most detail relates to the cartoon.

64. A. As chief executive, a president can issue executive orders to spell out the details of policies such as desegregating the armed forces.

65. D. Weak party voters are likely to switch their votes to the rival party's candidates from time to time—they are more influenced by issues and the candidates than they are by party loyalty. In 1992, Ross Perot was the independent candidate, and he won many of the independent votes, but not *all* of them. Independent voters are voters who think of themselves as neither Republicans nor Democrats, so D is the correct answer.

66. C. Implied powers are powers that the government requires to carry out the expressed constitutional powers. Expressed powers are powers that are directly stated in the Constitution. Inherent powers are powers that the national government may exercise simply because it is a government. Reserved means "set aside," so reserved powers are powers that are set aside to belong strictly to the states. So, the correct answer is C.

67. A. Look at the chart carefully. The group that saw the largest increase in Internet use was 10- to 13-year-olds, so A is the correct answer.

68. A. The first clause of the first amendment is the establishment clause, and it states that "Congress shall make no law respecting an establishment or religion." The First Amendment does not protect defamatory speech, or false speech that damages a person's good name, character, or reputation. Defamatory speech falls into two categories: Slander is spoken and libel is written. The Constitution of the United States guarantees basic rights in the Bill of Rights, which is composed of the first 10 amendments, and in several additional amendments. Therefore, A is the correct answer.

69. C. The main reason the colonists revolted was because they were being taxed but not represented—taxation without representation. Choice C is the correct answer.

70. D. When an amendment is proposed, Congress chooses one of two methods for states to approve it. One way is for legislatures in three-fourths of the states to ratify the amendment. The other is for each state to call a special ratifying convention. The amendment becomes part of the Constitution when three-fourths of these conventions approve it. Therefore, the correct answer is D.

71. D. In most cases the difference between federal and state court jurisdiction is clear. In some instances, however, both federal and state courts have jurisdiction, a situation known as concurrent jurisdiction. Concurrent jurisdiction exists in a case involving citizens of different states in a dispute concerning more than $75,000. Therefore, D is the correct answer.

72. C. Look carefully at your answer choices and the question. The question is asking for *supporters* of presidential primaries, so people who are *in favor* of them. Choices A, B, and D are all negative, or criticisms of the primary system. The only choice that is positive is C, so the correct answer is C.

73. C. Using the process of elimination is the best way to answer this question. You can rule out choice A because a budget deficit, or unbalanced budget, is a budget that is in debt. Choice B can be ruled out because the national debt is the total amount of money the government owes at any given time. You can eliminate choice D because a free-enterprise system is an economic system based on private ownership of the means of production—the capital—an on individual economic freedom. The correct answer is C, because the gross national product (GNP) is the sum of all goods and services produced in a nation in a year.

74. D. The General Services Administration (GSA) is responsible for constructing and maintaining all government buildings. It also supplies equipment for federal offices. The Central Intelligence Agency (CIA) gathers information about what is going on in other countries, evaluates it, and passes it on to the president and other foreign-policy decision makers. The CIA uses its own secret agents, paid informers, foreign news sources, and friendly governments to collect such information. So the correct answer is D.

75. C. The first step in the legislative process is proposing and introducing a new bill. The ideas for new bills come from private citizens, interest groups, the president, or officials in the executive branch. Various people may write new bills, such as lawmakers or their staffs, lawyers from a Senate of House committee, a White House staff member, or even an interest group itself. Only a member of Congress, however, can introduce a bill in either house of Congress. Therefore, C is the correct answer.

76. A. Under categorical-formula grants, federal funds go to all the states on the basis of a formula, often depending on the state's wealth. Lotteries are another way to raise revenue. A block grant is a large grant of money to a state or local government to be used for a general purpose, such as public health or crime control. A bond is a contractual promise on the part of the borrower to repay a certain sum plus interest by a specified date. In most states voters must be asked to approve new bond issues. So, the correct answer is A.

77. B. In selecting their department heads, presidents must balance many political, social, and management considerations. An appointee must meet more specific needs geared toward the department he or she will head. The secretary of commerce is expected to have a good reputation with business and industry, so B is the correct answer.

78. A. A campaign manager is responsible for overall strategy and planning. In the national office, individuals handle relations with television, radio, and the print media and manage finances, advertising, opinion polls, and campaign materials. On the state and local levels, the state party chairperson usually coordinates a campaign, which includes getting local party officials and field workers to contact voters, hold rallies, and distribute campaign literature. Field workers ring doorbells and canvass voters by telephone. But the campaign manager is responsible for the overall strategy and planning, so the correct answer is A.

79. C. Due process of law is the principle in the Fifth Amendment stating that the government must follow proper constitutional procedures in trials and in other actions it takes against individuals. The adversary system is a judicial system in which opposing lawyers present their strongest cases. The presumption of innocence assumes that someone is innocent until proven guilty. Equal justice under the law refers to the goal of the American court system to treat all persons alike. Therefore, C is the correct answer.

Section 4: Geography

80. B. You are looking for the exception in this question, so you will want to find the answer choice that is *not* a geographic zone or element of Africa. The only zone that is not a distinct zone is Central Africa as a cold climate. The equator goes through Central Africa, and it is not cold around the equator. So the correct answer is B.

81. A. Because you are finding the exception, as you think of what a human geographer does, you can think through the answer choices and choose the one that the geographer would most likely *not* use. A geographic information system (GIS) would not be as helpful as the other three choices for a human geographer, so A is the best answer.

82. A. The best answer choice is the one that offers *the most* correct information in response to the question; therefore, the answer is A.

83. A. In order to understand any type of graph, look carefully around the graph for keys that show how it is organized. On this bar graph, the numbers along the left side represent the exact number shown. You do not have to multiply by millions or billions to find the number of metric tons.

84. D. Remember to read each answer choice carefully. Some answer choices may not answer what the question asks. Sometimes, more than one answer may seem correct. Therefore, closely study the question so that you are sure of what it is asking, and then choose the answer choice that best answers that question; in this case, D.

85. C. You are looking for the exception in this question—one method that is *not* used by geographers. While it is possible that geographers address art issues, art is really a part of culture, and culture is a more inclusive answer, so the correct answer is C.

86. B. Study the information about land use in the table. Then think about climate regions in the selected countries. Notice similarities or differences between figures for the four countries. Choice C is not relevant, so it can be eliminated.

87. C. Make sure you are looking for the *fact*. Opinions usually contain phrases with the words (or their synonyms or antonyms) *good, like, think,* or *important*. Also, beware of words that have broad generalizations such as *every, all,* or *never*. With these criteria, the correct answer is C.

88. C. You should be looking for the *best* answer to the question. The best answer contains the most precise information for answering the question. Therefore, C is the correct answer.

89. B. If you know that GPS technology deals with precise positioning data, you can eliminate choices C and D, then you can choose the best answer from A and B. Of the two choices, B is the best.

90. B. Read the question carefully to determine what is being asked. Look for the key words and phrases that will help you identify the correct answer, such as *rapid population growth*. Sometimes more than one answer choice seems correct. You must find the answer choice that is the *best*. The answer that makes the best sense for this question is B.

91. C. Study the title and the labels on the graph to see what information is being presented. Note the important facts, and look at the relationships among the countries. Remember, an answer choice that may be true cannot be the correct answer if there is no information to support it in the graph. Therefore, C is the correct answer.

92. C. First determine what choices you can eliminate. Since Southeast Asia has a diverse physical geography and many outside contacts, choices B and D do not apply. Of the two remaining choices, the best answer is C.

93. D. You are looking for the exception in this question, so you want to find the one answer that is *not* a type of migration. You can use the process of elimination on this question. Choices A, B, and C can be ruled out, because all of these types of migration occur in the Latin American region. While many cities and small islands have high populations, high population is not a type of migration, so, D is the only answer left, and it is the one that makes the most sense.

94. B. Charts and tables may reveal patterns or trends. Look for similarities in groups of numbers before you draw conclusions. In addition, numbers need not be exactly alike in a question such as this one. For example, although both China and South Korea have the same percentage for Services under Economic Activity, the other figures vary widely.

95. B. First determine what choices you can eliminate. Since petroleum products are transported through pipelines, choices A and C do not apply and can be eliminated. Choose the best answer from the remaining options. That answer is B.

96. C. Reread the title and x- and y-axis labels of the graph to determine the information the graph shows. Notice that Guatemala, Nicaragua, and Panama all fall short of the regional average. Tackle each answer choice one by one, eliminating those that contain even one country that has a lower rate than the regional average.

97. D. Return to the passage and note the parts that represent decisions Xingjian had to make or actions Xingjian had to take. Based on what you note, try to summarize the government's role in Xingjian's life. Read the answer choices, eliminating those that you know are incorrect. Then determine an answer from the choices that remain. This makes D the correct answer.

98. A. Read the chart and become familiar with the information. Then read through each answer choice and use the process of elimination to narrow down the choices.

Section 5: Economics

99. A. For something to have value, economists decided, it must be scarce *and* have utility. This is the solution to the paradox of value—the paradox of value is the situation where some necessities, such as water, have little monetary value, whereas some non-necessities, such as diamonds, have a much higher value. Diamonds are scarce and have utility—and therefore they possess a value that can be stated in monetary terms. Water has utility, but is not scarce enough in most places to give it much value. Therefore, water is less expensive, or has less value, than diamonds. So, the correct answer is A.

100. C. You are looking for the annual costs due to damage from collisions. The average cost per month is $6,000. So, multiply $6,000 by 12 months, and you get $72,000. Therefore, C is the correct answer.

101. A. Fixing the potholes is a better economic choice since for every dollar spent, the city would get $1.56 back in benefits. For every dollar spent in directing traffic at intersections, the city would get $0.72 in benefits. Doing both is not affordable and doing neither is not responsible, so the correct answer is A.

102. D. A command economy is an economic system characterized by a central authority that makes most of the major economic decisions. A market economy is an economic system in which supply, demand, and the price system help people make decisions and allocate resources. A traditional economy is an economic system in which the allocation of scarce resources and other economic activity is the result of ritual, habit, or custom. Therefore, D is the correct answer.

103. D. The Law of Supply is the rule stating that more will be offered for sale at high prices than at lower prices. So, the quantity supplied varies directly with its price—choice D.

104. B. Supporters of the minimum wage argue that these objectives—equity and security—are consistent with the economic goals of the United States. Besides, they also say, the wage is not very high in the first place. Opponents of the minimum wage object to it on the grounds of economic freedom—another U.S. economic goal. Opponents also believe that the wage discriminates against young people and is one of the reasons that many teenagers cannot find jobs. Therefore, B is the correct answer.

105. C. You are looking for the exception in this question, so you need to identify the one way the national debt may *not* impact the economy. The federal debt can have a significant impact on the distribution of income within the economy and the purchasing power of the economy; it can transfer power from the private to the public sector; it can cut down on the incentive to work, save, and invest; and it can cause a rise in interest rates. It does not necessarily affect individuals' debt, so the correct answer is C.

106. B. When economists measure income rather than output, they use Gross National Product (GNP)—the dollar value of all final goods, services, and structures produced in one year with labor and property supplied by a country's residents—so B is the correct answer.

107. C. A country has an absolute advantage when it can produce a product more efficiently (that is, with greater output per unit of input) than can another country. Therefore, Beta, which can produce 12 apples, has the absolute advantage over Alpha, which can produce only 10 apples. So, the correct answer is C.

108. B. Technology is the use of science to develop new products and new methods for producing and distributing goods and services. Mechanization is combined labor of people and machines. An assembly line is a production system in which the good being produced moves on a conveyor belt past workers who perform individual tasks in assembling it. Division of labor is the breaking down of a job into small tasks performed by different workers. Automation is a production process in which machines do the work and people oversee them. Robotics is sophisticated, computer-controlled machinery that operates an assembly line. So, because the assembly line results in more efficient use of machines and labor, the costs of production are greatly increased, and the correct answer is B.

109. A. Again you are looking for the exception, so you need to find the answer choice that is *not* as important for a firm to know when it is considering where to sell its products. Where a product should be sold is an important decision of the marketing department. Should it be sold through the mail, by telephone, in department stores, in specialty shops, in supermarkets, in discount stores, door-to-door, or on the Internet? Usually the answer is obvious because of past experience with similar products. A cereal company, for example, would most likely market a new cereal in supermarkets. Another company might decide that its goods would appeal to a limited market, so it may choose to sell them only in specialty shops and on the Internet. It is not typical for a company to get its start by using direct-mail advertising and wait for calls from potential consumers, so choice A is the correct answer.

110. D. Workers in the United States are categorized in several ways. Unskilled workers are people whose jobs require no specialized training. Semiskilled workers are people whose jobs require some training, often using modern technology. Skilled workers are people who have learned a trade or craft either through a vocational school or as an apprentice to an experienced worker. Professionals are highly educated individuals with college degrees and usually additional education or training. Therefore, the correct answer is D.

111. C. You are looking for the exception—the one thing that is *not* a drawback of electronic banking. Electronic banking began in the late 1970s with the introduction of the computer. One of the most common features is automated teller machines (ATMs). These units let consumers do their banking without the help of a teller. On the Internet, you can see your account balances, transfer funds from a savings account to a checking account, and often even apply for a loan. Therefore, C is the correct answer.

112. A. Exchanging one thing for the use of another is called a trade-off. The result of a trade-off is what you give up in order to get or do something else. If your community gave up a fitness center, you would probably have fewer fit and healthy people. So, the correct answer is A.

113. D. The three basic economic questions that all nations face are: What should be produced? How should it be produced? And for whom should it be produced? Therefore, D is the correct answer.

114. B. You are looking for the pair that would *not* substitute. The substitution effect is the economic rule stating that if two items satisfy the same need and the price of one rises, people will buy the other. It is possible that you could substitute the exercise bicycle for the fitness center membership. You could also substitute home perms for salon hair styling. And you could substitute movie rentals for concert tickets. But you can't really substitute broccoli for pizza. So, the correct answer is B.

115. D. You are looking for the exception—the one thing an entrepreneur does *not* have to do. An entrepreneur is a person who organizes, manages, and assumes the risks of a business in order to gain profits. An entrepreneur is willing to take a risk. After making the decision to start a business, entrepreneurs must gather the relevant factors of production to produce their goods or service and decide on the form of business organization that best suits their purposes. Anyone hoping to become an entrepreneur must also learn as much as possible about the business he or she plans to starts. This process includes learning about the laws, regulations, and tax codes that will apply to the business. An entrepreneur does not *have* to do all the work him- or herself. Therefore, D is the correct answer.

116. **B.** Perfect competition is a market situation in which there are numerous buyers and sellers, and no single buyer or seller can affect price. Few perfectly competitive industries exist in the United States. The one that perhaps comes closest is the agricultural market. It is often used as an example of perfect competition because individual farmers have almost no control over the market price of their goods. No single farmer has any great influence on price. The interaction of supply and demand determines the price of wheat. Individual wheat farmers have to accept the market price. Wheat is an inelastic demand—a situation in which a product's price change has little impact on the quantity demanded by consumers. So, the correct answer is B.

117. **A.** You are looking for the exception, so you need to identify the one way that improved telecommunications *have not* affected global integration. Telecommunications is long-distance communication, usually electronic, using communications satellites and fiber-optic cables. Telecommunications have affected global integration in a variety of ways, giving nations "windows" into other nations, spanning from fashion to more of the world's people wanting to learn English as a second language. Telecommunications have not increased the cost of computing, so A is the correct answer.

Section 6: Behavioral Sciences

118. **B.** You are looking for the exception here, so you need to identify the one answer choice that is *not* a cause of cultural change. Cultures changes for three reasons. One cause is discovery, the process of finding something that already exists. The second cause is invention, the creation of something new. A third cause is diffusion, the borrowing of aspects of culture from other cultures. Therefore, the correct answer is B.

119. **D.** The hidden curriculum is the curriculum that teaches the informal and unofficial aspects of culture to prepare children for life. Therefore, D is the correct answer.

120. **A.** It might be easiest to use the process of elimination for this question. Usually situations such as this one do not work themselves out, so you can eliminate choice B. You can rule out choice C because it is not fair to Lynn. Having a rematch is not ideal, either, so you can eliminate choice D. The *best* possible solution is to create a policy that could be enacted to guarantee that Tony could get a fair chance.

121. **D.** Sexism is a set of beliefs, attitudes, norms, and values used to justify sexual inequality. Cultural bias is the unfair measurement of the cognitive abilities of people in some social categories. Meritocracy is a society in which social status is based on ability and achievement. The self-fulfilling prophecy is a predication that results in behavior that makes the predication come true. So, D is the correct answer.

122. **C.** The psychologist would be concerned with the mind and behavior of the athlete, so C is the correct answer.

123. **D.** The sociologist would be concerned with the social structure of the group; in this case the tennis players as a whole, or the nation, so the correct answer is D.

124. **B.** Age, body shape, personal adornment, and especially facial appearance are usually the major focus. However, personality, education, wealth, and other individual characteristics may be important as well. Therefore, the correct answer is B.

125. **A.** Marriage and descent are what mainly hold kinship groups together. Fictive kinship is of secondary importance at most. Laws are often enacted to reinforce the bonds of marriage, but laws alone would be weak bonds for holding a family together. So, A is the correct answer.

126. **B.** A child who demonstrates secure attachment balances the need to explore and the need to be close. The child welcomes the mother back when she leaves and is free of anger. In avoidant attachment, the child avoids or ignores the mother when she leaves and returns. A child with resistant attachment is not upset when the mother leaves but rejects her or acts angrily when she returns. A child with disorganized attachment behaves inconsistently. The child seems confused and acts in contradictory ways. Therefore, the correct answer is B.

127. **A.** Cliques are small, exclusive groups of people within a larger group. The main reason adolescents join cliques is to be close to others and to define themselves. Cliques may help adolescents achieve self-confidence, develop a sense of independence, clarify values, and experiment with new roles. Most core values and beliefs, though, are set by adolescents' parents. Therefore, A is the best answer.

128. B. B.F. Skinner is the theorist associated with behaviorism. He believed that behavior is motivated by reinforcement.

129. A. You should try to do well on the first test. The primacy effect is at work in this situation. This is the tendency for people to form opinions about others based on first impressions.

130. D. The cognitive theory assumes aggression is learned in childhood by observing and imitating the behavior of models, so the correct answer is D.

References for Additional Study

If you want even more information about the subject areas covered on the Praxis II Social Studies Content Knowledge Test, consider reviewing the following books:

Appleby, J., Brinkley, A., Broussard, A. S., McPherson, J. M., and Ritchie, D. A. *The American Vision*. McGraw Hill, 2005.

Baerwald, T., and Fraser, C. *World Geography: Building a Global Perspective*. Prentice Hall, 2007.

Bernstein, P. and Nash, P. *Essentials of Psychology*. McDougall Littell, 2004.

Boehm, R. G. *World Geography*. McGraw Hill, 2005.

Boyes, W. and Melvin, M. *Economics*. McDougall Littell, 2005.

Clayton, G. E. *Economics: Principles and Practices*. McGraw Hill, 2005.

Davidson, J. W., and Stoff, M. B. *America: History of Our Nation*. Prentice Hall, 2007.

Davis, J. E., Fernlund, P., and Woll, P. *Civics: Government and Economics in Action*. Prentice Hall, 2007.

Ellis, G. E., and Esler, A. *World History*. Prentice Hall, 2007.

Kasschau, R. A. *Understanding Psychology*. McGraw Hill, 2003.

Kesselman, M., Krieger, J., and Joseph, W. A. *Introduction to Comparative Politics*. McDougall Littell, 2003.

Miller, R. L. *Economics: Today and Tomorrow*. McGraw Hill, 2005.

O'Sullivan, A., and Sheffrin, S. M. *Economics: Principles in Action*. Prentice Hall, 2007.

Parsons, J. *Geography of the World*. DK Children, 2005

Remy, R. C. *United States Government: Democracy in Action*. McGraw Hill, 2006.

Shepard, J. M., and Greene, R. W. *Sociology and You*. McGraw Hill, 2003.

Spielvogel, J. J. *World History*. McGraw Hill, 2005.

Zimbardo, Johnson, Weber, Gruber. *Psychology*. Prentice Hall, 2007.